Growing Old in *El Barrio*

Edmundo Morales

Emiliana Moreno
1901–1995
In Memoriam

Judith Noemí Freidenberg

GROWING
OLD IN
EL BARRIO

New York University Press

New York and London

NEW YORK UNIVERSITY PRESS
New York and London

Library of Congress Cataloging-in-Publication Data
Freidenberg, Judith.
Growing old in El Barrio / Judith Noemí Freidenberg.
p. cm.
Includes bibliographical references and index.
ISBN 0-8147-2702-6 (cloth : alk. paper) —
ISBN 0-8147-2703-4 (pbk. : alk. paper)
1. Aged—New York (State)—New York. 2. Aged—
New York (State)—New York—Economic conditions.
3. Puerto Ricans—New York (State)—New York.
4. Harlem (New York, N.Y.). I. Title.
HQ1064.U6 N463 2000
305.26'09747—dc21   00-056001

New York University Press books are printed on acid-free paper,
and their binding materials are chosen for strength and durability.

Manufactured in the United States of America

10 9 8 7 6 5 4 3 2 1

To my children, Gabriela, Sebastián, and Julián;
and to Emiliana Moreno and the people of *El Barrio*.

CONTENTS

Acknowledgments   ix

Preface   xi

Introduction: Contexts of Immigrant Experience:
Aging in Place   1

PART I: **Growing Old**   11

1. From New Harlem to *El Barrio de Nueva York*: A Social
History of East Harlem, 1658–1948   12

2. *"Yo Aprendí de Todo Gracias a la Providencia"* (I Learned to Do
Everything Thanks to Providence): Growing Up a
Manual Laborer in an Export-Oriented
Economy (1902–1948)   20

PART II: **Growing Old in** *El Barrio*   45

3. *"Buscando Ambiente"*: Searching for a Better Life in a *Barrio*
in the United States   46

4. *"El Barrio de Nueva York"*: From the 1950s to the 1990s   66

5. *"Aquí Yo Me Maté Trabajando"* (Here I Killed Myself Working):
Work Trajectories and Experiences in the
Labor Structure   73

PART III: **Being Old in** *El Barrio*   99

6. *"La Edad Es Segun la Persona"* (Age Depends on the Person):
The Meanings of Being Old   100

Contents

7. *"Los Doctores No Pueden Curar Todas las Enfermedades"*
(Doctors Cannot Cure All Illnesses): Illness of
the Soul and of the Body   123

8. *"Usted Sabe Lo Triste Que Es Eso? No Tener Quien Vele por Uno?"*
(Do You Know How Sad That Is? Not Having Someone
Watch Out There for You?): Connections and
Illness of the Soul   153

9. *"Estamos Pobres de Dinero Pero Somos Todos Ricos"* (We Are Poor in
Money, But We Are All Rich): Coping with Economic
Constraints in Daily Life   178

PART IV: **Policy Ethnography of Aging in** *El Barrio*   205

10. *El Barrio*: A Metaphor for Social Issues in New York City   208

11. *"Nadie Sabe Donde Va a Parar El Barrio"* (Nobody Knows Where
El Barrio Will End Up): Local-Level Policy-Making   240

Ethnographic Findings and Policy Recommendations   267

Notes   275

References   283

Author Index   295

Subject Index   299

About the Author   310

ACKNOWLEDGMENTS

Among the many people who nurtured the project at various stages, special thanks go to Marcos Pantelis, Edith Masuelli, Patricia Gómez, Kathleen Benson, Muriel Hammer, Ivonne Jiménez Velázquez, Mercedes Doretti, Carlos Tobal, Consuelo Corretjer, Nancy Bonvillain, Linda Winston, Linda Kaljee, Harvey Pitkin, Cristina Puentes, Joan Montbach, Fabio Loaiza, June Nash, Frank Bonilla, Maria Vesperi, Jay Sokolovsky, Edmundo Morales, Michel Craig, Louis Caraballo, Jaime Davidovich, Peter Harris, William Kornblum, Joan Mencher, Eric Wolf, and Delmos Jones. I want to thank the principal informants, Emiliana Moreno, Susana Martínez, Dora Delorisses, and Petra Allende. I also want to thank my colleagues at the Mount Sinai School of Medicine and the Center for Urban Research, City University of New York; the Museum of the City of New York; the New York Academy of Sciences; and the University of Maryland. Funding for various phases of this project was provided by the National Institute on Aging; National Science Foundation; the Mount Sinai Hospital; the Wenner-Gren Foundation for Anthropological Research; Social Science Research Council; and Deans Awards, College of Behavioral and Social Sciences, University of Maryland at College Park.

PREFACE

Over the course of several years, many people in *El Barrio* shared their concerns with me about the daily lives of the elderly. In this book, those voices speak through me, and I—as narrator, communicator, and interpreter—am one among many voices in the conversation.

I wrote about those voices to my professional colleagues, to policymakers, to service providers, and to the general public in a variety of spaces. More voices joined the choir in reaction to the museum exhibit *Growing Old In Spanish Harlem* at the Museum of the City of New York, which I curated to depict the meaning of growing old in *El Barrio* on the basis of the informants' oral response to photographs.

I decided that I wanted to write the book for Emiliana and the people her experience embodied. This book is not Emiliana's life history, but through her voice the life stories of countless others emerge. If their stories are not told, we will continue to hear only our own voices. And in order to be truly human, we need to hear many more.

Emiliana, *dénos la bendición* [bless us].

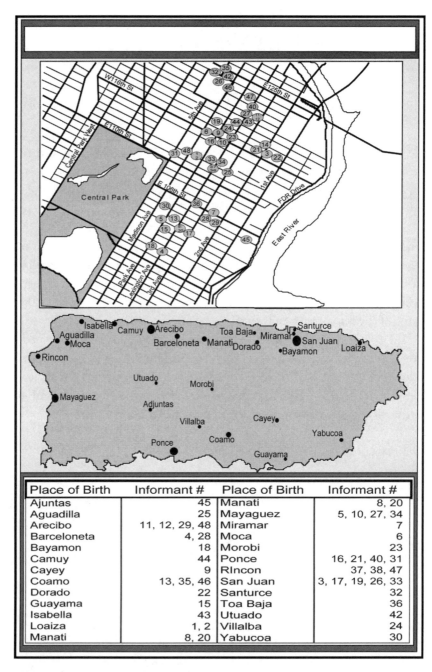

Place of Birth	Informant #	Place of Birth	Informant #
Ajuntas	45	Manati	8, 20
Aguadilla	25	Mayaguez	5, 10, 27, 34
Arecibo	11, 12, 29, 48	Miramar	7
Barceloneta	4, 28	Moca	6
Bayamon	18	Morobi	23
Camuy	44	Ponce	16, 21, 40, 31
Cayey	9	RIncon	37, 38, 47
Coamo	13, 35, 46	San Juan	3, 17, 19, 26, 33
Dorado	22	Santurce	32
Guayama	15	Toa Baja	36
Isabella	43	Utuado	42
Loaiza	1, 2	Villalba	24
Manati	8, 20	Yabucoa	30

Geographical distribution of informants, by place of birth (Puerto Rico) and residence at time of study (United States).

INTRODUCTION

Contexts of Immigrant Experience

Aging in Place

In the 1940s and 1950s, Emiliana, Jovino, Petra, Susana, Antonio, and many other elderly Latinos moved from Puerto Rico straight to *El Barrio*, in East Harlem, New York City. In the process, these newcomers came to experience what it meant to be a New Yorker, and how being in a given space relates to having a place in a society. This book is the story of those growing old in *El Barrio*, and about how living in a low-income urban enclave throughout most of the life-course colors an immigrant's experience of aging.

Space and social placement are different sides of the same coin. By examining a place, we come to know its people—we feel their sorrows and are exalted by their dreams. Space can be taken as a metaphor of social placement, a theater where the social issues of daily life unfold. Thus, *El Barrio* is a social, cultural, and political space, and its inhabitants are the local historians.

Doña María is an eighty-two-year-old woman. She lives in an apartment a little below street level in a tenement where the front door has been forced open so many times that at night the tenants seal it with wood planks to prevent intruders from breaking in. María cannot afford a telephone, so the only way I can let her know that I am there to see her is to shout her name from the street until she hears me. She is glad to have a visitor to tell her troubles to, which she does while caressing her three little dogs. María never married. She sold a plot of land and animals in her native Puerto Rico when she came to the United States to work as a seamstress in a factory. Unaware of work benefits that she was entitled to and, like many newcomers, prey to unfair employment practices,

María was left without a pension. In her old age, she receives money from Social Security, Supplementary Security Income, and Food Stamps to pay for daily expenses, but it is not enough. Sometimes, María confides, she feels dizzy from hunger. Although she reportedly lives alone, she is raising her deceased godson's daughter and she never hesitates to shelter, feed, or make her washing machine available to her three brothers. María supplements her meager income by caring for yet another godchild in the mornings. She also sews for a neighbor, a fortuneteller who announces herself on a street sign as a "card reader and adviser," and who reciprocates with cooked meals.

Down the street lives Don Juan, almost seventy. Like 40 percent of East Harlem's elderly, he lives alone. Juan pays his sister-in-law to cook for him on weekends; during the week he buys food and eats it on the job. He lives in a basement apartment. A window overlooks the yard, but he doesn't open it for fear of robbers coming in. The lack of ventilation and the humidity in his apartment worsen his asthma, he says, so he often goes to Mount Sinai Hospital's emergency room to spend the night. Although he has tried several times to find better housing, he gets discouraged by the lack of a personal connection in addressing his housing needs. Every time he goes to the Housing Authority office downtown to inquire about his application, he feels disconcerted about having to start from scratch with a clerk who seems to him "surprisingly" unfamiliar with his case. The process leading to better housing is so lengthy he has almost given up hope. Juan makes ends meet by working for a betting business that "the police should not know about" during the evenings: he earns $100 a week for announcing the arrival of the police to the bettors in the area. María has her dogs for company; Juan has his faith. He makes special efforts to attract good luck. Juan has placed statuettes of saints, among his belongings in his studio apartment closet, and inside his kitchen sink he lights a large candle for them that he buys at the *botánica* [herbal store].

María and Juan's stories mirror those of many others who came to New York from Puerto Rico with the intention of making a better life. What is daily life like for these elderly people whose income barely covers their basic needs? How are their lives constrained by living in the same low-income enclave to which they migrated decades ago? How do national policies and programs affect their daily lives? This book addresses the connections between public policies and private lives through the life histories, daily experiences, and concerns of those growing old in *El Barrio,* as Puerto Rican newcomers labeled East Harlem when Spanish became the neighborhood's lingua franca during the 1950s. Despite their geographical proximity to wealth and power, these people have been little noticed by those concerned with urban issues such as minority aging, immigration, and the increase of Latinos[1] in New York City.

The minority aged, the fastest-growing population in the nation, are expected to soar from 14 percent of the total elderly population in 1995 to a predicted 30 percent in 2050. Elderly Hispanics, estimated at about 4 percent of the total elderly population in 1995, are expected to make up 15 percent of elderly Americans by 2050. In 1995, 6 percent of the total Hispanic population was sixty-five years and older; this is expected to increase to 12 percent by 2030 and 14 percent by 2050 (Administration on Aging 1996). Since the Hispanic population grows by immigration as well as by births, it is inherently diverse in terms of income levels, national origin, and regional concentration. The poverty rate for elderly Hispanics has been estimated at two times that for elderly Whites (Hooyman and Kiyak 1996). The largest contingents, born in Mexico, Puerto Rico, and Cuba, are currently concentrated in the West, Northeast, and South, respectively. Eighty-five percent of elderly Hispanics live in metropolitan areas; New York has the fourth-largest concentration of elderly Hispanics in the United States.

Because most newcomers move as children or young adults, the aged born outside of the continental United States have only recently begun to receive attention. And yet Latino elderly in New York City increased from 8 percent to 13 percent between 1980 and 1990. They are poorer and more impaired than Whites and African-Americans.[2]

While the poverty rate for all Hispanics was estimated at close to 30 percent by the 1990 Census, it was 75 percent for elderly Hispanics living alone. The largest contingent of Latino elderly in New York City are Puerto Ricans, who constitute 59 percent of New York City's Latinos. Two-thirds of the non–Puerto Rican population were born in the Dominican Republic and a third in other Latin American countries, mainly Cuba (New York Center for Policy on Aging 1993).

Immigrant aging reflects the intersection of class, race, and ethnicity, both in the United States (Omi and Winant 1988, San Juan 1992), and the transnational networks that link migrants to their countries of origin (Basch, Glick-Schiller, and Blanc 1994; Glick-Schiller 1997).

Immigrant aging needs to be understood as transnational social mobility, the expectation luring newcomers to the continental United States. Many arrive believing they will return to their native country after achieving their goals, but the global political economy of migration conspires against materializing individual plans. Others measure upward mobility against the transnational networks that link migrants to their countries of origin. Whatever the reasons for their lifelong sojourn, many Latinos will remain in the United States as they age. Already the second-largest minority in the United States after African-Americans (in 1996, estimated at 10.7 percent of the U.S. population and 24.7 percent of the New York City population—U.S. Bureau of the Census), Latino aging is a U.S. public policy issue (Sotomayor and Garcia 1993; Applewhite 1988; Maldonado 1979; Torres-Gil and Stanford 1992; Brink 1992), and yet their needs are poorly understood.

How do these historical and socioeconomic factors affect Latinos who are currently growing old in East Harlem? In 1980, census data placed the total population of East Harlem at 114,569 persons. According to the Bureau of the Census's categorizations, the ethnic distribution was as follows: 8.5 percent Non-Hispanic White, 43 percent were Non-Hispanic Black, 47.1 percent Hispanics, and 1.4 percent Asian/other. The census data for 1990 indicate a 3.5 percent decrease in the total population to 110,508, with an ethnic distribution of 7.1 percent White Non-Hispanic, 38.9 percent Non-Hispanic Black, 51.9 percent Hispanic (40.9 percent Puerto Rican), and 2 percent Asian/other. East Harlem's elderly population increased from 10 percent in 1980 to 11.5 percent in 1990 (as compared to 13 percent for the United States). In both 1980 and 1990, about one-third of Hispanics in East Harlem had incomes below the poverty level, and 39 percent lived alone. Compared to the population of Manhattan, the East Harlem population was a bit younger, was twice as poor, and contained six times more Hispanic elderly. While median income for East Harlem was $14,882 in 1990, it was $32,262 for the rest of Manhattan (City of New York, Department of City Planning 1992).

How can the stories of María and Juan enhance our understanding of minority aging, immigration to New York City, and Latinos residing in low-income urban enclaves? This study advocates that an ethnographic understanding of social issues should inform the development and implementation of social policy. From this perspective, anthropological "informants" not only "inform," but also participate in the policy debate. Policymakers often draw plans for action on the basis of statistical profiles of population, while anthropologists provide ethnographic readings of local knowledge—like María and Juan's—that contribute to understanding the impact of policy. Yet "outside" and "inside" readings of population needs are usually not combined in program planning, as if they depicted different domains of knowledge. On the one hand, even when "informants" are consulted, their opinions have only a limited chance of being heard, as interpretations freeze lived experience. On the other hand, policymakers are usually unaware of the process by which social issues become culturally constructed at the local level.

By providing information about local populations and comparing them to larger populations, anthropologists can act as consultants to policymakers. Policies that both retain a general-population perspective and are tailor-made to a specific population, that are sensitive to the general and to the particular simultaneously, and that are responsive to culture can be more cost-effective. In this light, effective policies for the elderly Puerto Ricans of East Harlem, a subset of a population at risk—Latinos residing in low-income urban enclaves in the United States—are those that satisfy both the needs assessed by outside agencies (such as the Census Bureau) and the perceived needs of those who live in the neighborhood. If anthropologists have much to gain by understanding the larger society from the viewpoint of localized populations, policymakers can profit from learning how vulnerable populations cope with structural constraints to address their perceived needs. Thinking locally can also help us to act globally.

The goal of my research was to understand the life conditions of the Latino aged in low-income urban enclaves so as to ascertain their needs, both addressed and unaddressed, and offer policy recommendations. I found a theoretical framework that combined historical, political, economic and ethnographic perspectives useful in understanding policy issues affecting the aged. First, I needed to understand the historical, political and economic conditions affecting an ethnographic sample's life courses. But to understand the diversity of life experiences, viewed from the eyes of the people of *El Barrio*, an ethnographic approach was essential. In a sense, *El Barrio* became a prototypical environment from which to understand the elderly residents' daily lives; the policy implications of these realities, and the larger policy issues and debates, such as minority aging, migration to New York, and Latinos in low-income urban enclaves.

This is the way the story is told. Part I deals with premigratory life experiences: the social history of immigrant East Harlem, where the study population would grow old, provides the context to understand the personal histories of the prospective immigrants as Puerto Rico and the mainland United States became intertwined by a flow of capital, commodities, and people. The subjects of this story grew up in Puerto Rico and arrived in El Barrio "*buscando ambiente*," searching for a better life. Part II deals with the period from migration until retirement age. The concerns of the people of East Harlem since the 1950s (when the bulk of the informants came from Puerto Rico), particularly housing and employment, are mirrored in the personal concerns and occupational trajectories of the informants. Part III analyzes the social issues of concern to the study population since retirement age: the use of time and space in daily life; health conditions; and access to health care, social networks, and personal income. In Part IV, the informants express the daily problems they experience in private and public space and suggest solutions to policymakers.

Bearing testimony to the ethnic and class arrangements of space in New York, the Hispanic elderly of East Harlem are concentrated in six contiguous census tracts. The sample I originally designed was diverse in age, gender, and living arrangements and was intended to be representative of the 1980 Census for Community District 11, or East Harlem. Since only two informants recruited with these specifications were Cuban, too few to make meaningful comparisons, the analyses reported here apply to forty six Puerto Rican informants.

All of the informants were long-time residents of *El Barrio* recruited at service agencies such as hospital clinics, senior citizen centers, nutrition programs, offices of private physicians, and housing projects for the elderly; at neighborhood stores such as *bodegas*,[3] *botánicas*, and McDonald's restaurants; on the street, by talking to domino players and

Table I.1. Sample Population (1989) vs. East Harlem (1980, 1990) by Relative Age, Household Composition, and Gender

For 60 Years and Over (N = 41)

	Sample Population		1980 East Harlem		1990 East Harlem	
	N	Percent	N	Percent	N	Percent
Relative Age						
60 to 64	4	10	4,710	28	4,568	26
65 to 74	12	29	7,523	45	7,433	43
75 to 84	21	51	3,469	21	3,985	23
85 and over	4	10	925	6	1,299	8
Total	41[a]	100	16,627	100	17,285	100
Household Composition						
Alone	23	56	4,643	39	4,962	39
Not alone	18	44	7,274	61	7,755	61
Total	41	100	11,917	100	12,717	100
Gender						
Females	26	63	7,938	67	8,362	66
Males	15	37	3,979	33	4,355	34
Total	41	100	11,917	100	12,717	100

[a] Missing information for five informants.

Source: *Demographic Profiles: A Portrait of New York City's Community Districts from 1980 & 1990 Census of Population and Housing.* City of New York, Department of City Planning, August 1992, pp. 206–9.

superintendents; at community centers such as Casabe Housing for the Elderly; and in public forums at the Museum of the City of New York. As can be seen in Table I.1, the ethnographic sample turned out to be representative of the Census data only in gender. While the other two variables were also taken into account during the recruitment phase, in the course of the first month of ethnographic fieldwork the validity of the information provided by informants during the recruitment phase needed to be questioned. Regarding living arrangements, for example, although many informants had reported living alone during the recruitment phase, often in reality consanguineal, affinal, and fictive kin slept, cooked, shared meals, and used facilities for laundering or bathing at the informant's residence. This caused me to question the concept of "living alone." Does having permanent or transient guests sleeping over, sharing meals, and using facilities qualify an informant as living alone? Is an individual (the respondent) or a population (a social network or a household) approach more valid to determine living arrangements? What are effective ways to detect false positives and false negatives when attempting to ensure that ethnographic samples represent the larger population? This is one of the areas in which anthropologists and policymakers could collaborate to ensure more accurate demographic assessments.

Initially, I worked with these forty-six informants during a study of health-seeking processes, using life histories, ethnographic interviews (ranging from conversational to projective to closed), and surveys. The central voice, a Puerto Rican woman residing in *El Barrio* since 1948, provided testimony as one who "bears witness" (Behar 1993) for a collective voice (Benmayor 1991), once her experiences were compared to her cohort. The people conversed while developing a friendship; responding to photographs of themselves, of their homes, and the neighborhood; answering interview questions about specific dimensions of their lives in *El Barrio*. The informants also drew me into their daily lives and culture: reciting poetry, teaching me to pray, pointing out the joys and dangers of the streets of *El Barrio*, instructing me on the meaning of valued possessions they sheltered in their homes, and inviting me to share their food. Conversations took place over *arroz, frijoles,* and *plátanos fritos* (rice, beans, and fried plantains) and other familiar homemade dishes. By sharing the private as well as the public domains of their lives, they offered me insights into how critical social issues in the U.S. national culture played out in their daily lives. By taking me along on occasions when they used medical and social services and explaining on other occasions why they would not include me, they enlarged my understanding of the connections between public policies and private lives.

As interviewees gradually became informants and friends, I grew increasingly determined to draw public attention to their life circumstances through a bilingual anthropological exhibit at a museum in the neighborhood,[4] and other methods were needed to convey information to a variety of audiences. Photography was used as a documentary and research tool in portraying aspects of private and public space in *El Barrio*, and particularly their impact on daily life; to validate oral ethnographic information; and as a projective interviewing technique to motivate informants to discuss, without using direct questions, the issues that affect daily life. Using "visual instruments" to reinterview a sample and combining visual anthropology (Collier and Collier 1986) and ethnographic photojournalism (Penn 1990; Salgado 1986; Richards 1990) yielded information presented in the anthropological exhibition that could not have been elicited by verbal prompts alone.

Other interviews were conducted while collecting material culture at their homes: artifacts identified as significant symbolized the informants' spiritual connection to daily life as lived in the country of origin (for example, a coconut shell used to drink coffee in the informant's native Puerto Rico) and as experienced in their present country of residence (for example, a handmade altar constructed by an informant around a statue of Saint Lazarus bought at a local *botánica*).

The meaning of the informants' daily lives in the private and public domain of *El Barrio* was also captured through videotapes depicting the issues that affect aging in *El Barrio* from the perspective of elderly Latinos and the social groups that anchor them in the neighborhood, such as local service providers, street domino players, and musicians in social clubs.

Views on growing old in *El Barrio* were also elicited from museum audiences, who were asked to express in writing their opinions on the issues that it raised. These writings were recorded in a special binder in which they were also asked to provide information on their age, gender, country of birth, and present residence. The general public and specialized audiences were also invited to participate in discussion and debate at four public forums. Two of these forums, involving the neighboring community, policymakers, and providers, were organized with informants; the third brought together providers and researchers involved with East Harlem; and the fourth, urban ethnographers.

After five years of fieldwork, I had developed many different constructs of the meaning of growing old in *El Barrio*. My analyses are presented using secondary sources to contextualize the ethnographic information. Historical research on East Harlem[5] allows for understanding the connections between personal biography and neighborhood history (Bertaux 1981; Balán and Jelín 1979; Mintz 1996). Changes in the social environment that impact on the gendered experiences in the labor structure emerge from the life histories. The narrative of the central figure, Emiliana, who lived in *El Barrio* from her arrival in 1948 until her death in 1995, is compared to that of the other forty five informants, highlighting similarities and differences in qualitative and quantitative analyses of their experiences. When possible, the ethnographic data is compared to larger samples at three levels: the neighborhood level (Community District 11), the city (New York City) and the nation (the United States). The largest source in compiling these data was the decennial census of the general population undertaken by the United States Census Bureau. While government sources on the general population can be extrapolated to smaller areas, such as census tracts, surveys undertaken by private foundations, service agencies, and research centers were also useful for exploring the extent to which national data on general populations depicted the specific needs of identifiable population groups.[6]

By taking a view of the aging process from, as well as of, *El Barrio* (Peattie, 1968), this study contributes to understanding policy issues affecting aging processes. Given the growth and diversity of the minority aged, there is justifiable concern about how their service needs will be addressed (Angel and Angel 1997; Wydle and Ford 1999; Gelfand 1994). In addition, the immigrant minority elderly, including Latinos (Sánchez-Ayéndez 1988; Applewhite 1988; Miranda 1991; Sotomayor and García 1993; Sotomayor 1991), face special life circumstances. Although Latino elders are both economically and socially at risk (Markides and Miranda 1997), particularly in inner cities (DeLeaire 1994), few studies have been conducted in New York (Paulino 1998; Barsa 1997; Cantor, Brennan, and Sainz 1994; Freidenberg and Hammer 1998).

Using a retrospective longitudinal approach to understand immigrant life courses and placing their life histories in the context of the political economy, this ethnography contributes to visualizing how the local is embedded in the global. Although New York is an immigrant city and Latinos are second to African-Americans as a minority, the contemporary Latino experience in New York is only recently receiving more attention (Jones-Correa 1998; Haslip-Viera and Baver 1996). Although there is a rich ethnographic interest in New York Latinos,[7] recent ethnographies have not focused on the aged in low-income urban enclaves. Poverty—a defining feature of the Latino condition (Delgado and Stefancic 1998)— needs to be understood in time and place. The following analyses are offered as a contribution to the history and ethnography of *El Barrio* (Bourgois 1996; Rodríguez 1994; Thomas 1972; Benmayor, Torruellas, and Juarbe 1992), to the cultural history of New York City, and to critical policy issues faced by the nation.

PART I

Growing Old

Aging is that stage of life in which we make an inventory of our past in order to define our present identity. What are the interrelationships among social space, social status, and social issues in daily life? This question will be addressed through three axes—aging as life-course transition, immigration as relocalization, and urban poverty as historical formation—from the perspectives of social and biographical history and political economy.

Part I focuses on the informants' lives in Puerto Rico before migration, as well as the history and development of *El Barrio* before the arrival of the subjects of this study, using Emiliana's experiences as a lens to compare and contrast those of others. Tracing the social history of the neighborhood situates the life histories and current concerns of the aging study population within the context of the larger society: Chapter 1 illustrates New York City's ethnic and class structure through secondary sources on the social history of East Harlem. Historical information reveals how access (or lack of access) to housing and employment has affected successive waves of newcomers to East Harlem, resulting in the emergence of *El Barrio* as increasing numbers of displaced workers from Puerto Rico began to arrive and settle in what became a low-income enclave in New York.

Chapter 2 interweaves the historical with the biographical by exploring the life histories of the informants in Puerto Rico up until the time they migrated to the continental United States. As we will see, Puerto Rico and the continental United States were interconnected long before these people migrated.

ONE

From New Harlem to *El Barrio de Nueva York*

A Social History of East Harlem, 1658–1948

> The history of Harlem contains a curious continuity. . . . It has always, for someone, meant Utopia. It has always, for someone, signified the end of a journey.
>
> —Wakefield 1959, 35

The history of East Harlem is the history of migration to New York City, and it serves as a metaphor for the city's ethnic and class residential arrangements. Immigrant communities imprinted the urban landscape with visible signs of their diverse national, regional, and social class origins. In the process of pursuing upward mobility, migrant populations reaffirmed ethnicity as a political ideology and as the discourse for expressing social class and racial differences. Different ethnic groups competed with one another for access to two major resources: housing and jobs.

Housing was an issue with both economic and political aspects. On the one hand, construction of new housing virtually stopped during major economic recessions. On the other hand, housing has always been an issue not only of class stratification but also of residential segregation—tenements were built to house the poor in cheap, quickly built structures. Ethnic groups could only expand into areas where they would encounter minimal social discrimination. Entry into a previously forbidden, off-limits space meant that newcomers had to be willing to fight for space, block by block.

Since the eighteenth century, a variety of social groups have danced their way in and out of Harlem in a process of discovering themselves and their place in society. The original inhabitants, the Weckquaesgek Indians, part of the Delaware nation, were skillful hunters, trappers, and fishermen. New Harlem was the first name given to the area by the Dutch, as they recorded the establishment of commercial relationships with Weckquaesgek in 1658 (Stewart 1972).

During the eighteenth century, East Harlem was a residential haven for both rich and poor. The rich, inhabitants of downtown Manhattan, either moved permanently or purchased summer homes in what they then called "the rich Happy Valley of Harlem" (Wakefield 1959, 35), then a suburb. The poor, crowded in shantytowns or tenements, also sensed opportunity in Harlem.

During the middle of the century, population pressure and incipient industrialization changed the social articulation of East Harlem to the rest of New York City. For New Yorkers, housing conditions mattered less than moving to a known social space. The result was that people settled among others they recognized socially and who could possibly help them find employment. This gave rise to circumscribed ethnic enclaves.

Toward the end of the century, populations moving to the area began to include migrants from Europe, recent arrivals facing housing scarcity in the Lower East Side of Manhattan. The contrast between poverty niches and the oases of Dutch–style churches, hunting grounds, and country estates of the very rich, as well as restaurants, theaters, and the like (Stewart 1972), must have been as startling as crossing the border today from well-to-do Yorkville to poor East Harlem. But there was also an incipient lower middle class, mainly Irish and German, making its way into affordable row houses that were built quickly during the expansion of the housing construction and railroad industries (Stewart 1972). By the 1890s, when the population reached 241,000, East Harlem ranked second only to the Lower East Side among New York City's most densely populated areas, making it a tenement district (Benson n.d.). Then, as now, housing was a major social issue. As early as 1885, a rent strike was organized by the Irish to protest high rents in tenements.

By the turn of the century, the area received its first African-Americans, both from Midtown Manhattan and from the American South (Ernst 1949). Residential segregation, however, kept this movement to a trickle until the railroad company bought out the residential area in order to build a larger station and relocated its inhabitants to row houses in what is now Central Harlem (Lenox Avenue and 138th Street). This population displacement attracted more African-Americans, and by 1910, Harlem came to be associated with this group (Wakefield 1959). Although many White real estate owners attempted to slow down the sudden influx of African-Americans, their efforts were unsuccessful.

While the African-Americans moved progressively west and the Irish and Germans moved east, alongside the East River, the area between Fifth Avenue and the East River was peopled by Eastern European Jews, Italians, and Irish. There was also a large Cuban colony whose members specialized in cigar-making (Colón 1975), a profession also overrepresented among the first contingent of Puerto Rican migrants.

Eastern Europeans, mostly Russian Jews, settled in Harlem during the late nineteenth century in increasing numbers, following the ethnic and social class divide of the new land (Los Amigos del Museo del Barrio 1974; Gurock 1979). Better-off Jews lived on Lenox Avenue, where they owned real estate and large stores, while the poorer among them made their homes on Park Avenue, where they worked out of retail stores or peddled merchandise at the market under the elevated tracks. This Jewish Harlem (Gurock 1979) changed dramatically after the First World War, when many moved to better quarters—primarily to the Bronx—after the construction of the Lexington Avenue subway in 1919.

Eastern European Jews were replaced by incoming Italians. First housed at the Mount Morris Race Track stables, they moved to shanties at 106th Street and First Avenue and later, as the Irish had done, settled in shantytowns on the waterfront (Stewart 1972). The size of ethnic neighborhoods corresponded to their settlement history: thus, the Italians first nucleated around 106th Street whereas the Irish, having arrived earlier, extended from 74th to 104th Streets. By 1910, when the population of East Harlem grew to 341,000, Italian Harlem extended as far north as 113th Street (Los Amigos del Museo del Barrio 1974); by the 1920s, it had reached 116th Street. At its peak, a large part of Harlem—extending to about 104th Street to the south, Third Avenue to the west, 120th Street to the north, and east to the river—was, in fact, Italian (Orsi 1985, 17). By 1930, Harlem contained the largest Italian population in the United States.[1]

Although Eastern Europeans and Italians were the major immigrant groups to East Harlem, at the turn of the century, a skilled workforce representative of a leftist intelligentsia[2] from Puerto Rico, Cuba, and other Latin American nations started arriving in increasing numbers.

During the First World War, when the stream of immigrants from Europe slowed and New York was expanding, primarily to the North: some Eastern European Jews and Italians who could afford it took the opportunity to move out of *El Barrio* to the other City boroughs and to Westchester in upstate New York. Thus, having choices regarding housing and work is only in part a function of ethnicity—if ethnicity is an equalizer, social class is a divider.

It was to this conflicted multiethnic urban landscape that Puerto Ricans started arriving after the First World War.[3] Like prior groups of newcomers, arriving Puerto Ricans were the poorest population in the neighborhood. They faced social discrimination in housing that prevented them from sharing space with earlier and smaller groups of Latino arrivals, such as Cubans, Spaniards, and Dominicans, who had managed to settle in the southern part of East Harlem. Like all poor immigrants, they had to resign themselves to accepting the worst housing available—tenement houses. Very soon after their entry, finding no room in the east (the point of entry for most newcomers), Puerto Ricans occupied a niche centering around Third Avenue and 101st Street that was bounded by African-Americans to the north, Italians to the east, and by a high rent area to the south; thus, they could only expand west or share quarters (Handlin 1965; Wakefield 1959; Sánchez Korrol 1983; Chenault 1938). By the 1930s, 22 percent of the Puerto Ricans in New York lived in *El Barrio*, around two major settlement nodes at 101st Street and 116th Street.

A recession in 1922 conspired against the gains of the new immigrants. Overcrowding and unemployment were rampant.

> They appeared to be more crowded than ever in the apartments. I have the impression that there was about a dozen people—men, women, and children—by room. (Iglesias 1984, 163)

Despite these harsh economic realities, Puerto Ricans kept coming to fulfill their dream of a better life.

> In the Latin Quarter and in Harlem, in general, everyday seemed holidays. The streets were always full of people. Unemployment was rampant.

Almost daily, a Puertorrican family was thrown out with furniture and all.
. . . But our people did not seem to despair with economic depression. The
fact that the crisis extended to all the U.S. made it easier to bear for those
who had always lived on the fringe of misery. (Iglesias 1984, 207)

However, heavy immigration coupled with the housing shortage lit the
fire that resulted in the so-called Harlem riots of 1926, in which all Spanish-speaking groups participated in a street protest against perceived
housing discrimination from both the more established residents, who
prevented the Spanish-speaking immigrants from expanding their neighborhoods, and landlords, who were negligent in observing maintenance
housing codes.

Despite these invisible barriers, throughout the 1920s Puerto Ricans
managed to superimpose themselves residentially on the Eastern European Jews and later on the Italians further south, but they were prevented from moving east by the claims to "ethnic turf" from established
Italian and Russian Jewish settlements.

Since housing and employment were the most important needs of
the newcomers, it is not surprising to find they were also pivotal in
Barrio politics. Starting in 1927, Congressman Fiorello La Guardia[4]
understood the political importance of these issues at both the neighborhood and the national level, a concern later shared by Congressman Vito Marcantonio.[5] At the local level, Marcantonio gave back to
his native East Harlem by initiating slum clearance projects and creating an enclosed market (called *La Marqueta* by Puerto Ricans) to
house street merchants under the elevated tracks on Park Avenue.
Marcantonio's staff was approached by residents to redress housing
code violations at existing housing sites or to obtain space in public
housing projects (Meyer 1989).[6]

Finding work was not easy either, and the Puerto Ricans fared no different than previous newcomers. The first contingent of migrants were
literate, urban, semiskilled or skilled workers employed in manufacturing
industries (Meyer 1992, 68). Others came with capital to start businesses
such as boarding houses, butcher shops, *botánicas*, small pharmacies,
barbershops, and, as the migration stream progressed, restaurants and
nightclubs.

Negotiating the labor market was more difficult for those who came with few or no skills, but it also affected those who came with skills that did not easily transfer to the new setting. Many actually suffered downward mobility with the move. In fact,

> *El Barrio*'s Puertorrican population experienced extremely little success in the labor market. They were—when able to find work at all—concentrated in low-paying manufacturing and service jobs. The Great Depression dealt them a devastating blow, because even those jobs were fiercely competed for. (Meyer 1992, 68)

The 1930s were particularly difficult for Harlem. Although the New York piers employed a sizable proportion of the men, the virtual halt of the construction industry that had attracted many newcomers to the area had major effects on housing and employment. In addition, the economic downturn was accompanied by increased migration from Puerto Rico and of African-Americans from the South (Stewart 1972). The entry of these two immigrant contingents accelerated the exodus of Italians and the consolidation of the Harlem landscape for the newer entrants; African-Americans tended to settle to the west, and the Spanish-speaking population to the east. By 1929, in the recollections of the Puerto Rican socialist Bernardo Vega, *El Barrio* was firmly established (see Iglesias 1984). The vibrant street life of its center—bounded by Madison Avenue, Lenox Avenue, 110th Street, and 116th Street—attracted many of the cigar-makers who lived further south. The face of Harlem changed:"Italian groceries became *bodegas.* Synagogues became Pentecostal churches with signs of services printed in Spanish" (Wakefield 1959, 43).

Iglesias (1984) recollects dismal stories of trying to find a job, but paints a picture of Harlem where the difficulties in finding work and housing were offset by the camaraderie of political work at the labor unions and participation in political, social, and hometown clubs (Freidenberg 1978).[7] Iglesias sees East Harlem as a socialist center, where the status of Puerto Ricans—as migrants rather than immigrants—and the connections between the island and the mainland were discussed. Pedro Albizu Campus, elected president of the Puerto Rican Nationalist Party in 1931, was one of the many socialist orators who addressed people at clubs and sometimes in the streets.

Worsening housing conditions in the 1930s gave Harlem the look it has carried into more recent times: vacant lots, tenements in disrepair, homelessness. Chenault (1938), compiling statistics from the New York Real Property Inventory of 1934 and the Census of 1930, estimated the prevalence of families living together or "doubling up" in East Harlem, at least temporarily, as twice that of Manhattan. However, Chenault traces this practice to times before the Depression.

> Several years prior to the Depression, one large social agency described that: "Every available resource is utilized. Sometimes a bed occupied at night by one person is rented to another for the day time hours. It is not a question of renting of rooms, but rather beds, in many cases." (1938, 103)

By 1938, tenements, which had been built quickly during the 1900s in response to rapid population growth, still comprised 90 percent of East Harlem's housing stock (Meyer 1992, 68). It is thus not surprising that housing became an issue around which people rallied not only for more and less costly facilities, but also for acceptable standards of occupancy. Access to larger living quarters was not necessarily a solution to the housing problem. Some of the informants were pressured into sharing their household space with extended family members and boarders, something they did not need to do in Puerto Rico.

By 1936, there were about 20,000 Puerto Ricans in East Harlem. There were streets where only Spanish was spoken. Although *El Barrio* had spread to 120th Street to the north and Lexington to the east, night life centered on 116th Street and was visible in the sidewalks and alleys.

> When the good weather comes, the chairs and tables come out to the sidewalk for checkers games and dominoes and sometimes cards, and the kids come out, the younger ones playing in the vacant lots, the older ones huddled by candy stores and late at night in hallways. But the street comes most alive in the late afternoon when the men return home from work and the kids are home from school. (Wakefield 1959, 43)

Although the migration was steady, Puerto Ricans did not come to New York in large numbers until the late 1940s and early 1950s, at a time when they were already the largest ethnic population in East Harlem. Social networks were already in place to help incoming migrants find housing and jobs. In comparison to Puerto Rico, where the government encouraged outmigration, New York represented quintessential opportunity. Some came timidly, to try their luck—*buscando ambiente* (looking for a better life). Others came more decidedly, to settle with their families. They arrived in Harlem at a time when Eastern European Jews and Italians were moving up and out; when immigration restrictions were being implemented against foreign immigrants; when the United States, enjoying a postwar economic boom, became involved in the Cold War and the Korean War; and at the beginning of the McCarthy period. But they also arrived, as many foreign poor had, to settle in the neighborhood where others before them, now more familiar with the terrain, had rooted themselves. East Harlem was, is, and probably will always be an ethnic enclave that epitomizes hopeful opportunity and human despair, both paving the same streets.

The social history of the immigrant enclave provides the background to understand the human condition of the Puerto Ricans of *El Barrio* during the 1980s and 1990s. But to fully understand how they grew old, their experiences in the society in which they grew up need to be recalled. In the next chapter, their life histories bridge past to present, and Puerto Rico to *El Barrio*.

TWO

"Yo Aprendí de Todo Gracias a la Providencia"
(I Learned to Do Everything Thanks to Providence)

Growing Up a Manual Laborer in an Export-Oriented Economy (1902–1948)

> I am on the bus going to Emiliana's for the first time since our arrangement for me to come back with a tape recorder. I am a bit nervous, as if I were to interview her for the first time. And yet I know that I got stuck on how to start telling the story—as it happened to me so many times—and that sitting with her will do it. She tells me about her mother, about her life of suffering, that she is ninety-two years old. She encourages me to have faith in God and to hope that He will help me. She tells me stories about how she was here before coming here.
>
> —Author's diary, February 2, 1993

> He [her husband] always worked in sugar cane there. Sugar cane to ship from Rincón, Puerto Rico. And I worked in the workshops sewing American clothing, embroidering [*bordando a realce*].
>
> —Emiliana

Emiliana and the other informants currently growing old in *El Barrio* were born at the beginning of the twentieth century when Puerto Rico and the mainland United States had become interconnected by colonial capitalism. In Puerto Rico, most of the industries that employed prospective migrants relied heavily on U.S. capital investment to produce commodities for export to mainland markets. In time, this political and economic presence in Puerto Rico contributed to internal social and cultural restructuring that generated population displacements. As with other Latin American migrations to the United States, a "pro-migration cycle" was set in motion:

> The rise of Spanish-speaking working-class communities in the Southwest and Northeast was . . . less the outcome of economic gaps and individualistic calculations of gain than the dialectical consequence of the past expansion of the United States into its periphery. (Portes and Rumbaut 1990, 228)

Unlike other Latin Americans on the mainland, Puerto Ricans have been classified as U.S. citizens since 1917. The migration of Puerto Ricans is similar to the displacement of southern African-Americans to the Northeast in that their entry is unencumbered by immigration legislation. Yet, as for other Latin American migrants, the construction of a Puerto Rican identity is intimately tied to the politics and culture of the region of origin (López and Petras 1974).[1]

The history of the United States' presence in Puerto Rico provides a context for understanding the influence of these larger processes on daily life. Focusing on the household level of decision-making helps us understand the extent to which this presence colored prospective migrants' lives and unveils factors that accounted for their displacement.

I engaged in casual conversations with Emiliana and came back with a wealth of material to reconstruct her life trajectory from birth to migration; I went back to the informants and persuaded them to tell me their life histories. To help them reminisce, I would often ask them to show me their old photos when I brought pictures of them I had recently taken. I compared their personal and collective stories to survey data collected on the forty six Puerto Rican informants who comprised the study population.

I organized the life histories chronologically: before and after coming to *El Barrio.* Emiliana told me her story in stages marked by what she believed to be turning points in her life. The memories she had of her experiences were pregnant with themes that resonated through other voices, but with some variations. I could then situate differences and similarities in life course experiences within a political-economic and historical context.

Emiliana's life history in Puerto Rico will guide us into the collective premigratory experiences of the Puerto Rican informants aging in *El Barrio* today. Together, their voices will address the apparent contradiction between being "here" (in the United States) while they were "there" (in Puerto Rico) and demonstrate how growing up in Puerto Rico has much more to do with aging in *El Barrio* than meets the eye.

The Story of Emiliana's Life before Migration

Birth to Age Eleven (1902–1914): Growing Up in an Agricultural Economy (Rincón)

Emiliana was born in Rincón, in northwest Puerto Rico. Since the labor of all household members was needed, she grew up helping out in the household and on the farm:

> I was born on January 5 of 1902 in Rincón, Puerto Rico, not inside the town, outside of the town. That was towards the north. There we were born, there we were raised, and there we stayed until I was twelve or thirteen. My grandfather had a cane mill to obtain sugar honey [*melao de azúcar*] with oxen—a very big house, with all kinds of food. The same in my father's house. At home we never had a need, never.

But Emiliana was also interested in learning new skills and, despite her parents' disapproval, managed to obtain some schooling due to her own persistence:

> And I went to school because I found a cousin of mine who was a teacher and he enrolled me without telling my family, and because I enrolled in school they spanked me [*me dieron una pela*]. . . . [My cousin] came to fetch me every day, so much so that one day they told him: "Take her!" And they told me: "You have to be up at five in the morning because if not, you cannot go to school." They told me in front of the teacher: "She has to help her father in the morning to milk the cows, to bring the sheep, to take the pigs to the field and take care of those in the corrals . . . and get *gandules* from those large containers, so that she can go to school, because that is her work." I agreed, and I rose at five and worked till eight; then I bathed, got dressed, and went to school. They used to tell me: "Do not dare tear your suit, do not dare get it dirty, because if you bring that suit back dirty, you know you will not be allowed to go to school." I loved

| 22 |

school more than home. My mother was overjoyed because I had learned to read and write so soon.

But school was unimportant—particularly for a girl—when the family's economic survival was at stake:

I entered school at age seven, but at nine they brought me home to work. At that time, father sold fruits [*comerciante de frutos menores*]. He worked a lot and he needed somebody to help him. And my father said: "I need her to work here with me." So I left school to go to work! But I had to do jobs fit for men and women, *señora*! At home there were eight day laborers [*peones*] working, and I had to help those eight. And my older sisters were in the kitchen, cooking for all those people. You came from school, you took your clothes off. Nobody had to order you around. You knew what you had to do. That was the way it was in the past. Now the children do not work; now the children do not know what work is. But the young in the past did not know what childhood was.

For Emiliana, staying in school would have made an important difference in the turn her life took:

Look at me! If they would have left me in school, I would have learned something. When I was in school they taught English and Spanish. In the morning, you had to say "good morning," in the afternoon, "good afternoon." They taught you an hour in English and an hour in Spanish.

Yet Emiliana was very enterprising and, at age nine, attempted to get work skills:

When they took me out of school, I enrolled in a sewing workshop behind their backs again. At age nine, I went to town and there was a sewing workshop. I liked to work with needles and such, and I enrolled there. You should have seen them [her parents]! They told me: "You cannot go to study that. You cannot go to that workshop." But I told them: "But they accepted my sample and they say I can do it, that I can go." "No, you cannot go, you have to work here." "Please, let me go at least in the morning, since they already approved my sample, they enrolled me, I was able to work with the needle and do their work." They had to let me go.

Ever since that event, Emiliana has combined work at home with outside employment to contribute to the economy of a household that expands its sources of income by selling labor or produce in the market. In Puerto Rico, that market extended to the mainland United States:

That is where I learned for the first time to do the embroidering [*el realce del festón*][2] on shirts that came from here [the United States] and that were sent there [to Puerto Rico]. That is how I learned, pushing [*a la brava*]. That is how I learned to do all kinds of handiwork at the workshop [*taller*]. I stayed at the workshop until three in the afternoon, and then I came back home to work in whatever they needed me for. Because my father also made starch—the one that you sell—they came to buy it from the towns. My father worked a lot. He also sowed rice. Because he had as much land to plant as he wanted. Because we lived in a place owned by a *corso*.[3] In between the rice, we planted maize or beans because those you can harvest soon. We sowed, and when it was time to harvest, we were harvesting all day, a brigade of women and men. You should have seen the work there was at home! At home nobody was idle. And at night, you shook out the grain from the maize on a stone [*había una piedra de hacerles así a las mazorcas de maíz y ahí lo desgranaba*]."[4]

There were clear gender differences in the type and location of work:

At home, there was a male [Emiliana's brother], but with him you could not fiddle because he was in school. Then [there were] my older sisters, who with mother's sisters and other women had to prepare food for all those people [the farm workers]. You also cooked all kinds of vegetables in big wooden trays—*papas, yautía, guineo, plátano* and *ñame*.[5] These they boiled separately. Then, a man or two or three [farm workers] helped take lunch to the fields. You should have seen all the work we had at home! Every day. The year started and ended [the same]. Taking lunch to the people at twelve. And in the morning they bought three bags of bread to take to the workers with coffee.

Several economic strategies helped maximize profits in the peasant household economy. The most important was to concentrate labor and avoid its dispersal, for example, through marriage or schooling. Courtship for marriage started at an early age, yet the risk of losing labor through marriage and establishing residence outside the household was seriously balanced against the need for work hands:

When we began to mature [became young ladies, *señoritas*], around the age of ten, men started coming around the house because four sisters were there. And at home they did not want any of us to fall in love because they wanted us to work! And at home we worked a lot.

In addition to marriage, another threat to the household economy was attending school:

The only one who went to school of the sisters was me, because I enrolled behind their back; otherwise I would not have gone either!

The most predictable strategy was accumulating profits through savings:

They [her parents] kept the profit in boxes . . . full of silver, gold, pearls, diamonds, *azabache* [black pearl]. Father worked in agriculture [*trabajaba la agricultura*],[6] and he had to pay all the persons that he hired to work at my house.

To maximize earnings, savings could be invested in economic ventures elsewhere. This strategy, hypothetically more profitable than savings, also carried more risks: there were human costs, since household members needed to engage in circular migration; and economic costs, since investments could be lost. Emiliana saddens as she remembers that "from one day to the next, our earnings left us."

Ages Twelve to Fifteen (1915–1917): Trying to Make Better as Sharecroppers in a Coffee Plantation (Moca)

Despite the hard work, Emiliana remembers her early childhood as full of internal predictability and meaningfulness. Laughing with delight, she recollects:

We were doing very well at home [in Rincón]. You should have seen the friendship we had with doctors and policemen and teachers! Father worked hard, we worked hard, and mother also worked hard. At home, there was a pair of oxen, a cart, a horse, a pantry. We were well-off at home.

Suddenly, everything changed. When Emiliana turned twelve, the family abruptly made a decision to work a coffee farm located in Moca, east of Rincón. Against her will, Emiliana had to leave her hometown, where she felt she was making progress:

> One day, a teacher who saw how our home prospered and who loved my parents very much told my father: "I want you to go to a farm [*una finca*] that I have in Moca. There is nobody to take care of it. I would like you and your people to go and work it." That is what the teacher told my father.

In Emiliana's recollection, the family was well-off and did not need to move for self-subsistence. But she was only twelve years old and was not expected to participate in family decision-making. When the offer to share the proceeds of working the farm was accepted, her father moved the family in two stages. First, he invested a portion of his savings in coffee, plantains, bananas, and oranges and trained his brother and son to implement his production plan. Emiliana begged to stay, but to no avail:

> I asked him: "Let's not go there: it is bad around there!" That was Moca, in the middle of the island: on one side there were woods, on the other, woods and hills. It was a large farm [*una fincota*], *señora*, larger than from here [112th] to 140th! You cannot imagine! That was far from Rincón. But mother went and he went because there was a lot of land, and they liked agriculture. They liked it so much that father took his brother and son, and organized them to work the land.

After six months, the father took the rest of the family to inspect the farm. Any hopes Emiliana might have entertained about staying in Rincón instantly vanished:

> When he [her father] tells us "go and pack up so that you all see how pretty the farm is," that was like sending us to our death [*eso fue cortarnos a nosotros la mortaja*]. We were getting big already, I had already gone to learn sewing in a workshop [*taller de costura*], where I did embroidering, raised work, drawn work, grilled work, and embossed work. I still keep samples.

To everybody's consternation, the father found that the ranch had been poorly managed:

They [Emiliana's brother and uncle] did not work. They stayed to enjoy their youth. My father had given them money to work the farm [and had instructed them] to pay and keep the leftover money. When we went back [to the Moca farm], we cried bitterly. They had worked some things and others they had not. What they did the most was to pick up coffee because, although it was a lot of work, they did not have to work, they could hire people.

Despite the visible failure, Emiliana's father resisted giving up on the new venture. Instead, he invested their remaining money on expanding the number of paid workers:

We lost a lot of money because the farm gave us nothing. The only thing that grew there was coffee. And after a strong wind, all the plantains and the bananas and the oranges and the tangerines—everything was lost. There was some money left because they [her brother and uncle) were not given all of it. They had spent money on *mujeres cabronas*, you know, women who are after men. Then my dad started to work again, but the money was not enough to pay the workers. The youth [the brother and the uncle] left, one to work in the trains and the other to work in Rincón, and we stayed there alone.

Given the new financial constraints, it became even more necessary to hold onto family hands to do the work. Emiliana's parents would have preferred their daughters not to marry, even if their suitors made a good living, but rather to help with the farm work:

My father, God have him in His glory, told me: "Look, daughter, if you want to please me, here in this village of Moca do not fall in love." Here [in Moca], people went barefoot, spoke badly, you could not understand them. Then a gentleman who worked in the railroads fell in love with one of my sisters. He dressed well and had good manners. My father did not want him around, but as he came by often and was a good man, he married my sister and brought her to Aguadilla. Then the other sister fell in love with a man who made a good living. Ay! my dear girl! He [her father] could not be convinced to let this one get married either! [*No quería ni a tiros!*] because he was from Moca and yet, look, even millionaires, moneyed people came to our house. I was afraid of men. Ay, my girl, I did not know anybody there! But I did not want to get involved with any man. And yet those men dressed well, they came dressed up, adorned. And when I saw they approached the house—since they came by horse because there were no carts—and they gave a letter to my father, and he came to give it to me, I would tell him: "No, tell him no, thanks." Then they would understand the woman was not interested. If the man came three times, and none of the letters were accepted, he would never come back. I would never open a letter, never, because I wanted to be good to my father. I was good to him till the end. So all the sisters—except for me—got married with people from Moca but then left for the cities.

The move to Moca, an economic strategy expected to maximize earnings and improve the family's well-being, resulted in an increased workload for Emiliana once the enterprise failed. To make matters worse, Emiliana's father's unexpected sickness aborted all projected plans:

> You cannot imagine how much I worked in Moca! We had to get up at four in the morning to pick coffee far, far away, whether it rained or not. Father was sick, so he could not do anything. I had to pick coffee so that my mother would not suffer, because I gave my mother everything she wanted. Then, everything went wrong: my father got sicker and the money went . . . puff! We were in Moca for only three years, but had we not left quickly, we would all have died!

Ages Sixteen to Twenty-five: (1918–1927): Industries of the U.S. Mainland in Puerto Rico (Aguada)

Despite all efforts, the family's savings had dissipated. The family moved to Aguada, where Emiliana's father died.

> My brother bought us a house and we went to live in Aguada, that is to say, closer to Aguada than to Rincón. I had to work very hard, señora [*Tenía que trabajar hasta con las uñas*],[7] but I was used to it and I can tell you that if my brother would not have come for us [in Moca], my father would have died there because he fell ill and his legs became swollen. When we moved [to Aguada], my father was already unable to work. He then had a pain and a fever, a double pneumonia, and he died.

As the oldest female, Emiliana helped her widowed mother run the household and raise the youngest children by working at any task she could master in agriculture and sewing:

I was the oldest daughter. Mother still had three small ones to raise. I was [like] the mother of the two youngest. I worked to raise them because the girl was one and the boy three. I worked for my mother, I worked for them, and for another younger sister. And, look, work does not kill you; look where I am today! Work does not kill, suffering does not kill—otherwise I would be dead! I knew how to embroider those samples that came already cut up. First, I embroidered them and then I sewed them, because I also learned to sew. I learned everything, thanks to Providence. [*Yo aprendí de todo gracias a la Providencia.*][8] Girls today do not take to anything, but I learned everything I could. Do you want to know how many things I know how to do? Nobody believes me! But I know how to sow beans, even sugar cane, I know how to sow maize, I know how to take out coal. I tell you, I know all kinds of work. Agriculture and embroidery. I know how to sew trousers, I know how to sew shirts, I know how to sew suits, I know how to sew everything, curtains, everything, everything. Everything I watched, I tried . . . I learned to do a lot of things because of the way I am.

The sewing was destined for the growing manufacturing industry in the Northeast, at a time when hand sewing was commissioned at sites where labor was cheapest:

I went to town to take the work I had embroidered with these hands, in silk, to send here. Yes, for this country. The work that was done there in Rincón was to send to the United States. All of it. There was a lot: it was a very large workshop. The Americans came to get the work. The owner was an American married to a Hispanic.

For Emiliana to accomplish these tasks and enjoy her independence, marriage was out of the question:

My mother never suffered with me. All my sisters got married, and I remained single. I did not want to get married because somebody had to take care of my mother. I did not want to have boyfriends or anything, but I dedicated myself to going dancing. There were distinguished dances.[9] They sent for us and mother took me to the dances. I did not want to fall in love because I wanted to go dancing; boyfriends do not allow you to go dancing. Every two weeks I went to the dances. This man [now her husband] came with us because he was our neighbor, and he was always at our house.

| 29 |

Marriage only became an economic possibility for Emiliana when a suitor appeared who did not prevent her from remaining at home with her mother:

> Then this one [her husband] appeared. I told him: "No man can take me away from this house. Of course I want a man because I am a young woman, but the man who addresses me has to be responsible for both me and my mother, because I cannot leave my mother. I have to work for her and for my three siblings." I tell you, it was either that or nothing. He was hard-working. And when he went to speak to mother, mother told him: "She never wanted to fall in love or anything, because she wants to take care of me. But if you love her, you have to marry her before six months have passed." Because she thought that talking to him this way, he would say he could not and he had to leave. He told her: "So, I will marry her." And mother told me: "Look, I told him that and this is what he said, that he will marry you now."

Emiliana was the only daughter who married with her mother's approval and under her rules:

> We got married and he came to live at home as we had arranged, since I lived with my mother. We married in the Catholic church. He was good to my mother and respected her. She lived with us for twelve years and then started visiting her other daughters. One would come to fetch her from San Juan, another from Coloso, the next from Caguas. My mother spent her life visiting! But I was the one who sewed her clothes, who bought her clothes. And he [the husband] would never interfere.

Ages Twenty-six to Forty-six (1928–1948): Working for Export: Agriculture and Sewing (Aguada)

For the next twenty years, until she came to the United States, Emiliana and her family lived on an American-owned sugar cane plantation and made a living from its expanding operations:

> He [her husband] worked the land and worked the sugar at Central Coloso, pushing wheelbarrows of sugar. The factory was very large, you would get in there and would hear nothing. It was owned by people from here [the United States] that had that factory there [in Puerto Rico]. . . .

Then they [the Americans] got another that they called Guánica, another that they called Aguirre.

In Emiliana's eyes, life was good there. They had shelter they could call their own and, although they did not own the land, they could keep its produce. And that was enough to meet their expectations in making a living:

We had everything—more than we needed. We had our house, we had cows, we had pigs, we had goats. One of our goats gave us a liter of milk every day in the morning. And the cow gave twelve liters of milk. We had everything, everything! We only needed to buy oil and meat. Look, girl, at home we sowed radishes, sweet potatoes, two varieties of *yautía*, two varieties of yams, sweet potatoes of various classes: there was one that was called *batata ramira*, another that they called *batata yoya*, another that they called *batata metancora*, there were all those classes. There were gourds [*patilla, bollombó*]. I also planted potatoes. Now to the grains: I sowed rice, but a lot! I sowed *gandules* [pigeon peas]. But a lot! I sowed *habichuelas* [beans] of all varieties. I sowed *yuca*.[10] I tell you, wherever you set foot in the patio of my house it was full of flowers—flowers around the house, a lot of flowers. Then, in the center, there was a space to dry the grains. At home there was *pana de pepita, aguacate, namey*.[11] You could have all the land you wanted to sow, you did not need to buy it. The owners themselves would tell you: "Whoever wants to work the land can wherever, and as much as they want." The owners of the land were very rich people, they owned the sugar plantation, it was called the Central Coloso. . . . Look, the Central Coloso gave life to millions of men and women. I worked for the Central Coloso as well, mind you. At home, I sewed the bags where they put the sugar. And my husband carried one hundred pounds of those bags on a wheelbarrow.

A good life was defined by more than simply economic parameters, such as the availability of employment. The social value of work, which reaffirmed a person's place within the larger society, was also crucial:

Ave María Purísima![12] What a good life! You were never without work! Listen, never! We did own the house, we bought it. The house of the manager was about First and 122nd Street [i.e., about as far from her home as her apartment wass from First Avenue and 122nd Street). He kept coming and saying: "You are a good *agricultor* [farmer], God bless you and give

you a good life!" The head of agriculture of Central Coloso came by to inspect the farm we planted, my husband and I, and even brought us people
to help.

Raising children was a difficult task for Emiliana and her husband, but
the couple persevered in raising three children by the norms of their culture. Their first daughter, raised in the world they knew, fulfilled all their
expectations:

> When my oldest daughter was eleven years old, she was in a program called
> Club 4-H, because there [in Puerto Rico], they taught the children to
> work after school. She brought home all the money she made. I told her
> to keep it, but she would go and buy sheets, furniture, everything for the
> house. She would go to school on Saturdays and then stay all day at that
> club, working. By the time she was a young lady, I took her along with my
> husband to dances in town. You know, elegant ones [*de etiqueta*].[13] Soci-
> ety dances, do you know what those are? Dances where society people go.
> I took her to those, not to any dance.

But in raising her first child, Emiliana was also replaying her childhood
experiences by contesting cultural norms that imposed strict gender
roles. Emiliana managed to create her own life within the limitations of
the historical period of her childhood. She helped her daughter escape
rigidity, even at the cost of migration. What Emiliana could not control
was being caught up in the growing tide of people who flocked to the
U.S. mainland, lured by the impression that life conditions could be altered drastically by moving to another setting.

Emiliana and the Ethnographic Sample: Structural Factors in Life Experience

An individual's life course is affected by the socioeconomic predicaments
of class and by the historicity of culture. And yet, in creating a life, personal experiences—like Foucault's pendulum—oscillate. How typical or
atypical is Emiliana's life experience? Three themes run through the premigratory testimonies she passed on to me: the struggle for economic
survival, the employment of children, and the gendering of work and education. What are the other informants' experiences?

Although everybody had to work, work was available and provided for what, in their eyes, was a decent life:

> I had to work in Puerto Rico and earned forty cents a week, taking milk very far. In 1936, I earned twenty five cents a day in a bakery. With twenty five cents you could buy a shirt! It was a nice life.
>
> —Antonio

Prospective Puerto Rican migrants worked for industries with export interests on the mainland, especially sugar and sewing. Their occupations varied by gender. Most of the men worked for sugar cane plantations, cutting, transporting, or processing cane:

> I was born in Puerto Rico, in Barceloneta, a little village in the north. We were six brothers. . . . I went to school up to fourth grade. I worked in the Centrales Azucareras, right next to the village. I worked in the testing of sugar cane [*lograba la prueba de grado de azúcar de la caña*]. And that was the measure used to set the price paid to the sharecroppers for the sugar [*y por eso le valoraban el precio del azúcar a los colonos*] and that is what they paid them. When it was not harvest time, I was a repairs mechanic for Centrales Azucareras.
>
> —Florentino

Most of the women engaged in the home-based small shop production of goods for the needlework industry.

> In those times a lot of work came from Puerto Rico to be made by hand and so I learned to do everything and I went to work to help my father.
>
> —Matilde

Although the informants tended to concentrate in those two industries, people were poor and from an early age everybody was required to work:

> I had eight brothers. Morovis is a little village [*un pueblito*]. I was brought up by my parents. There were no resources for everybody. They would send us all up to second grade. My parents were very poor [*pobrecitos*]. By age eleven, I had completed second grade and gone to work at a family home. I worked like that, doing the laundry and stuff, for a long time. [By the time I met my future husband] I was working in

a family home in Santurce. My husband was working in the railroads. We got married in Santurce when I was twenty two and I stopped working. I had four children there.

—Josefa

Child labor was an important strategy for subsistence. When Emiliana prompted her husband to tell me the story of his life—"*Ella quiere saber cómo se llevó la vida tuya desde que ya conocías hasta después que fuiste grande*" ["She wants to know how your life was lived, from the time when you had discernment until you were grown up"]—he summarized:

My life was to cut weeds, to raise cows at home, and to work in agriculture. That was my life. I know how to sow everything; rice, maize, beans, yams, *guineos* [large bananas], plantains, *yuca, yautía*. Every kind of vegetable. I know how to sow sweet potatoes, because everything has its way of being cultivated. I learned from the time I was ten. Then I left agriculture when we came to New York in 1948.

—Jovino

Children were expected to help out, whether in or out of the household. In rare cases, children were employed at live-in jobs outside the household, like Josefa or Pura, who recalls:

When I was young there in Puerto Rico I devoted myself to taking care of children. My mother lived with a daughter of hers and I lived with a family; they gave me clothing, food, and I took care of the children.

Although children were expected to work, only a few remember abusive childhoods that prompted them to become self-employed:

And after a while, father started drinking and mistreated my mother, and hit me a lot [*me pegaba mucho a mí*] because what I did wrong is that I played at a tree a lot. If he would see me there and not fetching water, he would hit me a lot but I never gave in! [*me daba una pela! A azote limpio conmigo y yo con la lata pa'arriba*]. And then came the separation of my mother and him. I was twelve. My mother called me and my sister and told us: "Look, I cannot live with your father so I will go live with mother, and you two stay here and you behave yourselves." But one day I arrived and could stand it no longer; it was five in the afternoon and he was about to hit me. So I slept outside because I was not silly [*yo no era muy taimado*] and on the next day I saw some lads selling washbowls and I worked some time with them then; we made some pennies [*reunimos unos chavitos*].

—Monchito

Pura also had bad experiences as a child that prompted her to move away:

It happened that somebody did my father an evil [*le hicieron un daño*] and he turned mad and burned the house and cut all the trees, because there was tobacco, onions—and all that he cut. And a very good lady kept my mother and a younger brother and me in a house in town and we lived some four years there and then she took us out to another place.

While both Emiliana and her husband Jovino were taken out of school to help out in the household economy, there were clear gender differences in education and work. All males attended elementary school, in contrast to 80 percent of the females. The informants' families either did not send children to school or took them out of school when they were needed at home. Emiliana said of her husband, "He was [in school] until the eighth grade. They took him out to work in a *bodega.*" The other informants' experiences were similar.

I was a young girl who only got to fifth grade in school because my parents were very poor. They could not keep me in school any longer and I felt a great love for my parents.

—Matilde

I went to first grade in Puerto Rico. I could not go because I had to take care of my mother who was sick.

—Augustina

Parents placed greater importance on training children for manual work that would earn them a living than on providing them with a formal education:

When I was about to start the second grade, they took me out to work and gather wood. I had to take an ax and fell wood to make charcoal. I was eleven years old. I was taught how to sow *gandules*, maize, vegetables and then take wood up there so they could cook, and how to run errands, fetch water, go to the store with a little note and be told "to see if so and so sends me these things." So I went with that little paper there, and I did not know how to write.

—Monchito

Going to school was a great hardship for the few who combined it with work outside of the home:

So in Puerto Rico, I was in an elementary school, José Julián Acosta. I studied, I went to the library and, to help my mother (we were five) I went to a factory. I was seven and I worked making buttons. After school I would go and learn. That way, when I came here [the United States], things were easier. I knew how to operate many machines and I knew how to work by hand: I knew how to embroider, how to sew . . . and I learned all that in Puerto Rico as a child.

—Dora

While most women continued to earn an income by working outside or bringing piecework home, some gave up their outside jobs for house-keeping upon marriage:

No, in Puerto Rico I did not work, because in those times the women got married and the men did not allow them to work. At home they had to do the laundry, iron, cook, mend. I worked a lot.

—Julia

A few of the women were heads of households, yet their labor at home was not regarded as work:

I am from Puerto Rico, I was born in San Juan, in Puerta de Tierra, in a *barrio*. My father worked in the docks; he had a truck to deliver ships' cargoes. I am the youngest of four. Mother did not work, she was at home [*era casera*]. My father abandoned us when I was three, and she supported us doing laundry. He came by two or three times and I never saw him again. I worked as a messenger in a *colmado* [grocery store].

—Juan

Education was contested by parents, who undervalued it in comparison to their need for children to help out. The meaning of formal education varied for the informants. To a few, it was a promise of upward mobility in a society where income differences were insurmountable barriers:

I thought about the present and the future, as did my sister. From an early age we had the capacity for learning. We got it from my mother and father—we are all like that. We thought beyond the present and the progress we could have in Puerto Rico. Because in Puerto Rico in those times, whoever had money, and it is still like that, had greater opportunity, so I applied myself in school. I never missed school. I even had awards because if I did not find what I was looking for I went to the library, and I came knowing English from there.

—Dora

Only a few families sent children to high school:

I was born in Puerto Rico on July 20, 1916, in a humble family. My parents worked. Two sisters were boarded at a convent of Catholic nuns. I went up to third year of high school.

—Dora

Most families, like Juan's, did not believe education would lead to better jobs, especially during a period when they were in limited supply:

I went to school up to the fourth grade, not more because at that time [the 1930s] with the depression people did not believe an education was important in Puerto Rico. Those were the days when the United States was not as involved in Puerto Rico.

To some extent, it did not matter whether one went to school or not; what mattered was to learn to work. That was the most important value taught children in Puerto Rico, says Luz María:

I am stupid. I do not know how to read or write. The only thing I was taught was to work like a mule [*a trabajar como una burra*].

Naturally, access to a school was crucial to obtaining an education. For example, Luz María was born in the countryside, so she defines herself as "*jíbara, del campo.*"[14]

Some informants construed marriage, like employment, as an economic survival strategy in which it was culturally appropriate to invest:

After I had that job I got married at age twenty five with a gentleman because, as he had a house and everything, then I married him. He had a grown daughter and son, his wife had died and I had two daughters. I lived with him nine years and he came to New York.

—Pura

Interpreting marriage as long-term security, some female informants actually invested in seeking a suitable partner. María, for example, bought a house and animals with money earned in the lottery to increase her marriage chances, although she managed to avoid marriage as cultural prescription:

> My sisters got married and as their husbands mistreated them so much I told my father that I would not give up his name ever. I danced, I attended the patron saints' holidays [*fiestas patronales*], I hung out, I paid attention to them [men], but I did not want to get married. When I got close to saying "yes," I said "no" [*cuando llegaba al puntito de sí, yo pues no*].

How Does Emiliana's Premigratory Experience Compare to That of the Study Population?

Emiliana's story exemplifies the interrelatedness of age, gender, household composition, occupation, and education in premigratory career paths. When compared to those of the other informants, Emiliana's story clearly indicates that, beyond the similarities resulting from growing up in the same society, occupation and education are conditioned by a person's age, gender, and position in the family. By tracing these variables, I was able to find common trends: for example, the concentration of females in household occupations and/or sewing, and of males in agriculture or other unskilled occupations. But I also found diversity in the age, direction, and permanency of the moves made before coming to *El Barrio*. Although the turning points in Emiliana's life are used to structure the narration, I have grouped the experiences of the study population by decades in my analyses of the frequency distribution of their premigratory occupation (see Figure 2.1), residential changes, and education by age and gender.

The informants were born between 1898 and 1929. About a third were born in large cities, while others came from rural areas, small towns [*pueblos*], or villages [*aldeas*]. Growing up was a family affair. During their first decade (birth to nine years of age), life was with large families—

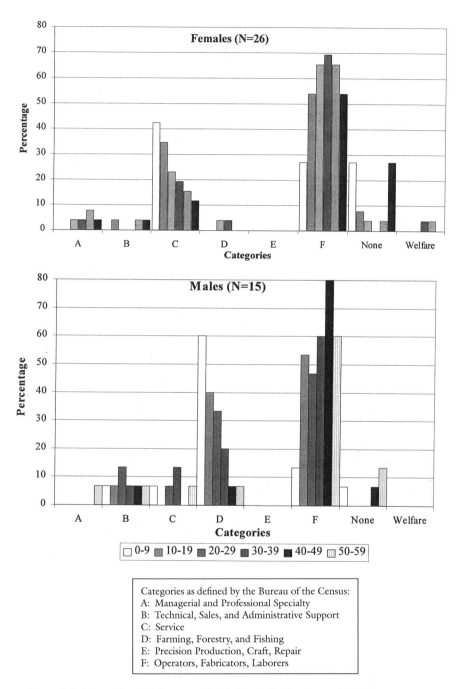

Figure 2.1. Occupational Trajectory of Study Population by Age and Gender

parents and siblings (as many as fourteen), grandparents, or other persons responsible for raising the child (such as *padres* or *madres de crianza,*[15] when biological parents were deceased or unavailable). With the exception of one girl brought to New York at age three, the informants lived in the place of their birth during this stage in life.

The informants were expected to help out at home from very young ages, as young as five years old. The occupational experiences tended to vary by gender: girls were expected to contribute to household chores such as fetching water, carrying wood, and caring for infants, and to perform tasks in support of farm work such as taking food to field laborers. Yet girls also supplemented family income by working for manufacturing industries, particularly in sewing jobs. They embroidered at home as young as five years of age; by age nine, some of these girls worked part-time at sewing workshops [*talleres de costura*] or took piecework home.

Boys were also expected to perform some domestic chores such as keeping the courtyard clean, or fetching water, but were more likely to be put to work in agricultural activities, most often in sugar cane fields. They performed tasks ranging from general farm work to cutting cane at ages as young as eight. Only one was a helper in a small business: he swept a *bodega.*

The myriad family obligations of children did not prevent them from attending school, even if sporadically. In fact, with the exception of a rural-born girl raised in a small village by a *familia de crianza*, all the informants received some schooling, even if in some cases it was only for a year or two.

In their second decade of life, most informants remained in their hometown, but some had moved to larger cities. Three had moved to San Juan and one to Ponce, in Puerto Rico; six had come to the U.S. mainland (five had made it straight to *El Barrio* while one had made a three-year stopover in the Boston area working as a farm laborer). Only one, Emiliana, had moved from a small town to a rural area. Living within large households continued to be the norm, although a few had established independent households upon marriage.

During this decade, the division of labor by gender became even more structured. While females continued to be responsible for household chores and for helping out on the farm and/or in family occupations, they increasingly started seeing the world through the eye of a needle, either as seamstresses pedaling sewing machines at workshops [*taller de costura*], or as mistresses of the needle at home—but only after completing domestic chores. Their handiwork was destined for the manufacturing markets in the United States, a response to the growing demand for finishing tasks offshore—sewing buttons on soldiers' uniforms, embroidering women's dresses and blouses, or engaging in such time-consuming tasks as making wedding dresses, scarves, and gloves. Although women's work continued to be concentrated in the apparel industry, a few women had also started work in other manufacturing industries such as tobacco, and in domestic work in private homes or hotels.

The nine women who had married and/or had children by the end of this decade stayed at home, though only one referred to her occupation as "housewife." While available opportunities to make extra money—such as caring for infants and doing laundry—were avidly grabbed regardless of marital status, the majority derived their income from selling sewing pieces and embroidered work [*labores para vender*], individually or through a *taller*. Only one woman held a white-collar job, as a secretary at City Hall [*Alcaldía*] in Cataño.

Males continued to work in agriculture, particularly in the sugar cane industry, cutting cane in the field or processing sugar at local plants. Yet they also engaged in a variety of manual occupations: at docks, at factories (jewelry, painting, welding, repairing), in small businesses (as bread makers in bakeries, serving customers in *bodegas*), or in the restaurant business (as busboys). Permanently attuned to work availability, the men who are now aging in *El Barrio* needed to be versatile, embracing opportunities to freelance as janitors, vendors, carpenters, and construction workers and, when everything else failed, delivering milk and water to private homes. Given the myriad demands on their lives, it is not surprising that formal education had been totally abandoned by this decade. Yet, for those who continued their schooling despite hardships, there were important differences by gender: of those making it to eighth grade, females outnumbered males (40 percent versus 20 percent).

By the time the informants were twenty to twenty-nine years old, twenty-seven of them had left their birthplaces for farm work or were living in urban centers. Sixteen had made it to *El Barrio*, either directly or through intermediate stops in other urban centers or in New York City boroughs. For those who remained in Puerto Rico, life offered few surprises: most continued to live in large households, either with their families of origin or with their own spouses and children. With three exceptions—a man who defines his occupation as a *"mecánico dental,"*[16] a women who was a teacher, and another woman who owned her own sewing workshop—most continued to hold unskilled occupations.

In Puerto Rico a discrepancy continued to obtain between the occupations of males and females. Men were employed by sugar cane enterprises in a variety of occupations; by small factories as mechanics; by small businesses; by construction industries in chores like mixing cement; and by the docks in loading tasks. During slow times either in the economy as a whole or in the industry that employed them (what the informants call *tiempo muerto*, or dead time), they hired themselves out for any available job. But they also resorted to their own creativity to make a living in the streets: for instance, they offered chopped wood, or fixed *piraguas*[17] for thirsty passersby. One man sought job security by enlisting in the army.

Women continued to concentrate in the sewing industry either at home or at small factories, sewing clothing and repairing sugar sacks for sugar cane plants. But they also worked at other factories or as domestics if single. Some married women whose husbands did not allow them to work outside the home, or who had made that decision on their own in order to raise their children, still sold products of their labor, particularly sewing, in the open market. With the exception of some training on the job, no education was pursued by the informants still living in their place of birth.

By the time they were between thirty and thirty-nine years old, another thirteen informants had left their birthplaces for the U.S. mainland, most of them coming directly to *El Barrio*, and a few through step-migration, by sojourning either in the United States or Puerto Rico. For example, Susana, who was born in a small town called Toa Baja, was raised in the much larger town of Bayamón and then moved at age fifteen to Cataño, where she remained until age thirty four. In the course of the next two years, she moved back and forth between Puerto Rico and *El Barrio*, where she remained for the rest of her life.

With the exception of one male and one female who lived alone, the pattern of living within a large household—with blood relatives or people who were "like family"—continued. The needle continued to absorb women's time when they were not occupied with house chores: they sewed by hand at home, or sold their labor at sewing factories. The exceptions were one teacher and a few who worked as domestics in private homes or hotels. Men combined work in the sugar cane industry with employment in other sectors of the economy: construction, transportation, and commerce. One was enrolled in the army, one bought a store. None of those remaining in Puerto Rico continued school.

Only three informants remained in their birthplaces after their next decade of life (forty to forty-nine years). A man in Barceloneta, who shared his life with a wife and eight children, was engaged in construction work. A male truck driver made a living at Ponce's docks. A never-married woman alternated between living on her own and with a niece.

There was only one informant who had never left Puerto Rico by age fifty. Most informants had by then settled in *El Barrio* or were making their way there. Some continued to hover around the land where they would grow old. The Rivera's, a couple in their late sixties, were first lured to retire in Pennsylvania by a daughter. A few, like Marta, continued to go back and forth between New York and Puerto Rico well into their seventies.

The elderly of *El Barrio* own a history. Without understanding their life experiences as they came of age in their society of origin, we cannot understand how they grew old in their society of destination. The historical period in which they grew up, as well as the political economy of Puerto Rico and its linkages to the U.S. mainland, affected individuals' life courses. By tracing their personal experiences from birth to their move to the U.S. mainland within that context, the informants help us visualize a world in which place of origin and place of destination are intimately interconnected.

PART II

Growing Old in *El Barrio*

In the case of immigrants, making an inventory of the past includes reflecting on the experiences growing up "there," in Puerto Rico, and "here," in New York City where the informants are growing old at present.

How has migration to a low-income urban enclave in the 1950's affected growing old in *El Barrio* in the nineties? Part II continues reviewing the informants' personal histories within a broader historical context, this time New York City rather than Puerto Rico. Housing and employment issues provide a perspective for understanding (1) the work patterns of the study population from the time of arrival in *El Barrio* through retirement from the labor force; and (2) how the structure of opportunity at the time they entered the New York City labor force influenced their work trajectories and the conditions under which they will grow old.

The informants' premigratory experiences influence their employability in the ethnic- and class-stratified labor markets, which in turn determines the structure of opportunities available during their working years. This background to their present lives enhances our understanding of the informants' personal experiences and limited upward mobility, but also of structural characteristics of the larger society, primarily the process of formation of immigrant niches in the labor market.

THREE

"Buscando Ambiente"

Searching for a Better Life in a *Barrio* in the United States

> I am walking to Emiliana's house when I realize that I have
> visited informants, eaten, shopped and used *El Barrio* but not
> behaved as an anthropologist there for a long time. The
> streets speak to me about a world different from the one I in-
> habit. And yet there is so much familiarity. I remember cor-
> ners, stores, buildings, people. The anthropologist in me re-
> minds me that, even if I dressed or walked differently, I would
> never pass, that I do not belong there. And yet I do. Am I
> going to start doing fieldwork all over again? Why do I keep
> coming to El Barrio? Does it remind me of my own first im-
> pressions when I came to New York from Argentina for what
> I thought would be a short stay? Where else do Emiliana and
> I meet in the realm of experience?
> —Author's diary, February 9, 1993

The personal experiences shared by Emiliana and the other informants
portray those of many Caribbean immigrants arriving to the mainland
United States during the middle of the twentieth century. A political-
economic and historical framework is needed to understand how their
personal experiences of uprootedness reflect larger trends. The regional
economic imbalances and the mobility of labor and capital (Wolf 1984;
Sassen 1990) informed the northward pull characterizing the informants' life prior to migration. What are the informants' perspectives on
the attraction of the financial and industrial center that invested in the industries employing them before moving to New York? How can these
personal histories be cast within the social histories of a specific geographical space, *El Barrio*?

Thirty-seven percent of my informants arrived between 1950 and 1954. They were not alone: an estimated 80 percent of Puerto Rican migrants to New York City arrived during that time (Centro de Estudios Puertorriqueños 1979). New York was the Mecca for thousands of people:

> And by the early 1950s, *El Mundo*, San Juan's leading Spanish-language newspaper, was referring to New York simply as *la urbe*, the metropolis, exactly the way people all over the Empire referred to Rome in its heyday. . . . New York, during the great Caribbean exodus following the war, became the metropolitan center and migration goal for Puerto Ricans of all kinds, but especially for the very poor. People from everywhere in the Caribbean flowed into New York in greater numbers, in fact, than into any other city in the world. But the Puerto Ricans have been the most conspicuous. (Mohr 1982, xi)

Those whose voices speak to us also came *buscando ambiente,* searching for a life better than the one they had—better in terms of the standards against which they measured their life in Puerto Rico. However, by the standards of New York, they had landed in a U.S. *barrio,* a low-income urban enclave peopled by a large number of Latinos. Unknowingly, they would contribute to the construction of *El Barrio,* a geographical space, as an extension of Latin American history. In *Puerto Rico in New York* (Galíndez 1969), it is asked:

> Where do you establish the differential borders between North America and Latin America? Where do they blur? It is in the Latin American proletariat in New York that Latin America truly begins. Latin America has displaced itself, breaking itself into pieces on geography; it has extended its human borders within the United States, but only on condition to earn, by itself and against all odds, its difficult right to history. (1969, 7–14, my translation)

The stories that follow describe the lives of a Latin American proletariat in the U.S. for immigrants who put down roots where they first landed. While living in a *barrio* conveys the image of not prospering in the larger society, there is no consensus among the informants as to whether they have done "better" or "worse" as they compare lifestyles in Puerto Rico to those in New York, more specifically, *El Barrio.* What were the stories that they told about coming? What was common and what different about their first experiences *buscando ambiente?*

Emiliana's Migration and First Year in *El Barrio* (1948–1949)

"What a Good life! You Were Never Out of Work, Never!":
The Good Life Was at Home

Emiliana was satisfied with life in her place of origin. Smilingly, she tells me: "*Mire, si en casa, a Dios gracias, estábamos muy bien en casa*" [Look, at home, thank God, we were doing well at home]:

> At home we did not suffer, never, for nothing. At home there were all kinds of grains, we harvested for the year. Either him [her husband] or I went to town, we took maize to grind [*moler*] and we brought back sacks of flour. The rice we harvested, we took it to town to shell the grain [*desgranar*] and we brought it back without shell [*cáscara*], in sacks. . . . At home you did not suffer for anything . . . because there were all kinds of vegetables.

Since she thought she had a good life in Puerto Rico, Emiliana was not curious about other ways of being, unlike many informants:

> I do not know how the situation was here [in the mainland United States]. Because at home [in Puerto Rico] there was everything. He [her husband] worked and I worked, I sewed, I did all kinds of work. He worked outside, and at home. I had workers at home so he could work outside and at home we lacked nothing.

To evaluate a good life, and conclude where it was better, she uses parameters from her region of origin to assess life in the United States. She claims, for example, that in Puerto Rico there was no need to hold on to a steady job in order to put food on the table:

> There [in Puerto Rico], there was food of all types and here [in the United States] you have to buy everything. There we had everything. The only things we had to buy were oil and meat.

When she finally migrated, she did not do so to make better for herself but for a member of her family:

I did not come looking for a better future because I had a good life there [*no vine buscando ambiente porque ambiente bueno tenía yo allá*]. I am poor no matter where I am, but there I was better off than here. Because there my husband hired people to work the farm, the farm gave you everything you planted.

"She Had to Look for Her Future, Because We Had Ours Already": Emilana's Daughter in Search of a Better Life in New York

In Puerto Rico, Emiliana was raising her family in a way that pleased her: hard-working children who helped parents make ends meet:

Ay! Daughter of my soul! That girl tore my life apart when she came, I could not rest. She was what we most loved at home. She was the first child, and she was vivacious and good, very, very good. She helped her father a lot.

Having been frustrated in her own hopes about education, Emiliana struggled to support her daughter's focus on education rather than marriage:

There was a man in love with her, who was a fool and wanted to order her around [*gobernar*]. . . . He did not want her to go to school. And I told him: "She will go to school, because I decide [*ordeno*] what she does." He said: "But in school another man will fall in love with her." So I told him: "It does not matter, she is only fifteen, and if someone falls in love with her, she will not love anyone [she will not reciprocate] because she is studying." Well, it got to a point that he distanced himself from the house. It was good that he did that, the best thing he did. Because she continued going to school even if he did not want her to.

But the constraints of culture conspired against her wishes, and Emiliana was confronted with the greatest challenge people face upon migration: how to alter their life circumstances "here" (in Puerto Rico where they were presently making a life) by being "there", by making "better" somewhere else (in her case in the United States). This immigrant dilemma opens a Pandora's box: as possibilities for change open up, the rules of the game also change considerably. Her daughter's boyfriend's persistence helped Emiliana realize that, in order to extricate her from his pressure, she would have to send her daughter to the United States, where she thought more options would be available to her. Reconsidering her resistance to previous efforts by her brother-in-law to have her husband move to *El Barrio*, "I told him that I did not want him [her husband] to come, that I wanted him to stay with me always."

The next time a ticket was sent, Emiliana artfully replaced one potential migrant with another:

> Yes, at that time many people came here and I did not want her to come but I was disgusted with the men who fell in love with her and would not let her go to school! In one year, he [the daughter's boyfriend] came back with the same foolishness, so . . . his brother [her uncle] said: "Send her over here, that here [in New York] she will work or study, or both, whatever she wants." And I told her: "Look, they are sending a ticket, do you want to go or stay here?" She said: "Ah, I will go with my uncle." I told her: "There, you will work or study." "Ah, so I will go to study," she said.

Emiliana wanted her daughter Vidalina to pursue an education according to her own wishes and not succumb to the pressures of a possible marriage partner. So she offered Vidalina options she could not have in Puerto Rico by giving her an opportunity to come to New York. Vidalina welcomed having choices, although she pursued a course different from the original plan: she worked first, then married, and later studied. But as a migrant, she embodied a collective paradox: while she had yearned to obtain an education "there" (in Puerto Rico) before marriage, she ended up doing "here" (in New York) what she was being pressured to do "there"—she got married.

Emiliana soon learned that her design for her daughter to complete an education before marriage would not materialize in either place.

> When she came here she was fifteen. She was a young lady already [ya es-taba señorita] and the uncle brought her to finish her studies here. And she went to study at night and to work during the day and that is how she got an accountant's diploma [contadora]. She came to study and work. She started to work immediately, she did not go to school. She fell in love with a man. He was known to the family; I did not know him. He was a neighbor of ours there [in Puerto Rico], but he lived

here [in New York]. He was very nice, but he was a drunk. He sent word that he wanted to keep her, and that she felt like loving him, because he was a good man, he had work, . . . well, thousands of things. Both of us were against it. And I asked her if she wanted me to send for her, and she told me not to.

For Vidalina, having options helped her sort out her own priorities: to work, then to study. In between, she fell in love and sought her parents' blessings to marry:

"Mother, this man loves me very much, he wants to marry me and I want you two to come so you can meet him, because if you do not get to know him I will not marry him and I will lose the opportunity because he is a very good man." It is true that he was very good, of a good family and everything, but we were not in agreement. I sent word that no, no, and no, but then his brother [her uncle] sent word that we should come to see for ourselves that she was in love and did not want to leave him.

The daughter's decision to stay was a great blow to Emiliana:

When she fell in love, I sent word for her not to fall in love, because she had come to study and look for a future [*buscar ambiente*] and that I hoped that she searched for a good *ambiente* [a good future].

Vidalina's case helps clarify the meaning of *ambiente*. When asked after telling the story what *ambiente* meant, Emiliana replied:

Ambiente means that she had come to complete studies so that she could get a diploma in something good. She needed to look for her future, we had ours [*el de nosotros estaba*]. But she wanted to come because she wanted to get a better future than the one she had at home.

Yet, as we will see below, although *buscar ambiente* is an individual decision, it encompasses whole networks.

Migrant Networks

When her daughter's decision to marry and stay in New York seemed final, Emiliana gave in. By then both her husband and older daughter had ties to New York. To follow the daughter, the trip needed to be financed by burning bridges back home:

> When we saw [realized] that she would stay here, we came immediately [*nos vinimos al hilo*], we sold everything we had and we came. We sold the house, we sold some animals, and we left. In 1948 we arrived here. Jovito and I came with a baby of six months, and the boy was six.

As is quite common with many migrants, what was planned as a temporary stay became a permanent move:

> Ay. We came here without thinking because I had my daughter here! Leaving Puerto Rico broke my heart [*me costó el alma*]. What's more, if it wasn't for my husband, I would not be here. We came to stay at the house of his brother for a while. . . . No, we did not come thinking we would live here, we did not think about that. We came, but we did not come to stay. "We will go, and we will come back" [we said to ourselves]. And we have been here for forty years!

Emiliana arrived at the house of her brother-in-law, who lived in an area heavily populated with Latinos:

> I came to live to 102nd and Madison, to 1476 Madison, in *El Barrio*, next to Mount Sinai Hospital, right there. Mount Sinai Hospital then was a little house, you should have seen it!

Just as she was settling into her new place, Emiliana's mother fell sick, forcing her to return to Puerto Rico for six months. But by then, Emiliana was trapped in the migrant's dilemma: she was neither "here" nor "there," but caught up in a network dispersed across the island and the mainland.

Unhappy about having to share living quarters with her brother-in-law in New York, she agreed to return from a long visit to her sick mother in Puerto Rico on the condition of having her own home:

> And then they bought an apartment here on Fifth Avenue, in a very good place, I liked living there, I am still sorry, because it was good living there: on 114th and Fifth Avenue. They bought a very good apartment, very large, very comfortable. It had a good balcony; it had everything. So we stayed there to live until we came here [to a housing project on Lexington Avenue].

"Here and There, Everywhere It Is the Same Thing": Comparing Life in the Region of Origin and of Destination

Emiliana compares what is better "here" and "there." There, she did not need to buy food and had access to most of her relatives. Here, her children obtained an education and she raised a caring family. In an attempt to corroborate my initial understanding, I asked Emiliana if it was better in New York at the time she arrived from Puerto Rico. She answered:

> No, because I liked it there. And all my family stayed there. Everybody there works with the government. . . . My children also studied here: one as a secretary, another as an accountant, another for trains. . . . But the children that I raised [in addition to my biological children] did not want to study. They got married before their time.

Emiliana attempts to solve the migrant's riddle—which place is better?—by philosophizing about global circumstances affecting the human condition:

> And I thank the Lord that I am here but, as I am told, things are bad everywhere. No matter where, because what you see here, is the same there, and over there, and over there. In some places worse and in some places better, but it is almost always the same thing.

And yet, she concludes that one should return to die where one was born:

> I tell you the truth, I am here because he [her husband] does not want to go to Puerto Rico, but if he tells me let's go, I go. But he does not want to go there. . . . He is afraid of planes. . . . I know that one day you die wherever you are. That is it. We should be living there now, because there is where we lived.

Jovino, Emiliana's husband, disagrees with her:

> *Jovino* [reassuring her]: If we were there, we would have died a long time ago.
> *Emiliana* [angry]: No, we would be dead here. [Turning to me] He wanted to come. He was crazy.
> *Jovino* [protesting]: You cannot compare the situation in Puerto Rico and here, Emiliana.

Emiliana: Why not? When you have what you need . . .
Jovino: When I got sick from the heart, if I had been in Puerto Rico I
would be dead already!
Emiliana [disagreeing]: You would not have died! There they operated
people from the heart as well. I had pneumonia there and I am still
alive!

Turning to me, she closes the argument with a sigh: "Look, in life I
am never satisfied."

"Looking for Something": The Social Construction of Immigrant Experience

What were the social experiences of the other informants as they moved
to *El Barrio?* Why did they come to *El Barrio?* What were they looking
for? How did they go about finding it? As they reminisce about their life
course, these become major existential questions. Packing up and leaving has left a huge imprint in their minds. Ninety-five-year-old Luz María
repeatedly tells me that she came to New York in 1922. She then elabo-
rates her answer with particular details, such as: "December 12, on the
ship *El Ponce.*" When I act surprised at her memory, she confirms the
centrality of the event by letting out a mocking laugh: "*Estoy vieja pero
loca no*" [I am old but not crazy]. Forgetting means losing more than
memory.

Everybody came looking for something, whether for themselves or for
members of their network. The informants' experiences were also similar in two other ways. First, they had never planned the move to be permanent—they saw migration as an exploration of change. If life was not
good in Puerto Rico, if something crucial was lacking in their region of
origin, it was only natural to attempt to change life circumstances by
searching elsewhere. That is what *ambiente* means—pursuing a better
place than where one is at present. What these informants share is their
hope that *El Barrio* would be a place where life conditions were better
than in Puerto Rico—although "better" means different things to different people. "Better" need not be limited to economic considerations:
"para mejorar condiciones de vida" [to enhance life conditions], *"para*

buscar trabajo" [to look for a job], *"para buscar fortuna"* [to seek fortune], *"para vivir mejor"* [to live better]. Second, informants also share the belief that the move was about social connections, rather than solely individuals, regardless of who actually initiated the move.

Searching for *Ambiente:* What Are Migrants Looking For?

The phrase *buscando ambiente* carries the understanding that the move enhances a person's opportunities and control over his or her future. But is *ambiente*, in and of itself, a "thing" one can own, trade, weigh against other "things"? *Ambiente* takes on a meaning in becoming rather than in being. In searching for it, the individuals make of it whatever their present needs are. *Ambiente*, thus, is not a tangible good, but rather becomes transformed into a good during the search for the better, and thus embodies an existential problem of the human condition. Searching for *ambiente*, then, needs to be understood as a social construct.

The informants searched for *ambiente* for a variety of needs: money, education, family reunification, change of lifestyle. Most talked about households where combined incomes were insufficient to support all family members; they needed to leave either to ease the pressure or because they felt compelled to provide for the household.

Although migration became one among many economic strategies, in weaving their stories, the informants placed more emphasis on the social than on the economic side of the equation. Thus, *buscando ambiente* was a network, rather than an individual, strategy to cope with economic constraints. There were different ways to do this.

One strategy was for youngsters to leave on their own. Many stories confirm that the economic situation was such that not all household members could be supported:

> I lived with my mother and three brothers. Things were bad. . . . I came hidden in a ship. Some friends who were sailors took me out. In two months I had a job.
>
> —Juan

Another strategy to ease the pressure on the household was to send youngsters to be raised by relatives elsewhere:

I was born in Puerto Rico, in Bayamón. We were seven siblings, two females. Here I came to live with an aunt in New York. She raised me. My
parents died and I learned afterwards.

—Telesforo

A third economic strategy to help network members was to enter into
new networks. This was the case for Matilde, who came to the United
States in 1925 to get married:

It was very hard [to make a living]. And I was the only one that could
earn anything [for the household], since I was the oldest child. I had
two younger brothers. And I remember that I asked . . . because it is
often said that we are the chosen ones from the belly of the Mother [the
Virgin Mary]. And from the little house of my parents, one day I spoke
with God. At that time, I did not know who God was, nor did I know
who Christ was, or anything. But I spoke to Him and I said: "Oh, God,
it is said that You are so great!" I will never forget those words that I
said: "They say You are so great! Why don't You get me a spouse so that
I can help my parents, so that they do not die of hunger!" And then,
from one day to the next, in about two weeks, I went to visit a friend
and there I found a man who had been in love with me for four years.
He was nineteen years older than I and I had never given him the opportunity to get near me. I was lucky to be in that house on the day
when he had gone to take leave because he was going to the United
States in two weeks. So as soon as the lady of the house went to fix us
coffee, as if he were a machine, he asked me in marriage. And, I would
have never thought I would do this in my life! I accepted him! Then it
was all automatic. He came. I did not see him again until two days before he left. As soon as he arrived in the United States, his sister wanted
to give me the ticket because she knew my family and he refused. He
wanted to bring me over when he had work. When he worked, he sent
me the ticket, and gifts and everything. He came in May and I came in
September of 1925. I went to live with his cousin for thirteen days.

If Matilde came to start her own family here, others, like Telesforo and
Julia, came already with families, looking for better work conditions:

I worked in Puerto Rico but there was no security: here they deduct for
security. I took my wife and five children . . . and when I finished with the

army [*me licencié*] in 1948, I came to see if I could change the situation. I wanted a change of life.

—Telesforo

At that time, my husband worked at the Ministry of the Interior, he was a mason's master [*maestro albañil*]. When the Partido Popular went out of power, he lost his job and said: "Well, I will go there, with my brother-in-law, to the north!" He started to work in Long Island.

—Julia

Ambiente does not necessarily result in increased income. It could also, as in the case of Emiliana's daughter, translate into other valued items such as an education. In those cases, an individual's motivation to study is combined with addressing a family need:

I came to progress, to have the possibility of having a profession that I could not finish in Puerto Rico. In spite of my intelligence, I had continued to advance to help my parents who also worked and my brother who were all in Puerto Rico. When I came here, I was in [my] third year [of high school], but since I always helped my mother, my aunt told my mother: "Look, how Dora seems to be intelligent, as you tell me." So my mother told her: "I would like my daughter to be a nurse here and it is difficult. Those who have no money cannot advance. I will send her there if you want her." I started high school here with that goal and I could never finish. I am still struggling to complete my diploma here!

—Dora

More often than not, there was a relative at the other end—in *El Barrio*—who lured the migrant with images of easier access to education, employment, or health care—for example, Emiliana's brother-in-law, Florentino's sister, or Monchito's daughter:

I came because my family was doing well here. I did not get along with my father. When my mother died, my sister came to visit. She told me that I would do better here, that I could find good jobs. She filled my head up and I came.

—Florentino

We came from Puerto Rico to Pennsylvania in 1985 and from Pennsylvania to New York in November 1987 because Pura was sick and my daughter was here.

—Monchito

Pura's story illustrates the many instances when the migrant follows a network member who, as the initiator of the move, is the one *buscando ambiente*. To cope with the network member's unaddressed need, the response is family reunification. This is the case for Emiliana, who followed her daughter, or Luz María, who followed her husband:

I came in December of 1922 because my husband was already here since August of the same year. He was born in Arecibo but worked in Vega Baja as a factory bookkeeper. He decided to come in August of 1922 because he lost his job and could not find one. He came in a ship called *Sagua*.

Finally, some of the migrants' reasons for coming in search of *ambiente* might be found simply in a change of lifestyle. For women, it is often the need to escape cultural constraints at home. In the case of Emiliana's daughter, it was the pressure from a traditional boyfriend who did not believe in women's education. For some other women, like Aurelia or Augustina, a divorce opened up the possibility of a new life, either on their own, like Aurelia, or with relatives, like Augustina or Josefa.

I came to New York in 1946 looking for a new life [*buscando nuevo ambiente*] and to make more money. I earned seven dollars a week in Mayaguez and twenty-eight dollars a week in New York.

—Aurelia

All my children were born in Puerto Rico. There I divorced my second husband. He was a womanizer [*muy enamoradizo*] and my oldest daughter sent for me. I came to live with her on 102nd Street.

—Augustina

I lived in Santurce until I separated and I came to the United States in 1953. I came because I had no *ambiente* and I had a bad life [*me daba mala vida*]. I came alone, with the two youngest children and I left the two oldest and with time I brought them. I have lived here since 1953. In

Puerto Rico, I had six children and my oldest daughter was married already. I came to live with a sister on 113th Street.

—Josefa

For yet others, like Dora, a new life opened up when they were forced to confront the racism of nonsupportive networks:

I came here when I was sixteen, alone, in the ship *Ponce.* I was sent for by my white aunt to continue my studies and work to help my mother. We lived on Madison. I came to study nursing and to work with children and the sick. I went to school at night. I have people in the family who are white and others who are colored. Well, not as much as my cousin who had blue eyes and was blonde. Anyway, it is not our fault to be like this. So my cousin was against me and another girl. We had to wake up and leave breakfast as if we were servants. I suffered a lot. And then they ate and left everything for us in the evening and they threw water on the food on the stove so we could not eat it. And one day I told her: "I will tell you something, I never ate like a pig at home, because my mother never treated us like pigs, so do not treat me like a pig." Then she asked a cousin, a brother of hers, to hit me and I told him: "You hit me and I burn you." Sometimes I would go to bed without eating. To make ten dollars I needed to work seven days. My aunt sent three dollars to my mother who worked in the Hospital Miramar. The white daughters threw me out because I was black [*prieta*]. A woman I met at Jehovah's Witnesses took me to a fire station where I was allowed to sleep, thanks to a Latino fireman. When the firemen were on duty, I would sleep in a bakery. Then I went to the home of Rafael Hernández, the composer who had a radio shop, to see if I could sleep there. Then I went to live with Mrs. Rose. She did not treat me as a boarder. She helped me as a daughter to continue working and studying. As time passed, I got better jobs. We helped each other. I continued sending money to my mother.

—Dora

Human curiosity about the infinite opportunities they imagined existed under the glittering lights of the town, and endless comparisons of lifestyle between "here" and "there," also attracted Puerto Ricans to the New York shores. Some informants simply say they came *"porque había más ambiente aquí"* [because there was a better future here], or *"por curiosidad"* [for curiosity], *"porque todo el mundo se venía"* [because everybody came].

Regardless of the stated reason for the move, within the many-layered meanings of *ambiente* was the search for a better fit between individual and society than the one the prospective migrant had at present. Social relationships anchored "here" and "there" became the means to implement these individual projects. They were also central in the migrants' immediate need to construct spaces of opportunity as they resettled and became key to establishing a household and obtaining a job. The informants came with their own family, lived with family members, or boarded with people they knew from home and made new acquaintances through the old ones. Even those who lived alone had network members come and go or even established networks with strangers:

> When I came from Puerto Rico, I lived on 116th Street. I gave *tecatos* [drug addicts] food. There were a lot. I left them here [outside the apartment] alone and went to work. At night I gave them a blanket to cover themselves. In the morning they shared the coffee I gave them. They would tell me: *"Mama,* do not worry. If somebody touches your door, we kill him."
>
> —Josefa

Migrating to make better can also be couched in network terms: *"para estar más cerca de la familia"* ["to be closer to family"], *"porque todos se iban a Estados Unidos"* ["because everybody went to the United States"], *"para criar mejor a los hijos"* ["to raise the children better"]. Migration, then, ties rather than separates and, contrary to what is often believed, becomes a mechanism to solidify social links. Migrants search for *ambiente* in *El Barrio* because that is where their established networks are.

Searching for *Ambiente* in *El Barrio*

Ambiente is a unit of measurement for individual life chances: one can have more or less of it. The migrants disagree on whether their life conditions or those of their networks were good or bad in absolute terms before they left searching for *ambiente*. While Emiliana felt the "good life" was at home, most informants were not so satisfied and tended to believe the geographical change would enhance their life chances [*mejorar las condiciones de vida*]:

I came to look for a better *ambiente*.

—Julia

I was doing well in Puerto Rico but when you are young you want to do better.

—Telesforo

Since geographical displacement is involved, moving as a strategy to get *ambiente* implies a comparison of regions to decide where it is geographically better to be: in Puerto Rico or in the mainland United States. On this point, one also needs to be specific: where in the United States? Visualizing a "there" inhabited by people one knows becomes at least as important as where one lands.

Those whose stories we've heard about searching for *ambiente* are now old. *Ambiente* also invites comparisons among different stages of the life course: did they have *ambiente* then, as they arrived? Do they have it now? And, the most central question of all: Did they get the *ambiente* they were initially searching for? Have they done better?

Some think they have:

I have not done badly because at least I have two checks and if I get sick I go to the Veterans [Hospital].

—Telesforo

Some think they have broken even:

When I came to this country I brought nothing. I get what they give me. I resign myself in life [*yo vivo la vida tan conforme*]. I am satisfied with God and the saints and the Virgin because thanks to God I do not lack a plate of food. I have my health and enough to pay electricity and gas. I am satisfied.

—Josefa

Others think they have not done better:

We came here to look for fortune, to feel better, but it turned out that it is worse. In Puerto Rico, I left my house, a large lot [*un solar bien grande*] where I had everything: maize, beans, bananas, sweet potato, *guanábana*, orange. . . . I left behind around a dozen chickens, I left two big pigs. I left a cow with a calf. I left all to my father.

—María

Many people believe that because one lives in New York one has money and lives like a king. Well, no, on the contrary, sometimes we live in misery or worse because sometimes the money one gets, like I get a check a month, is not enough for anything.

—Aurelia

Ambiente may just be a reminiscing mechanism of the migrant to evaluate and compare life course stages that result in space and time equations, such as depicted in the model below:

$$\frac{\text{Here (where I am growing old)}}{\text{Now (older)}} : \frac{\text{There (where I grew up)}}{\text{Then (younger)}}$$

All the migrant needs to add in this model are qualifiers such as "better," "the same," or "worse."

The answer to these personal queries is intimately tied to what was "here," in *El Barrio*, at the time they arrived that structured the opportunities available to them. Some needed to clarify their vision of the "here" by making repeated trials. Migration was rarely a once and forever event. People moved back and forth between New York and Puerto Rico, sometimes for extended stays at either end to visit relatives, to get over disappointments, to clarify where life was "better." For example, Antonio came for the first time in 1945, returned to Puerto Rico in 1968, and has made three or four other trips there since then. He is still unsure as to where he will grow old. For those who could not engage in these cyclical moves, imagining future and past scenarios became a way of dealing with the existential riddle of the present in the streets of *El Barrio*.

The Collective Experience: Emiliana in Trends and Figures

Emiliana arrived at the time of massive migration of Puerto Ricans to New York at the end of the Second World War. Galíndez portrays the dramatic increase thus: "If we take the median annual migration of the 1920–1929 period, it could be said that during the war the volume of migration grew by 145%, that in 1945 it reached 314%, and by 1946 to 515%" (1969, 23). The study population is representative of the general population of Puerto Rican migrants to New York City (Centro de Estudios Puertorriqueños 1979): although the distribution of the informants' time of arrival ranged from 1910 to 1969, about two-thirds of the study sample arrived between 1940 and 1960. Informants tended to arrive after the peak migration years, about forty percent making the move between 1950 and 1954. By the 1940s, when Emiliana moved, about half the females (54 percent) and 40 percent of the males had made it to *El Barrio.*

Emiliana was forty-six years old when she arrived, contesting the stereotype of the young migrant. By the fifth decade of their lives, the majority of the informants (over ninety percent) had already come to *El Barrio.* While a little over half of them migrated between the ages of twenty and forty, 31 percent of the females and 27 percent of the males migrated between the ages of forty and sixty.

The reasons for migration varied by gender: females reported family as the primary reason (40 percent), with work as the second; males favored work (30 percent) over "looking for a better life." But, whatever the reported pull, as Iglesias (1984) puts it, the newcomers sought company. If there was nobody they knew upon arrival, they soon found somebody to share quarters with. This strategy not only provided company but also helped land a job, as those who were already there could act as brokers in finding jobs for newcomers. They could also orient them to manage the urban landscape and translate the language of the new land. Migrants surely needed the help since knowledge of English was restricted to that learned in Puerto Rico.

> When I came to this country I knew how to say in English: "paper, pencil, book." *Agua* they say water. Yes, beans, bread, I knew how to say many things when I came here, that was because there they taught it [in Puerto Rico]. Later, they stopped teaching English.
>
> —Emiliana

> Those were the days when nobody spoke Spanish here. I got lost and could not ask anybody. When my husband-to-be wanted to take me to his

sister's apartment where he had the furniture he had bought on sale. But I, with those morals that mothers in Puerto Rico teach you, said to myself: "I will not go with that man because even if I know him from Puerto Rico and he is a good person, here in a country I do not know I will not be alone with him. He tells me his sister is at home but . . . if she is not?" So I offered him to go by myself and he told me I would get lost. He was right: . . . I got lost. I wanted to sit and cry because I had nobody to ask for directions because my English was bad.

—Elsie

Not everybody came directly to *El Barrio*. Antonio, for example, went to Chicago where he had family, worked in a restaurant for a year and a half, and then came to New York. Six other informants went first to other places in the United States, but the majority came directly to *El Barrio*, the port of entry, where their networks were:

The attraction of the city is fantastic; the Puerto Rican does not come to the United States, the Puerto Rican comes to New York. And almost all of them come to *El Barrio*; then they spread out. (Galíndez 1969, 29)

Residential segregation in *El Barrio* had to do with structures of opportunity available at the time of migration: people one knew directly or through network members lived there and were the brokers to the new society and jobs. The neighborhood, a dense settlement of Puerto Ricans, thus embodied the meaning and the context of daily life for the informants. But at the same time it symbolized the social issues confronted by New York City and the United States and, was a continuation of Puerto Rico, and of Latin America, in the United States.

Indisputably, individuals moved to make something better of their lives, whether it was their economic situation, family reunification, or curiosity about other ways of being. Yet, despite individual reasons for the move, migration as a process was a family strategy that involved network members back home and in *El Barrio*. Holding on to a geographically unbounded social world (Basch, Glick-Schiller, and Blanc 1994) enables persons to live "here" while referring back to their hopes "there." As migrants, their lives would forever become split between a "here" and a "there," blurring life-course reminiscing about a "before" and an "after." Their arrival would also be divided by their social class in the region of origin (Flores 1987), and further divided by their class placement in the region of destination: in looking to "make better" within the borders of *El Barrio,* they would train for marginality in the larger society.

The world of work provides another window to explore the social construction of marginality at the local level. How do the informants' stories tie into the neighborhood's history and available structure of opportunities? In the next two chapters, I will explore the social history of *El Barrio* as a context for the intricacies of exploitation and hope in the hard world of work that the informants encountered.

FOUR

"El Barrio de Nueva York"

From the 1950s to the 1990s

In Old San Juan was The New York Department Store; in Harlem, New York, is the San Juan Restaurant. The window of a coffee shop in old San Juan bore a sign advertising a flight to New York; the sign in a barbershop on Lexington Ave. advertised La Isla Encantada. "The Enchanted Island" was supposed to be New York, but it turns out to be Puerto Rico.
—Wakefield 1959, 17

The City's face and its future, with some of its scars enlarged, are there in Spanish Harlem. . . . All the big issues are there, along with the poor, the jobless, the dropouts, the violent, the desperate, and tens of thousands of normal people.
—Sexton 1965, vii

When Emiliana came to the United States, she came directly to *El Barrio*, the port of entry for the massive postwar (1945–1950) migration of Puerto Ricans. Like those of many others who made the move during those years, Emiliana's experiences of daily life[1] in *El Barrio* provide a lens to understand the different transformations experienced by sending and receiving society within the same time period. While Puerto Rico became the target of industralization plans orchestrated in the continental U.S., the displaced migrant was incorporated into the unregulated labor markets of New York's Harlem through ethnic brokerage mechanisms.[2] Thus, the influence of social class and ethnicity in a person's life is told through the history of a neighborhood.

Settling in dilapidated neighborhoods left behind by older immigrants, Puerto Ricans added a new flavor to the city's ethnic mix. East Harlem became Spanish Harlem. The consolidation of these ethnic communities represented the end point of a process that began with the acquisition and economic restructuring of Puerto Rico. (Portes and Rumbaut 1990, 228)

From Immigrant Broker to Established Settlement: *El Barrio* from the 1950s to the 1970s

By the 1950s,[3] *El Barrio* was already an established *colonia*,[4] a residential enclave transmitting information that would allow newcomers to cope with their most basic needs: housing and employment. Being able to make connections to a previously established social network—knowing somebody who had already made the trip and could effectively function as a broker to the larger society—rendered the available structure of opportunity meaningful and contextualized daily life for years to come (and, in the case of those growing old in *El Barrio*, throughout the life-course of the immigrant). It was a two-way street, since the new arrivals provided news and invigorating links to a place they were connected to through frequent visits and concern about its political fate.[5]

The population of East Harlem changed considerably between 1950 and 1957: in terms of ethnic composition, the percentage of Whites decreased by 10 percent;[6] the non-White population remained about the same at 18 percent; and Puerto Ricans increased by 10 percent the already dense Latino population.

In 1950 the census tract in El Barrio's center (bounded by East 106th Street on the south, Fifth Avenue on the west, and Park Avenue on the east) was almost 75 percent Puerto Rican. The five surrounding census tracts contained about 50 percent Puerto Ricans. A very large percentage of this community's non–Puerto Rican population consisted of other Hispanics, reinforcing the maintenance of the Spanish language and a Latino lifestyle. (Meyer 1992, 69)

During the 1950s, the Hispanic section of East Harlem extended from 96th Street to 116th Street, where it merged with African-American and Italian districts. The area east of Third Avenue, once an Italian neighborhood, was by then primarily Puerto Rican. Wakefield concludes:

"Most strictly speaking, then, Spanish Harlem today means most of East Harlem except for the upper or northern section" (1959, 17).

Housing conditions in East Harlem encountered by newcomers from Puerto Rico and African-Americans from the Deep South were much worse in the 1950s than in earlier decades of the century.[7] According to Wakefield: "By the mid-1950s, the roughly mile-square area of East Harlem was one of the world's most densely populated areas" (1959, 235). Housing was so scarce that many people, like Emiliana, "purchased" apartments—which, according to Padilla, meant obtaining a key to the door through

> a transaction between someone who needs an apartment and either the building superintendent or the tenant occupying the premises. It is defined as the sale of an apartment rather than as the payment of a fee, and among recent migrants it is accepted as one of the ways a private apartment can be obtained in this city. (1958, 4)

During the 1950s most people lived in tenements,[8] but these years also marked the beginning of urban renewal building projects.[9] From the perspective of the policymaker, these projects were designed to ease overcrowding; from that of the residents, they were designed to accommodate yet more people in less space, obliterating the known landscape (Wakefield 1959, 17) and separating families (Mencher 1958; 1995). Many a family had its members dispersed to all five boroughs.[10] Structurally, the rise of the projects replicated the tenements.

> How ironically close are the aims and results of the projects and the tenements! Both were built to accommodate the greatest numbers possible; both were built with mass-production, standard design, with no reference to the world they stand in. And yet the tenements were built for the benefit of landlords; the projects for the benefit of "the people." (Wakefield 1959, 244)

The efforts at urban renewal bypassed the human element, increasing the sense of alienation and dislocation from social and economic reality already experienced by people in East Harlem. The federal public housing law completely overlooked the household composition prevalent at the time (Mencher 1995), which was not necessarily a function of traditional culture but of the circumstances of migration into East Harlem.

Newcomers would seek an established household until they secured a job and settled independently. They all became "part of the family," unrecognized by a rigid legal structure, unaware of the impact of housing and employment on household organization and income.[11]

By the 1950s, the available jobs were in the unskilled and semiskilled sectors in factories and service industries such as restaurants, hospitals, laundries, and households (Padilla 1958, 6). According to the 1960 U.S. Census, the unemployment rate in East Harlem was 9 percent, as compared to the national rate of 3.7 percent. By 1966, 10.9 percent of all males aged twenty to sixty-four were out of the labor force, and the teenage unemployment rate was 25.1 percent (Los Amigos del Museo del Barrio 1974, 10).

In the 1960s, long-established Whites continued to move out, and Puerto Ricans and African-Americans continued to move in at a steady pace. By this decade, only 14 percent of the Whites were Italian, mostly elderly. Sexton provides the following ethnic breakdown:

> Puerto Ricans who have given it a Spanish accent (41 per cent), Negroes (38 per cent), Italians and others (21 per cent). In fact, eleven percent of the White population was 60 years of age and over (East Harlem Committee on Aging 1964) in the sixties. East Harlem is coming of age. (1965, 9)

During the 1960s and 1970s, growing public acknowledgment of long-unaddressed needs was voiced by community development activists of diverse ideological persuasions and tactics, ranging from accommodation to protest. Grassroots associations, organizing around issues of housing, occupied buildings and storefronts in *El Barrio* (Los Amigos del Museo del Barrio 1974, 10). About one hundred agencies later joined ranks, carving out sections of East Harlem (Johnson 1974), to successfully avail themselves of federal resources under the policies of the "War Against Poverty." Largely financed by antipoverty programs,[12] the new resource structure helped residents voice issues that affected their daily existence, such as public sanitation (Hamill 1973), and attempted to make the electoral process work for them. Although, unlike the immigrant groups that preceded them, the Puerto Ricans still held a transnational view of politics,[13] by the late 1960s, Puerto Ricans either joined Democratic clubs directly[14] or influenced ethnic politics indirectly. Yet, what engaged some informants in political participation was the vividness of local issues—such as housing and employment—and their belief in the importance of their participation from within *El Barrio* to address change.

From Transnational Migrant to Ethnic Enclave: *El Barrio* from the 1970s to the 1990s

Historically, East Harlem agglomerated the newest immigrant arrivals and segregated them residentially by ethnicity. These trends continued to be the norm in East Harlem during the 1970s and 1980s, as Puerto Ricans concentrated in the east and south and left the north and west to African-Americans.

In 1970, there were about 163,000 people residing in East Harlem (Johnson 1974), a decrease of 17,000 from 1960.[15] The Latino component (primarily from Puerto Rico) had increased to half of the East Harlem population, while a third were African-Americans from the South. Of the Whites, Italians outnumbered other nationalities and were overrepresented among the persons over sixty-five, a large proportion of whom lived alone and were female.

At that time, East Harlem continued to house a relatively low-income population, with the exception of three middle-income, high-rise projects that altered the urban landscape of the southwestern corner of the area along Fifth Avenue and the western blocks of East 97th and 96th Streets. The urban renewal policy implemented in the 1950s had by the early 1970s resulted in

> thirteen public and cooperative housing projects [that] shelter 53,000 people, not all of them originally natives of East Harlem, while two-thirds of the population continues to live in overcrowded tenements, inadequately protected by post-war rent control law. . . . Only a small fraction of tenement dwellers are admissible to public housing today. (Stewart 1972, 57)

Jobs available to the East Harlem population were concentrated in the service and manual sector. Only about half the population was employed, mostly men, and the percentage of the reported non-working population, mostly women, was higher than in the general population (Johnson 1974). When these figures are interpreted within the context of eco-

Do you want to know what I did here [at home]? I had my son's children, my son had a job that did not pay that much. You have to defend the life of your people and your own. So I took coconuts and made coconut jam, but a lot. I made coconut sweets and cod fritters. Look, I made platters big like this. I gave them to the children, and they sold them in La Marqueta[1] . . . they sold them outside. . . . There was a woman who had her shop inside . . . who said they were taking her customers away . . . and the policeman chased the children off. So I told them: "Do not worry, that tomorrow I will make more, and I will not violate any laws.". . . This I did in addition to working. I have never figured out how much I worked, I have never gotten tired, this is how I am. You can tell me something and I do not tell you I won't do it. I look for a way to do it. Look, I went with the two boys, one carrying fritters and another sweets. The policeman was there waiting for us. He asks me: "Are these your children?" I tell him: "These children are my grandchildren and I will tell you something, these children do not go inside La Marqueta to sell, and they have told me there is a policeman that wants to chase them away, but I will tell you something: I do not have a selling license. My license is that they are in school and one has to buy them clothes and shoes and I do not live off welfare, I have to work for their food and clothing. Because what my husband makes is not enough. And I will not go to welfare to waste my time, so I will leave them here selling, and nobody will bother them, because they are not bothering anyone." Look, the policeman told me: "Leave them around here." And I told him: "In a few moments, they will sell the food." In a few moments, they sold it!

The Tenth Job: Sewing Flowers at Home

And now that I am old, three years ago I learned to do flowers. Do you want to know how I learned that? I went to a wedding and they gave me one flower and I said: "Hum, how pretty it is! I wonder how you make it?". . . So would you believe that I undid it and that is how I learned? . . . And I learned how to make flowers! Look, I have learned many things, but [she] who does not learn is because [she] does not want to learn or because [she] does not have time or because [she] does not apply herself."

Working for a Living: The Experience of the Ethnographic Sample

To understand Emiliana's and the other informants' experiences more fully, we need to examine their work lives from within a historical and political-economic framework. How were Emiliana's stories similar to or different from the cohort's experience of the workplace? How do those experiences help us understand the meaning they invested in work? Does an inside understanding of the articulation of this labor force in the labor market enhance our comprehension of the historical period in which they were growing old in Spanish Harlem?

The informants' career trajectories during the years they worked in the local labor market clearly reveal an important point: everybody worked in one way or another. This migrant labor force showed an amazing perseverance in looking for a job and finding one. Their stories speak of resiliency and planning for the future:

> I worked making lenses for reading glasses and I had made a list of what I knew how to do [for the time] when I retired.
>
> —Telesforo

Most worked for a salary in the formal economy:

> I always did well here. I have always had jobs. I did everything. First, I worked in restaurants, then in repairing and painting boilers. I have worked as a super for the last twenty years, first with the City, in Metro North, until they retired me. I have been with this building [on 97th Street] for the last twenty or thirty years.
>
> —Florentino

The majority of informants worked at unskilled occupations in a variety of industries:

> I worked in factories. I worked at Macy's in good fancy jewelry, what they called rhinestone. That is why I use lenses. I also worked at St. Regis Hotel for nine or ten years. Then, in Flower Fifth Avenue Hospital with a salary. I was a volunteer for six years, first in the cafeteria part-time and then downstairs full-time. I worked on liquid diets and nutrition for abnormal

children. I worked there for over twenty years until I retired at age sixty-nine in 1982.

—Dora

Opportunities for mobility were sometimes restricted to the same industry:

I started packing, cleaning tables, cleaning the leather and such until I learned and I got to be an operator, you see? I learned to sew and then I had some more opportunity.

—Julia

Knowledge of English was perceived as a strategy for advancement on a par with other acquired skills:

Lucky me that I could learn some English, but I could not work at any other thing [than factory work] since I had no preparation.

—Julia

Lack of English proficiency was an obstacle to exercising citizenship in an environment characterized by work exploitation. María, for example, might have obtained benefits from the union (Local 25) had she read her job contract, but,

I refused to learn English. I lost them [the benefits] as an idiot [*por boba los perdí*]. I also lost my job contract.

The informants' experiences differed in terms of job permanency. Emiliana, for example, changed jobs seven times while she worked in the formal economy. Others had very stable work lives—Julia, for example, who worked for forty-two years at the same job, or Dora, who worked for Flower Fifth Avenue Hospital for over twenty years.

They varied, as well, in terms of the length of time they worked in the formal economy. Some, like Rosario, retired early for health reasons:

When I turned fifty I was already feeling bad so I stopped working.

Others waited until retirement age to stop working in the formal economy. And yet others worked past retirement age: Florentino, for example, started his story by saying: "I am retired . . . I work."

Many informants worked in the informal economy. Some did so throughout their lives, like Josefa who did laundry for neighbors as a means of supplementing income from welfare, or Emiliana, who sold food to help raise her grandchildren. Others earned money after retirement. Telesforo, for example, who retired at sixty-two "to get my retirement pension in case I died," fixes discarded radios and sells them; Juan guards the entry to illicit businesses.

Some women had no experience in the paid labor force before migrating:

> In Puerto Rico I did not work because in those times, women got married and men did not allow them to work. At home they had to wash, iron, cook, mend. I worked a lot.
>
> —Julia

All female informants found jobs upon arrival, with the exception of one: despite Julia's intentions, she was unable to work in a formal economy that provided no child-care. This constraint did not deter her from combining government subsidies with income earned informally:

> I stopped working when I got married [in Puerto Rico]. I lived there until I separated and came to the United States. I came with two [children] and, in time, brought the other two. I came to live with a sister on 113th Street. I came here to look for a job, but since I brought four children I could never find a job and they gave me public assistance. I could not work because the children were small, and I went on welfare. I never worked outside of the house. . . . I had to take them to school and watch them [*velarlos*]. When I brought the other two I got my own apartment. I could live on welfare and I did laundry and ironing and with that I made a living [*me lograba la vida*]. When the children grew up I stayed on welfare because I started to get sick.
>
> —Pura

But for the rest, to work was an honor, while to be on welfare was an indelible mark of social inadequacy:

> And that is what I tell my children, that work is an honor, even if that is not how the world sees it, but it is how they should see it. I have worked

even when I was sick, crying hard [*llorando a lágrima viva*], but I never skipped work.

—Emiliana

Success in landing a job often related to one's connections, whether family, friends, or political brokers:

Olga Méndez's [an elected official] father-in-law helped me get into hospitals to take nursing courses.

—Dora

Connections were embedded in systems of reciprocity where the more fortunate aided those with fewer connections in obtaining occupational training and securing jobs. That help included training for occupations in demand in the current labor market, such as sewing; understanding the city's transportation system; and circumventing hiring practices that favored U.S. citizens. Emiliana is against job discrimination among Latinos:

Do you think that I walked little? I went near Jamaica here in New York, looking for work for me and looking for work for all those who came from Puerto Rico and everywhere. Here I looked for work for some people who came from Colombia, and I thank the Lord, because they did not give work to anybody who came from there. I do not know why, so I took them, I only spoke for that woman and said: "I have her living at home, she has no job and cannot pay me and here I bring her so that she is given work, so she can pay her rent in my home, because she did not pay me anything, she wanted to pay, but had no money." The same day they hired her! Yes, the situation was difficult, and they did not want to hire those who came from abroad. I said they were Puerto Rican and they hired them. . . . To Puerto Ricans they gave work as soon as they arrived, be it day or night! The ones they did not want were from El Salvador, Colombia, Peru, all those places from there, they did not want to give them work. Us, they did, because we belong to the Americans, yes.

I taught them even the few words that I knew of English, and also I taught them to sew in the electric machines . . . all those who came, I had my machine and I sat them to it saying: "Come, pay attention, so that you get a job sewing.

I tell you, I taught them everything. They came from Puerto Rico, sometimes I would take three to work and they would hire them, one to cut thread, another to sew buttonholes, and another to fold. That is the way I taught people, because my husband and my brother-in-law taught me.

I would tell them: "Look, at this stop, look, write it down, this is where you get off, you go out here, and there is no work here, so you get back on the same train, and you continue going downtown." Because you had to show them where was downtown and where was uptown, and you know that they got lost! They got to Brooklyn, around there. I took everybody to work!

For these working-class households making a living in *El Barrio*, being employed while raising a family required a twenty-four-hour-a-day continuum of work that demanded energy, creativity, and sharing of tasks.

Life is all work. My husband came at three and I left to work. Nowadays most people have a grandmother to help take care [of the children]. I did not have anybody to care for them. I worked from four to twelve. I got up at seven for breakfast and school. Then I fixed lunch and left dinner ready.

—Dominga

Informants distinguished between the economic and social value of work. Work is an individual activity that generates income. But work is also taking care of a family. Caring for a family constrains one's present lifestyle.

The place where I lived before was fine—it had three comfortable rooms. But when I brought the kids [children of her stepson], I had to switch.

—María

Caring for a family also represents a good future investment:

Well, I had and I did not have, because I have my children . . . because once your children end up being educated, hard working, respectful, they study, that is happiness. . . . Thank God, I have two children now, I have grandchildren, they do things for me, they always come, they want to know how I am. If they have something, they bring it to me.

—Emiliana

I raised my six children here in New York, as poor children. In those times, one had no money to buy toys, but I had them in the living room playing with boxes filled with candy, and they would run around and in that way, they were raised and they studied what they could.

—Matilde

Matilde was among the women whose husbands expected them to stop working outside of the home upon marriage:

While we were preparing the wedding, he told me at once: "If you accept to live poorly, you will not work outside [the home]. I want my wife to stay at home." I started to think and said to myself: "*Ay bendito*, how will I help my parents?" So I told him calmly: "Look, my son [*Mira, m'hijo*]: I will tell you something I had not told you before. I asked God to help my parents and now you tell me I cannot work. How will I help them?" "I will help you send them money every week," he said. "But that will not solve the problem." So I started to work. When their needs were met, I stopped.

—Matilde

Although Matilde worked until she could meet her family obligations, and then stopped at her husband's request, other women went back to work only after separating from their husbands:

I worked in beauty. I got married and the fights started right away. He did not want me to work, he used to say that the woman is of the house [*la mujer es de la casa*]. I had seven children with him. When we divorced I went to work.

—Rosario

Families, however, were not restricted to the informants' children but to all members' consanguinal or fictive ties wherever they resided. The informants' contractual obligation to their networks ranged from sponsoring travel, to securing jobs, to finding them living quarters:

Around the fifties, forty-eight or fifty, I brought my mother. She lived with me but then I got her an apartment because I liked to live alone and because she had my brother with her and I did not like the things he did.

—Dora

So we saved enough to send a ticket to my brother who was eighteen. I brought him here and immediately he [her husband] got him work in

Brooklyn in a factory. Since he knew about carpentry, that is where he started to work. We sent money together to feed my parents and sent one ticket to my father, who came in November. Then we lived with my sister-in-law in a large house on 388 Manhattan Avenue. My mother came in March with a seven-year-old child. Thank God both of them were working soon. He got a job in a hotel folding sheets and such. So then they could get their own apartment because there were three working already. So he [her husband] told me: "Well, no more work. Now, any [extra] need they [the parents] might have, we will share because they can now cover their needs.

—Matilde

Earning a living, then, was not distinct from taking care of one's connections and reaffirming one's rights to reciprocity:

I never hired anybody to take care of my children, no. My husband worked at night, and I worked by day, and he took care of them [the children] by day. And that is the way we did it. And that is the way we crossed each other, he took care of them, took the girl to school and went to sleep. At three he got up to pick up the children from school, yes. And I came, I cooked and we ate, then back to work. No, we shared life very well!

—Emiliana

I rose at dawn, I did my work, I took them [the grandchildren] to school, I came back, I went to work, and if I had none, I would pick up piecework at a factory. But I told them [the grandchildren]: when you get out of school, you wait for me up here. And they did that, they waited at my house, thanks I give to the Lord, God of the Armies, because God has been so good. And, one way or another, I worked, and I went to see my mother every year, if she fell sick, I went three times a year to see her, so she did not suffer. That is how I was.

—Emiliana

So that she [my oldest daughter] could work, I raised three of her children, and three of my son's.

—Emiliana

I came here because an aunt on my mothers' side came here to progress, to help her children she had there [in Puerto Rico], most of whom graduated. So I came to live with her and she helped me a lot so I could start by living at her house. Many of us lived there in her apartment, about seven rooms. And as she worked cleaning government offices, all of us found work soon. My first job was in men's pajamas in a factory at a time when I still did not dare speak English. There I made little, little, little [money], but the point was to make enough to help my aunt so I could stay there. And in those times with ten cents you traveled across New York. . . . I started to work because my mother struggled for us. . . . My father was a train operator [*maquinista*], and there was a landslide and he died, and my sister and I were left, and my mother always worked in a clinic with doctors' uniforms. It is hard when you do not have a person. . . . I started school. I worked to make a *peso* daily. I worked Sundays to get eight or nine *pesos*. Do you know what that is? Then she [the aunt] would give me the bucks [*chavos*] for the subway, and she would send some money to my mother, and she would keep the rest, and she manipulated all the money, and I went to school at night. When I went to the [political] workshops, I got interested, I found out that I wanted to struggle and to learn and my goal was [to get my nursing diploma, but] I will die and I will never get my diploma! Nevertheless, all the jobs I had after the factory were in hospitals and I retired from a hospital.

—Dora

Even at times when some women were out of work, households could apparently be supported without their cash contributions. According to the informants' recollections, although earnings were meager, they were sufficient to afford housing and other living expenses in *El Barrio* in those times:

One made fifteen *pesos* a week, but everything was cheap then. You could get a house for twenty-four *pesos*, twenty *pesos*—not like now, six hundred, seven hundred *pesos* in rent.

—Matilde

So I went to a multimillionaire who asked me three *pesos* a week [to live there]. The refrigerator we had was like this and it had a little box inside and I had to buy the ice and then she would put in her milk. And there was only one bathroom. It [the house] had four floors and today it is a project [there is a housing project there].

—Dora

Emiliana: There [where they lived, on Fifth Avenue and 114th Street] . . . everything was beautiful.
Jovito: We paid thirty-four dollars a month.

Work was a means of asserting one's place in a social environment and thus meant a combination of earning income, maintaining social ties, and rooting oneself in *El Barrio*. A person's identity was defined occupationally, socially, and spatially:

The mother of my nephew lost her mind and gave him up and I took him to welfare. So a *sin vergüenza* [scoundrel] in the welfare office, a Latina who spoke good English because she was born here [on the mainland], said that instead of going to welfare I should go to Fifth Avenue.[2] She thought I did not understand English. I asked her: "What do you mind?" [She meant to say: mind your own business.] "Ah", she told me, "so you speak English." "No, I am letting you speak so I can answer you because it seems to me you have the only job on Fifth Avenue because if you are sending me there, you must be able to get me a man to go to bed with because I have not come here to get men [*a coger hombres*] like you have." And I broke her head [*le rajé la cabeza*] and they put me in jail for a day. I told her: "You are here, but I am from *El Barrio* and I know how to handle things there. I have never left *El Barrio*." ["*Tu estás aquí, yo estoy allá, yo soy de la barriada y yo sé como se bate el merengue aquí. Yo no he salido nunca de El Barrio.*"]

—Dora

But when they came to demolish all those old houses there [, they moved us here]. They told me that we had to go live in Queens, and I told them that I would not go to Queens. Then they told me Brooklyn, and I told them that I would not go to Brooklyn! They asked me for the reasons, and I told them. And then they sent me another appointment and they wanted to force me to live in Coney Island, and I would tell them that I was not going to live in Coney Island. They would ask me why. And I would tell them that I did not live there, that I lived here. . . . I would tell them: "I want to live here in Manhattan, and in those projects down there, in *El Barrio*, because there are empty projects." They would tell me that they were filled up, I would tell them: "So when one gets empty, you give it to me, but I do not leave this area. I will leave this area, you know when? The day I die, because when I came from Puerto Rico, I came to live in this area and in this area I will stay, so if you are kind enough, you give me here in this area, because I need to live in the area that I came to live in when I came here from Puerto Rico." "Yes, ma'am, but you cannot stay where you want." I would tell them: "It is useless to have me go live where you want, because I won't; you take my apartment here, which I paid for, you have to give me [a place] where I want to live, and not where you want, because this is my house." "Ah, but we have to demolish it." And I said: "So demolish it, but you give me where I tell you I want; otherwise you cannot demolish it, because with me inside you cannot demolish it . . ." "So the police will take you out." "Not even the police, because to take me out from here they have to give me a house to live, because this cost me money and they have to give me money to buy another one, you find someplace where I want to go live, and I go." They had to give me here [i.e., the Housing Authority had to give her an apartment in this building].

—Emiliana

The informants' career trajectories need to be understood within the context of historical changes affecting the structure of labor markets in both Puerto Rico and the U.S. mainland. Their work experiences vividly show how the past affects the present: because most of them had worked at any available job before migration, they were well prepared to respond to labor market demands in New York. But by contributing to the increase in low-skill labor supply, they unknowingly reaffirmed the exploitative characteristics of the industries that employed them, such as low pay and gender disparity in earnings.

I earned ten dollars a week for forty hours of work.

—Julia

Then all you could make was fifteen dollars, sewing. You only made fifteen *pesos* a week in those times! One made very little money then. In those times, men made twelve *pesos* and women made six or eight.

—Matilde

High mobility was another labor market characteristic that affected the industries employing the informants. Often, as Emiliana made clear, owners closed factories in one location and reopened them elsewhere to avoid inspection. Workers also had minimum job security and were often left without social benefits.

Exploitation during their working years resulted in limited access to work benefits that would translate into entitlements, such as social security or pensions, during old age.

I was never left with a pension. Do you want to know what social security I am given? His [her husband]! In his pension, they add $242 for me. Nothing is mine, and with all that I worked! Nothing, so that you know. Neither what I worked there [in Puerto Rico] nor what I worked here [in New York] was counted. So that you know the crooks [*los pillos*] from there are here. In this country, there are more crooks than anywhere else. What happens is that one does not open one's eyes [*lo que pasa es que uno no se espabila*].

—Emiliana

Here there were many sewing factories and I went to sew, and [government] people asked [about work contracts] and nobody said anything, but we arrived there [one day] and they [government officials] asked us [again] and we had to say that they had not given us any papers, and they [factory owners] fired us for that. . . . That is why I did not get my social security. You know how much I should have? Five thousand dollars in earnings! And I only have $3,500 . . . because that man we worked for . . . took our money and did not put us down [report our earnings to government]. They [factory owners] did not let us punch a card nor give us that money [government contributions], they only gave us the money, no envelope, no receipt, nothing. Now, they have to give social security to anybody who works.

—Emiliana

[In the third job] I tell you, it still hurts . . . I was so silly! . . . When a man [from the government] arrived she [the boss] told us: "Be careful, do not say anything, no speaking, no speaking" [she touches her lips with her fingers]. So the man came and ordered the people to stop working, a man from the government, he did not let us work anymore. But in a few days they [the boss] called us again, so those of us who were working talked among ourselves and we said: "We will say that they are not paying us by the job" because if you worked by the job they paid you more . . . if you worked better. So the boss asked us to leave, they closed! That was the end of the job.

—Emiliana

Most workers resigned themselves to abusive work conditions, equating migration with powerlessness. Some spoke up for the human right to help oneself and one's household members, as when Emiliana encouraged her grandchildren to sell outside La Marqueta, or sheltered unemployed relatives, or volunteered for the Democratic Party:

> My son was responsible for his children because their mother had left them, so I took care of them, and I asked him [the building manager] for five rooms: upstairs we had been given four. But if not [if I did not push], they throw me to . . . look, they dispersed [*las regaron*] all my friends: some to Queens, some to Coney Island, some to the Bronx. Yes, you have to try the good way [*a las buenas se saca el cimarrón del monte*][3]: if you speak well to people, you reason with them, everybody agrees with you. And they help you! So you want to know what happened? Here I had a friend of the judge, a politician who had power [*mandaba*]—I do not know whether you have heard Olga Méndez[4] mentioned, those people supported me, because I am political too. I liked politics, . . . because I struggled. So I hang out with them, went to work for them, my daughters too, to fill out papers, to stuff envelopes and stamp them, well, I worked in the club they had at night. We helped them quite a bit and Méndez was very good to us, and Isabel, his wife. . . . If it was not for that and for . . . Danny Caballero, he worked in the courts and he helped me in all of that. . . . So with good manners I won the case and I won the apartment, you see, I am still here. Yes, you have to know how to speak, because if you do not know how to speak, you lose. Here I had my rent in arrears, I had a stepson with two daughters and his wife, I had my stepdaughter, with a bunch of girls, living with me in this same apartment. So the manager heard about it. . . . So one day the manager came here. I am a brute because I do not know English but I know how to express myself. So I told him: "Yes sir, it is true. I have the house full of people. . . . I have them here because they do not have another place and they do not have work. And they do not have a house because they had to give in their house because they were left without work, but I have them here and I will not let them sleep in the street. . . . The government cannot be against me for doing that. Because here there is no discrimination and if I do not have them here, I would discriminate . . . you have to excuse me, but I would go to the Supreme Court if I have to. . . . They will tell me that when they [the guests] find work, they can leave. And that is what they have to tell me here too.

> —Emiliana

Like Emiliana, other informants reacted to these work conditions through political activity. A few volunteered with organizations to change living conditions for the next generation, like Susana in the education field, and Petra, Dora, and many others in organizations supporting the rights of immigrant Latin Americans.

> At night, during the war, at 6 A.M., I would go to a place where I would volunteer. . . . I said: "Ay, my God, I hope Roosevelt wins the elections because the man has good principles, because we work and earn a pittance [*ganamos una miseria*] so it is good to get something for tomorrow." That is what I said [recently] at a conference: "I am enjoying what I earned" because I earned it since the war started and I worked when Roosevelt was president. One of the first persons to get social security here was I. I am one of the pioneers here, which meant I worked to have the benefits of my work tomorrow.
>
> —Dora

Postmigratory Occupational Trajectories: Informants' Experiences

Holding on to a job was, in most cases, a means of holding on to a family. What was the economic (as production) and social (as reproduction) value of work? How did the study sample distribute occupationally? How did this distribution relate to the overall economic picture for New York City and the nation? To relate the informants' personal experiences to structural issues, I first analyzed the life history material and documented the informants' occupational histories on the basis of the language they used to describe their jobs, beginning with the first job in the United States to their retirement from the labor force. My analysis revealed the following generalizations:

1. Most migrants (65 percent of the females and 73 percent of the males) entered the New York labor force after their thirties, decreasing their work accumulation toward retirement benefits in comparison to the general population, whose initial labor participation occurs earlier in life.

2. Like the general population, the majority of the sample retired between ages sixty and sixty-nine, but there are gender differences. About 20 percent of the women retired early, during their fifth decade, primarily due to health reasons; about 30 percent of the men retired late, during their seventh decade. For those continuing to work beyond the official retirement age, women tended to bring sewing home, while men

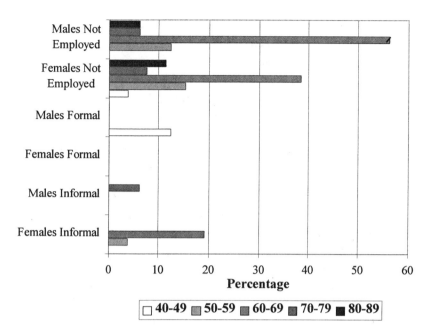

Figure 5.1. Post-Retirement Employment Status by Age and Gender (Females = 26, Males = 16)

engaged in short-term contracts, primarily construction work (see Figure 5.1).

3. The informants held a limited number of occupations during their working years in the U.S. labor force. Over half were employed in only one industry throughout their careers; only 5 percent held four different occupations.

4. The majority (76 percent) worked between three and five decades.

5. Although the sample participated in the U.S. labor force from the 1920s through the 1980s, the majority worked during the 1950s, 1960s, and 1970s. By the 1950s, almost 90 percent of the study population was in the labor force. More than two-thirds held blue-collar jobs,[5] and only two persons were white-collar workers (a male dental technician and a female office administrator). The few cases of upward mobility from blue- to white-collar jobs throughout their careers were women.[6]

Second, I classified the informants' labels according to U.S. census categories: they had worked as machine operators, laborers, and helpers. This allowed me to compare their occupational distribution to that of the population of District 11 (East Harlem) and the U.S. Census of Population for the years they worked.

Third, the same procedure was used to place the sample's labor force participation within the sector of the economy they had worked in: manufacturing and service industries. By grouping their occupational participation by industry, I was able to relate their occupational patterns to the global picture and estimate whether they had any prospects of mobility during their careers. Women were heavily concentrated in manufacturing and, within that industry, in the apparel sector. Men were overrepresented in services, although they had worked for a variety of industries, such as transportation, manufacturing, health services, construction, agriculture, retail trade, and business.

I interpreted the occupational profile of the sample's experiences within the context of economic systems of their past and present work sites. At the time my sample arrived in *El Barrio*, employment in agriculture still occupied between one-third and one-half of the population of Puerto Rico. While employment in agriculture decreased, employment in manufacturing increased.[7] Since the garment industry had employed a large number of women in Puerto Rico, it is not surprising to find them occupying the same niches upon arrival in New York City (Ortiz 1996), and the profile for the sample corresponds to trends documented for both the district and the city (Waldinger 1985). During the 1950s, the available jobs in *El Barrio* for men were in low-skill service occupations (Mencher 1995). During the 1960s, Puerto Rican workers still held blue-collar or service jobs requiring relatively little skill. Throughout the years the study sample participated in the labor force, Puerto Rican workers in New York City were heavily concentrated in manufacturing: two out of five of these workers held factory jobs (U.S. Department of Labor 1974). The manufacturing industries continued to attract a disproportionate number of New York's Puerto Rican female laborers.[8] The 1970 Census shows that in New York City, 47 percent of Puerto Rican women were working as operatives (Safa 1981, 241). Puerto Rican men were concentrated in blue-collar and service occupations.[9] Another disparity is noticeable at the upper echelons of the occupational structure: fewer than one-fifth of the male Puerto Rican labor force worked in professional and technical occupations, less than half the proportion for employed New York City men in general. Among women, the occupational distribution was similarly skewed for Puerto Ricans: only one-fourth of Puerto Rican females held clerical or sales occupations, as compared to half of all the city's women workers (U.S. Department of Labor 1974).

The structural characteristics and historical changes in the industries where this labor force worked help us better understand the impact of the economy on the cohort's structure of opportunity. Three noticeable changes during the 1960s and 1970s characterized the restructuring of New York's economy: the loss of manufacturing sector jobs, the loss of jobs at low skill levels within the industry, and the growth of sweatshops with an increase in piecework contracts for home work. While the manufacturing industry was a stable source of employment for migrant women who had skills transferable to that industry, it was a declining sector in New York City's economy. From 1960 to 1970, this sector experienced a 40 percent decline in jobs. The service and manufacturing industries, where this labor force was disproportionally concentrated, tended to have high unemployment rates and seasonal fluctuations in employment, particularly in the niches where the informants found employment. The underemployment of home workers, particularly sewing women—usually severely undercounted in surveys—was another labor market feature adversely affecting the people residing in low-income urban enclaves. A bleak picture emerged from a survey conducted in 1966:

> We find that the sub-employment rate for Puerto Ricans in low-income areas in New York enclaves is 33.1 per cent in contrast with the 10 per cent unemployment rate for the City as a whole. Indeed, in the area of major Puerto Rican concentration—East Harlem—this rate rises to 37 per cent. In other words, for every officially counted unemployed Puerto Rican worker, there are at least two others who have a very real problem in terms of labor force maladjustment. (U.S. Department of Labor 1974, 382)

The structural characteristics of the labor market and the social conditions of employment not only adversely affected the informants during their working years, but also during their retirement years, as they had difficulty perceiving accrued worker benefits as entitlements. As a labor force, they were disciplined, unorganized, unaware of the laws of the new land, and vulnerable to abuses. A common abuse, as Emiliana's story vividly demonstrates, was to fall prey to racket unions and employers that kept their earnings unreported. This situation was endemic even in the strongly unionized industries where many informants found employment;[10] they not only had no voice in union leadership to redress inequities in salaries and work conditions but could hardly believe they could articulate one.

Fourth, I analyzed the extent to which the informants had experienced permanency in the same industries to assess the impact of economic restructuring on their labor force participation. There was an above average concentration of informants in industries that lost employment during the decades they worked. The most dramatic losses were in manufacturing (from a 9 percent loss 1950–1960 to a 19 percent loss 1960–1970), particularly in the apparel sector (which suffered a 22 percent loss 1950–1960 and a 24 percent loss 1960–1970). But there were also dramatic changes during the 1960–1970 decade in the construction industry, which lost 12 percent of its jobs (U.S. Department of Labor 1970). Jobs declined by 517,000 in manufacturing between 1960 and 1984, by 32,000 in construction, by 81,000 in transportation, and by 114,000 in trade (Sassen 1990). During that period, the service sector maintained a steady growth, but not in the unskilled and semiskilled slots where the study population worked. Consolidating its central position in the globalization of economic activity, New York restructured its economy to accommodate the growth of both the formal and informal sectors:

> While overall employment and population in New York City declined in absolute terms, there was a 17 percent increase in employment in the nine major white collar industries. Similarly, while overall figures in manufacturing generally and garments particularly declined, there had in fact been a major expansion in manufacturing jobs but mostly in forms of organization of work that are not easily recorded in official figures, notably sweatshops and industrial homework. (Sassen 1990, 150)

Fifth, I analyzed the sample's career trajectory by gender. Before migration, most women had combined agricultural work with manufacturing. After migration, they continued to work in manufacturing, expanding from garments to other sectors of the industry. Men seemed to experience more occupational changes upon migration, moving primarily from agriculture to the service industries. It can be argued that women were thus better prepared than men for their new workplace, since their occupational shifts were not as drastic. Women also had advantages in terms of job availability, since their jobs were steadier and often paid more than the men's (Mencher 1995, 54).

Making a living in *El Barrio* required the efforts of every able worker whose experiences with the world of work related to the available structure of opportunities. The question asked in the previous chapter— whether they had found *ambiente*—can now be recast: Was there *ambiente* to be found? Where these older Puerto Ricans ended up is not at all where they expected to be when they migrated to U.S. mainland cities in the 1950s and 1960s, looking for a better life—*buscando ambiente*. Most believed they would return to their homeland once the goal of financial and social improvement had been attained. But the unexpected economic, political, and social obstacles they found on the mainland thwarted their efforts to create a better life and delayed their return home. Contrary to their youthful dreams, a great number of these immigrants are growing old in a mainland that seems in many ways just as foreign as it did thirty or forty years ago. Did what they found then condition the way they are aging now, and if so, how? Their current concerns will be related to social issues in the next few chapters.

PART III

Being Old in *El Barrio*

In *El Barrio*, the process of aging is in part conditioned by the socio-economic condition of the collaborators, as well as by the characteristics of the public space where they live. The lives of elders in *El Barrio* portray both their own diversity and the social issues that cut across larger populations (the aged, immigrants, Latinos, residents of low-income urban enclaves). The Puerto Ricans growing old in *El Barrio* in the 1990s provide a case to explore longitudinally the long-term consequences of residential segregation on daily life after sixty-five. The chapters that follow explore how having grown old in *El Barrio* affects the ways the informants structure activities of daily life, address health care problems, establish social connections, and allocate income within the household.

This analytical framework allows us to understand whether Emiliana's experiences typified others' experiences and to use this understanding to contribute to policy formulation. The chapters analyze policy issues using ethnographic and survey data and compare the study population to the elderly in New York City and in the United States.

| S I X |

"La Edad Es Según la Persona"
(Age Depends on the Person)

The Meanings of Being Old

I am in my ophthalmologist's office with Emiliana and her
daughter. We have come to get a second opinion on her vision problems. Emiliana desperately wants to see, but is
also afraid of medical interventions. Sometimes, she says
she will consent to surgery; sometimes, she is terrified of
an uncertain outcome. I am torn between pushing her to
be courageous, and supporting her to let things be. She is
torn between listening to her husband, who believes nothing this critical should be attempted at her age, and to her
daughter, who has learned from her mother that life is
about persistence. Emiliana's anguish over her loss of vision resonates with that of many other informants. It occurs to me that her disability means more than the actual
act of seeing, that loss of vision implies the elderly cannot
look out, into the world, when few people express interest
in looking into their lives, a stage when they are rendered
invisible to living society.

—Author's diary, May 1994

In the United States, as in many postindustrial economies experiencing
a demographic increase of the upper ranges of the age pyramid, the elderly are perceived as a population category constrained by a variety of
social and physical handicaps: for example, increased isolation, decreased
income, and deteriorating health. Policies address the state's concern
about the social costs of supporting a presumably unproductive popula-

tion. This ideology, which informs public policy and public opinion, is reflected in portrayals of the elderly as surplus populations. Cultural constructions of the aged in the United States tend to visualize their propensity to behave as consumers of goods and services, as passive recipients of programmatic actions, as receivers rather than givers. Based on these assumptions, most programs and policies are based on cost-containment of health and social services based on the disabilities and handicaps that increase with age.

The potential of this age sector to make social and economic contributions to society is either ignored or downplayed by service planners. Cultural constructs focus on economizing but disregard the economic potential of the aged. The healthy elderly are considered exceptional rarities of "successful" or "productive" aging, but their resources are understudied and remain untapped by public policy-makers.

To understand the meanings attributed to aging by a specific population growing old in a particular time and place, I will provide my informants' cultural constructs by asking: How do specific populations construe the meaning of aging? What are the individual differences within specific populations? How do individuals perceive their own aging? How does the social and cultural context affect how they view their own old age? How does the dominant social ideology of aging impact on their construction of daily life? What is daily life like for the elderly who reside in low-income urban enclaves? But I will also examine the cultural constructs implicit in public policy and contest the notion of homogeneity that disregards that individuals both age differently and cope with these cultural assumptions differently (Atchley 1997).

Moving from individual to collective experiences, I will attempt to understand aging from the perspective of individuals enmeshed in daily life within micro-environments, yet part of larger structures and social systems. To explore the human condition of aging in *El Barrio* as both a locally circumscribed cultural construct and a principle of social differentiation in American national culture, I will compare the meaning attributed to the process and state of aging by a specific population to the cultural constructions of the aged in the United States to contribute to the consideration of policy alternatives.

Emiliana's View of Aging

Like other stages in the life course, being old is structured by social and cultural values. How a particular person experiences age's challenges and constraints will thus be in part individual, in part social construction, rather than solely an outcome of biological age. Emiliana's view of aging is ageless: she emphasizes the centrality of work and of enjoyment in daily life.

"One's Life Is the Best if One Works"

For Emiliana, who has worked all her life, an idle life is hardly worth living. The aged who do not work have given up life and feel they are too close to death. In fact, she places the elderly in a continuum from "those who do everything" to those who "do not want to do anything":

> I think about aging, that there are many persons who are not even sixty and who are very discouraged, who believe they are about to die. And yet there are persons . . . well, myself! I am ninety two already and, were it not for my eyesight, I would do everything. . . . To be elderly . . . does not mean that you have no right, because there are persons who are already eighty and ninety—I have seen persons like that—that are still working, because when I was ninety, I was here sewing curtains, suits, household clothes, sewing tablecloths, cooking, taking care of everything in the house, but there are old people who do not want to do anything. I do not know whether it is because they do not want to or because they cannot, or because they believe they are about to die.

Work refers to more than simply activity in the workplace—it means being active. Productivity refers both to economic tasks and to social reproduction. Emiliana, for example, strongly believed in investing time to rear the younger generation, according to cultural traditions she approved of, even if it meant taking time away from making an income:

> Yes. I continued being here with them [the grandchildren]. I rose early and I took them to school, at fourteen! Don't believe that because I saw them big I abandoned them! And do you know where I took Sixto Junior [her grandson]? They had him in a school in the Bronx and I went to take him every day! And he was in eighth grade. Look to see if all grandmoth-

ers do that! No, not even the mothers do that. . . . I would take the kids to school and would leave them, and at ten in the morning I was already calling to see if they were at school, and that is how I learned that my granddaughter was not staying in school, how would I not know? I would leave her in school sitting at her desk, and I would come back, and she would leave as soon as I turned my back! . . . Lilian left school and . . . went to 105th [Street] and First Avenue to a club where her mother was and I would go get her and she would not want to come with me. Do you think that I have not suffered [*pasado trabajos*] with those grandchildren? You do not know how I have suffered!

Emiliana believed that a person should only stop activity due to sickness, not to age. Emiliana combined sewing at home with raising her own grandchildren and other *hijos de crianza* [stepchildren]:

No, I stopped working [bringing sewing from the workshop]. Do you want to know until what age I worked? Not even I can figure that out [*yo misma ni saco cuentas*]. I charged [for work I did] here, I was dedicated to sewing at the house and do you want to know how many children I raised? Look, I took care of Junior, I took care of Elen, I took care of Lilian, I took care of Emily, I took care of my daughter, and I took care of all those kids you see around here. I did all the work in this house, I took them all to the doctors, I took them all to school and I did everything. No, I did not work at the workshop any more. Only if they brought sewing to me, like if you brought me a suit, I did it, somebody else brought me another, I did it.

There is no retirement age for Emiliana, who cannot even remember when she actually stopped working. For her, remaining active is a sign of life, of vitality, of being in the world like a full human being:

Bringing sewing from the workshop? Until what time? Ah, I do not remember, I do not remember. I worked night and day here. And I also knitted some small things . . . I knew how to do those, I embroidered lace [*realce*] and all of that, and I thank this divine God that I could instruct myself in the works.

Emiliana believes she became old when she almost completely lost her eyesight the year prior to these reflections. Symbolically, partial blindness can be construed as a metaphor for having lost her vision in life: activity with a sense of purpose.

After that I did not work any more. Well, I was old! But I can tell you that if my vision was good, I would not feel old to work! No, I would not feel old to work, it is only that eyesight does not help me. But if I did not have bad vision, I would be here working, doing those flowers, or doing any job, sewing for people from outside. I cannot do anything for the last year. I cannot even thread a needle.

For Emiliana, eyesight is what lights up a human life; even when she is able to straighten up the house by relying on her sense of touch, she knows too well that she can no longer function independently, either in the household or in the outside world. Although she is affected by other chronic disabilities (arthritis, foot problems, unbalanced gait) in addition to impaired vision, she still believes in the value of individual effort to prevent disability from affecting normal life:

I spend the day picking up, vacuuming, dusting, I spend the time cleaning, picking up clothing that could be out of place. Even if I do not see it, I touch it, I know which is good, which is bad, which is clean, and which is torn. You have to make an effort [*Poner de su parte*]. You have to punish the body to be able to live. Because you cannot be pulled by what happens in the world, nor avarice, nor the times nor anybody. There, you hang in there. Here, where you see me sitting down, there are times that I cannot move. . . . But look! I do like this and do not say anything because . . . in the name of our Lord Jesus Christ! Like this, do you see me like this? Staggering like this? Well, this is the way I go on walking. I go look through the drawers and search . . . only to spend the time . . . but this is the way life goes by [*así uno pasa la vida*]. And you get angry when you are angry [*le dá coraje pasar coraje*][1] about what you are going through. But if you do not learn to live, you do not get anywhere.

"One's life is the best if one works," says Emiliana, because an activity—her definition of work—keeps you focused on daily life, like when one is tending to a child. No matter what it is, or where it takes place, or even how well one can carry it out, a project has to do with purpose. Only a meaningful life is worth living. Although she does not categorize her current activities as work, she at least conveys the same conviction in pursuing them: to be idle is synonymous with death.

But you learn to enjoy and suffer and, in one way or another, you live life. You are suffering, you know how to work, you look for a job and do it at home and in that way you think about what you have to do and forget your sufferings. That was me. Yes, work, because work is like a child, that you have to take care of: when you are watching that child, you do not pay attention to anything else.

Look, it is as I tell you, I do not get used to not working. I do not get used to being idle. . . . Yes, life is not bad, one's life is the best there is if one works.

Like many other elderly, Emiliana equates loss of vision with loss of independence, culturally defined as the inability to perform household chores:

If I had good eyesight, do you think I would have anybody cooking here? I would do everything! Why not! Because I . . . feel strong, I do not feel discouraged, and . . . my husband, until they sent somebody here to cook, was the one who did everything in the kitchen. He knows how to cook better than I, my husband.

It has been a year [since the couple's health condition deteriorated and they were assigned a home attendant] and he did things very well, but I tell myself that God might have sent me this in my eyes so that I rest, because I did not rest! I worked night and day here and teaching people what they do not know, because I like everybody to learn how to do housework. That is important, there are people who do not know how to prepare coffee, nor prepare a meal and that is important. . . . Nowadays, men are paying a lot of attention to that and instead of getting a girl who does not know how to do anything, they get a mature person, because she knows how to do everything. . . . I taught her [the home attendant] to cook and she is already fifty. . . . Now they say older or mature to refer to the elderly as well.

"One Has the Right to Be Happy"

Having work and companionship are basic human rights. A decrease in the availability of companionship drastically transforms the social environment. It is this social death, rather than biological death, that adversely affects the well-being of the elderly. The death of significant others has both emotional and structural connotations. But mourning loved ones, particularly one's children, is worse than fearing one's own death as one ages.

> Now I tell you, my husband is old, I do not want to see him die. I want God to pick me up before him, because that is the saddest thing in the world, to see a loved one die. And one way or another, the man is the hero of the house. I complain at night and, he gets up and comes to me.

> But thinking about old age, it does not matter, one can be happy, because in my case, if I was not mourning my daughter and my siblings, yesterday I would have sung . . . at church and at home. Last year I sang on the phone for the people who ask for somebody who can say something in a song. I sang that song called "Mother, I Am Far from You," I sang it on the radio on Mothers' Day. They asked me if I knew poetry, I told them that I knew some, and they told me: "You are ninety two and you re-member all that?" And I said: "Yes, I remember all that." And the man told me . . . "Have you talked to people in public?" I told him: "Yes, I spoke at church, and also at political gatherings."

Emiliana is convinced that the elderly, like other human beings, are knowledgeable, intelligent, and very useful to society. The elderly are normal people who can lead a normal life like everybody else: they can remember poetry, they can use the radio to reach out to others, they can be alert to danger in the household.

> An elderly person can still defend life because if there is a fire in a house, that older person [who] is intelligent . . . unplugs appliances quickly . . . and the fire is put out. I did that at home . . . there was no need to call the firemen.

Emiliana also makes a plea for remembering the human condition rather than the age of a person. The elderly, like everyone else, have the capacity to enjoy physical activity, to dance, have sex, and find ways to make themselves happy.

> I tell you that I enjoy dancing more than food, even being old as I am. *Ave María*! I enjoyed myself in the past at the dances, but I tell you the truth: that did not end for me. Now I am in mourning, but even if I am

old, I dance. I love dancing. I dance every time they play a pretty record here, but I cannot turn, do you know how I have the soles of my feet? The toes face upward, like this. . . . I knew an elderly woman who gave parties, and the first to go out to dance was her, with anybody, it [age] did not matter.

Yes, I believe all that about the elderly, and look, I also believe that an elderly man at eighty can have a woman. Yes, he can have a woman, and a lady of eighty can have a husband, because I have seen women of age who want to be with their husbands sexually. . . . But do not believe that an elderly person does not have a right.

Based on their long years of experience, the elderly should have a heightened ability to find paths to happiness and to minimize sorrow. In fact, exercising the capacity to enjoy life is not only a human right but an obligation to one's significant others.

The elderly have much to tell and have many desires to be happy, so let them be happy, let them enjoy their life. I tell my husband, do you wish to be happy? Be happy! Sing, dance, take a walk, because one has the right to be happy. Why should you be sad because you are old? No! The older you get, the happier [one should be], because God has given you the power of continuing to walk. I am old, but I go here, I go there. I want to be happy and enjoy the air, so I go get the air, so that God helps me even more to be healthy. And so on, but now the new persons [i.e., youths] have many problems in life, and get sad. But I thank God. You see me and you think that I am not sad [because] I do not show it. I always speak well [with happiness] because sorrow kills, when you are very sad, you let yourself down, and then you can drop dead, and your children lose their mother.

Self-awareness, planning for the future, and willingness to learn from their elders are values that the elderly, even those who could not attend school, can teach the young.

Age depends on the person. There are persons that have not gone to school as children, but have been intelligent and cautious. . . . It is hard for a cautious person to have something bad happen to them. . . . At home, mother was very intelligent, was always thinking about tomorrow. What she needed to do tomorrow, she prepared today. And I am like her. There are elderly who go out and cannot return home because they do not know the way. But the majority of youth today are not cautious . . . because they do not want to learn from what they hear or what they see. . . . The people from before knew more than now and yet there were no schools. Well, there were schools, but you had to pay to go to school . . . the poor people could not go to school. . . . My parents would tell us: "You do not know anything, we are older, when you get to be our age, you will see things never seen, you will astound in what you see.". . . My mother knew when it was summer, when spring was about to come; now, there are many people who do not know that, they know how to read and write but they do not know [those things].

Yet, concludes Emiliana, not all elderly are alike. Time alone does not teach; it only provides the background, the fabric on which a human being embroiders a life. But how one ages, says Emiliana, depends on the person [*la edad es según la persona*]. What do the other informants have to say?

Ethnographic Themes, Cultural Constructs

Aging is a process and thus relates to chronological time. But how the use of time is defined is a cultural construct. I will explore the use of time for Latino elderly after sixty-five, an age that in the United States signifies retirement from the labor force and entitlement to receive income benefits such as pension plans and social security programs, and medical services such as Medicare. I now turn to a comparison of the cultural constructs that inform aging policy to those of the study population.

What is the meaning of being old? Although the time and the place in which the process of aging occurs undoubtedly contextualize the experience, individuals provide a rich source of diversity. However, aging is more than an individual process of becoming in the course of time: the past informs the present. If selling their labor in the marketplace organized the informants' lives in the past, what role does this activity play in their present lives? What do they believe they should be doing at this stage in the life course? What do they actually do? What are the possibilities and constraints for doing what they say they want to do? Can we get glimpses of policy issues by looking into individual experience?

The themes that arise from an analysis of Emiliana's story relate to work, happiness, productivity, and participation in society. Her thoughts, which challenge many cultural constructs on aging, are reflected in numerous mirrors: the voices of some of the informants talking to me in private, their thoughts expressed in public settings, and museum audiences' reactions to their views.

Since work is a central value in the United States' national culture—the way we understand personal identity and connectedness, the way we structure time, the way we construe individual productivity within a collective—it is not surprising that most cultural constructs of aging have to do with work. How do they compare to the informants' beliefs about work?

The first cultural construct regarding work is the belief that the process of aging results in a marked decrease in activity and that the retired elderly are inactive. For society, work means gainful employment in the formal economy. An individual's work is translated into economic productivity for society as a whole. Yet retiring from the paid labor workforce does not mean a person is inactive. On the contrary, the informants associate activity with work. Although everybody wishes to be active, the informants' level of activity and ways of coping with disability can be placed in a continuum. Some are homebound due to disability and are very passive. Angela, a woman well into her nineties, who suffers from multiple disabilities including a serious heart condition, describes the limits on her activity:

> I go from here [the house] to the clinic and from the clinic here. When I am here, I move from the bed to the living room, and back . . . watching TV is my only entertainment.

Others who are homebound, also due to disabilities, do as much work at home as they can:

> I entertain myself doing any little thing with my hands and I sit and write and do little things [*cositas*] to entertain myself. Well, I did the dolly, I took a piece of fabric and entertained myself doing a suit for the doll to spend the time.
>
> —Matilde

And, finally, there are those who are extremely active. Here is an example of a typical day for Dora:

I wake up at 5 A.M. and I pray with my rosary and if I have to do something, I do it because I do everything in the morning. If I have laundry, if I have to clean, if I have to defrost the refrigerator. Then, before going down I pray another complete rosary. And then I go to walk from 7 to 7:30. I walk in the street. I stroll in the street [*doy una vuelta*], if I find somebody to chat with, I chat, if not I sit, I read, I buy the paper, I read *The Plain Truth*, I get coffee. Sometimes, I find people I have known for a long time, acquaintances or friends, many go out to walk early to take children to school or to shop in the supermarket, and we chat. I then call the Institute's [the Institute for Puerto Rican and Hispanic Elderly] office to see if somebody called in sick and then I go visit the people they would have checked on. I shop for them, take them shopping, bring them back home, and all of that I report there [at the Institute]. The Center [Senior Citizen Center] is open at 3:30. I go there. . . . Also these days, I have been going to church because we are praying for a boy who strangled himself due to drugs. I always go by McDonald's at 103rd Street. You ask them: "Have you seen *mama?*" There is where people who need me find me . . . for any favor they wish, ran an errand, go here, go there. Even Isabel Méndez [an elected official] says: "Look Dora up for me, if she is not at home, go to McDonald's."

—Dora

A second cultural construct regarding work is that purposeful activity needs to be remunerated. We tend to be conflicted about unpaid workers—the retired, housewives who take care of the elderly, unemployed youth. Do they really work if they are not paid? The informants say they do: they define work as being active, whether in activities related to their past skills or taking care of grandchildren so their own children can get ahead. Many work as volunteers:

I am very busy since the elections are near. I am for the Democrats. Yesterday, I went to a workshop in Astor Place in the morning where they invite representatives of both parties to answer questions. Then I went to the corner of my house on 103rd to distribute leaflets for the Democrats. People are very confused because they do not get face-to-face information.

—Dora

In the morning, I will work with the R.S.V.P. [Retired Service Volunteer Program] since I have been invited to talk and to recruit volunteers at senior citizen centers.

—Petra

By being active, the elderly respect themselves as independent actors who are more valued by a utilitarian society.

I was on vacation, but they [the management of the building where he works as super] called me because they need me. I am the only one that understands the boiler. Who else can they get?

—Florentino

My son stays to take care of me [overnight] because he says I am old. But I do my things, I do not like to be helped, I am independent. I do not want anybody here.

—Rosario

A third cultural construct regarding work is to categorize activities undertaken by the elderly as leisure or rest. The informants categorize activity as work, investing it with the same meaning as they would paid activity and organizing it according to a schedule. Purposeful activity, as defined by the informants, is awarded the same legitimacy as society's prescribed use of time. Defined as work, purposeful activity can be pleasure rather than obligation; payment can be rendered in emotional satisfaction rather than money; and well-being can be enhanced in or out of the workplace.

I went to the Church of the Good Neighbor. I prayed, I sang, I enjoyed myself. I then stayed to help take care of the old at its senior citizen center.

—Julia

I sing bingo at UPACA [Upper Park Avenue Community Association] on Wednesdays. I visit the sick. I am an active member of the Puerto Rican Institute. I go to Washington, I go to Albany. I like helping my people.

—Dora

A fourth cultural construct concerns our belief that it is up to the individual to find work, whether work is a means to earn a livelihood or pursued for noneconomic benefits. The informants disagree: work is a human right, a social benefit to which they are entitled. Thus, if there is no work available, the government has an unwritten social contract with the people it is meant to represent: the obligation to provide jobs, whether paid or unpaid, to anybody who wishes to work, regardless of age. If work is an entitlement, employment opportunities should not be categorized by age. The informants' beliefs challenge our common way of thinking of unemployment solely in relationship to youth, as if young people are the only ones in need of making a living.

A fifth cultural construct has to do with setting age restrictions upon work in the paid labor force. The informants believe that work, whether performed in the formal or informal economy, does not end at a set age.

> Today, I was very busy because I signed a contract with a manager on 125th Street to become the superintendent of two other buildings on Lexington.
>
> —Florentino

> I fix TVs, radios. I find them in the street and sell them well. I entertain myself with that, it's like a therapy.
>
> —Telesforo

> I work watching people playing dominoes and other betting games. My job is to announce the coming of the police. Meanwhile, I go out for fresh air [*cojo el aire*].
>
> —Juan

Neither aging nor lack of paid work are believed to be sufficient reasons to give up being a productive member of society.

> I work at home, on the [sewing] machine, but there is no more work for me. Work is slow now [*Estoy quieta ahora*]. Yesterday, I sewed a blouse for a lady who brings me food. She is good to me. I entertain myself a bit.
>
> —María

A sixth cultural construct regarding work is the overemphasis on income as retribution, so that work is equated with paid activity. Yet there is social value in work. According to the informants, work helps take their focus away from life's troubles.

> The elderly should look for an activity, something to do, something that helps rest one's mind, so that one is not thinking all the time.
>
> —Florentino

A seventh cultural construct assumes the elderly cannot work and therefore need assistance and entertainment. This attitude leads to programs that, based on assumptions of dependency, often infantilize the elderly. The informants however, feel that independent activity is necessary if they are to feel in control of managing their lives. Some of them resent the planned activities at senior citizen centers and other places where the elderly congregate.

> I go to Casita María [a Senior Citizen Center] but I do not like it because it is for the old [*es para viejos*].
>
> —Florentino

An eighth cultural construct is that the elderly contribute little or nothing to society. The informants, on the contrary, believe their work is useful to society.

> Youth is in the streets—they do not go to church, they do not work, they do drugs. So then, it is the old who are supporting the government.
>
> —Dora

There are various ways to engage in purposeful activity. Some informants are still engaged in the paid labor force. Some construe activity (doing/working) as housework. There are also other categories of activity that the informants engage in that transcend the private world. Many participate in church, in politics, in interest groups, and in community organizations. And most would welcome additional opportunities to become more involved with collective enterprises. For example, one informant says:

> I feel like sitting down to write and I write. I do not know why. I write on anything, on the good or on the bad. I do not know the reason why, but writing is my entertainment.
>
> —Susana

Susana[2] is one of the poets who collaborated in the staging of a poetry reading at a public museum. Although religious and spiritual themes about aging were invoked, poetry was used in a very practical way, since "*Allá donde vamos no se escriben poesías*" [Where we're going, no one writes poems]. Susana and her peers[3] used their passion for writing to form a group of resident poets in East Harlem who call themselves "Seniors in Action." Their goal is to remain active and productive, using poetry as a medium to provide social meaning to this stage in their lives—"to think about life troubles." This group of elderly poets regards the sociopolitical conditions of life for people of *El Barrio* as sources of inspiration. According to one of the members, poetry is the most important genre to express human feelings. Susana told me that the group represents the views of numerous elderly persons who continue to be active, and who do not believe that aging frees them from the responsibility to do what they wish to do in their lifetime. Ultimately, the existence of the group symbolizes that age is not a barrier.

Many informants play games, such as lotto, bingo, *bolita*, and dominoes, as a way of being visibly active in *El Barrio* as public space:

> The happiest time for us here [in *El Barrio*] is when we can have a beer and play dominoes, which is a very nice activity. . . . We play every day . . . for entertainment, to keep the mind busy with something.
>
> —A man interviewed in the street

Beyond their entertainment value, these activities help the elderly keep connected to the outside world. So when they are faced with constraints that prevent them from being so engaged—such as personal illness, crime, authorities forbidding some games, or the closing of facilities—a lot more than leisure is at stake.

> I would play dominoes all the time on 103rd Street. I had a fight . . . since then I got sicker. . . . I started to stay indoors twelve to fifteen days.
>
> —Juan

> I go to bingo . . . at 97th Street. . . . They took my purse. . . . It was my only entertainment.
>
> —Carmen

A few informants consider themselves civic activists and define productive activity as empowering the elderly and other disenfranchised populations to have a voice as social personae:

> My name is Petra Allende. I am a woman, a Puerto Rican and an American citizen born in the Island of Puerto Rico in 1920, and I'm loyal to the land where I first saw sunlight. I moved to *El Barrio* in New York City in the late 1940s and am the mother of six children, sixteen grandchildren,

and four great-grandchildren. I worked for many years in factories, in city government, and as an activist to abolish the literacy test for voters. Since 1982, I have dedicated my time to helping senior citizens, and working for the rights of senior citizens, and all those in need.

—Petra, quoted in New Museum of Contemporary Art 1994

Petra[4] collaborated with me in organizing a community program where representatives from government agencies, political officials, and the press were invited to hear the concerns voiced by the Latino elderly of Harlem.

While some suffer from disabilities that prevent their activity outdoors but, like Emiliana, remain active at home, others identify themselves with the cultural constructs regarding work, refusing to be active and becoming even more socially invisible:

To work helps, but to work you need health and *ánimo* [drive]. Maybe that is why they do not want the elderly in jobs, because they are tired and produce less. How could I work if I cannot go from here to the corner, if I cannot take a bus because I fall down? I say that the old are too tired, to do housework is enough for them. If they do not need to work, they should not work.

—Aurelia

Thus, there is diversity in the informants' approach to life regardless of their age. Those that have been "loners" as youngsters have a tendency to continue preferring being by themselves as they age, like Florentino who tells me when I call:

Here I am, watching TV. I have not gone out today [Saturday]. I am always locked up here. I have nowhere to go. I do not like to go out. I go to walk by myself. I stop at the corners. I never liked to visit, not even when I was young. I go to Santa Agonía [a church] every Sunday, I am not attracted to games or dances. I like it better like this.

—Monchito

This preference hardly means becoming socially isolated: when I walk the neighborhood with him, he stops at the streetcorners and on the sidewalk to talk to people who know him from the *bolita* (illegal lottery) game. Holding a regular paid job during the week, Florentino is hardly bored, unlike the "many elderly [who] get bored because they have nothing to do."

Because holding a work identity is so central in our culture, a cultural construct we subscribe to is that life has a dramatically different meaning once a person stops working. Yet many informants subscribe to the idea that what gives the person the strength to work is the same as what is needed to enjoy life: one needs to offset problems and to work at making life a positive experience. Being sick does not necessarily make a person unhappy. But being unhappy, Aurelia interprets from a photograph of an elderly woman in *El Barrio,* is not having food, housing, and somebody "who gives a hand," who cares—be it visitors, a home attendant, friends, or pets:

> This lady lives alone, I think. . . . She has a problem with her legs or her hips, but she is happy because she has a roof, food, and there is always a visitor.
>
> —Aurelia, looking at the photo that appears on page 169.

A ninth cultural construct maintains that the ability to be happy decreases with aging, that aging is a sad stage of life, that the aged feel hopeless. For some informants, age does matter:

> To get old . . . you cannot imagine what it is to get old [*ponerse viejo*]. One loses the senses, one gets tired.
>
> —Aurelia

> When you are old and sick, everybody is against you. [*Cuando usted está vieja y enferma, todos se le echan en contra.*]
>
> —Luz María

According to other informants, age is not a deterrent for continuing to lead a normal life, which includes having a clear vision of future:

> When you are old [*está en años*], age is not bothersome [*no son molestia*] to many people.
>
> —Monchito

> I do not feel old although I am of advanced age [*No me siento vieja aunque soy mayor de edad*].
>
> —Julia

He is thinking . . . about having a good life and prospering. Even if you are old you can think about the future; the future does not end until you die.

—Jovino, looking at a photograph of Florentino

A tenth cultural construct maintains that the elderly equate old age with end, death, despair, and absence. Some certainly do:

When we are old, we feel sick. Sometimes, we do not suffer from important things but the pains one feels of old age do not get cured ever. Since dawn, one is tired. What will happen to us tomorrow, to us who are alone, old and sick?

—Aurelia

Others, however, consider these beliefs to be related to an attitude toward life, not to advanced age:

How am I doing today? Quite well. I have rheumatic pains when it rains, but since that has no cure, I take two Tylenols and do not think.

—Matilde

Age does not bother me. [*Los años a mí no me estorban.*]

—Luz María

I can work, I get along with people.

—Monchito

This construct assumes that the elderly are not alive in a complete sense and need to give up joys such as sex, singing, or dancing. Some informants feel constrained by social prejudices regarding sex, confirming negative stereotypes:

Félix came yesterday. I do not want a man to be too friendly with me. What would people say?

—Aurelia

Others, however, maintain that happiness can actually increase with aging if they give way to their feelings.

Finally, our culture subscribes to the cultural construct that the elderly cease to participate in society at large once they are not fully engaged in the labor force. Several comments written in reaction to the museum exhibit attest to the fact that making the process of aging interchangeable with decreased participation in society can have serious consequences for the social fabric:

> All of us have wanted to tell an older person to hurry up or get out of the way.
>
> —A twenty-six-year-old man

> Our society abandons folks who are above a certain age, below a certain economic level, and outside of a certain ethnic, sexual or social persuasion. We need to STOP, reassess and change ourselves to be able to give to our children a picture of beauty and love towards elders.
>
> —A fifty-eight-year-old woman

Looking into our old age in the experiences of the elderly is a learning experience for our children and ourselves. In honoring our aged, we honor ourselves as we prepare for our own old age:

> Honor our aged. They are our teachers. They are our history.
>
> —A thirty-year-old woman

> We are a society of aging people whom our youth must learn to nurture, love and respect or they will be a generation of lost souls.
>
> —A sixty-one-year-old couple

Reflecting on the meanings of being aged provides continuity with cultural traditions:

> May we remember our culture, whether it is Hispanic or Black. We must continue to teach our young of our past!
>
> —A thirty-nine-year-old woman

And, in the case of those who were born outside of the region where they are currently aging, this continuity might project into future return migrations:

> It is very interesting to see that in a so-called first world country people would live under these conditions [the ones informants shared in the museum exhibit]. Unfortunately, there is no money but these people also lack enough education to live better. I believe there is a lot to do in this country when they [the informants] are [were] young but when they are old,

they are worth nothing. That is why Latinos who have worked in this country have to go back to their countries to be treated with dignity!

—A twenty-nine-year-old woman

Self-reflection leads to self-awareness and to politicization:

I believe my old age would also [like the informants'] be lonely and sad. One can see the rich always live better. The poor always live badly and are alone. Government should give us more consideration, us who have given our lives to the country, at the time we can no longer work and should not live so alone.

—A fifty-nine-year-old woman

School children should be taught that change is in their hands.

—A sixty-year-old woman

Beliefs and Practices in Time Use in Retirement

The informants' perceptions about being aged influence their beliefs about the impact of retirement on their self-fulfillment and level of activity. When and why did they retire? And now that they are retired, what do they actually do in the course of a regular day?

The informants retired from the labor force between their late forties and early eighties. The majority (74 percent) retired between ages fifty to sixty-nine, but four retired in their seventies and another four in their eighties. The major reasons for retirement were health conditions (almost 40 percent of the sample) such as asthma, heart ailment, and emotional problems, and having reached retirement age for the industry that employed them: eight collaborators (two males and six females) decided to stop working because "it was time," because they were "tired of working after two decades," or because they were aware of social security entitlements due to them if they left the workforce. A sixty-six-year-old female was laid off from a factory that closed down. One male, who worked in the agriculture, manufacturing, and services industries, reported retiring at age forty-eight because "he wanted to do something else": at the time of this study, he was working for a *botánica* as a clerk. After retirement, three males reentered the paid workforce while six females performed volunteer work for senior citizen centers or hospitals. But the majority (79 percent) stayed home: their perceived health problems made them feel more vulnerable to negotiate an unsafe public space.

But what do the elderly do all day? Is there diversity in the informants' use of time in daily life? Do men and women use time differently? Where do they carry out such activities? Who is around?[5] The ethnographic sample distributed their time in four major categories of activity: one related to the private space (praying, attending to pets, resting, and doing household chores), while three helped them interact with the outside world—via the media (listening to the radio, watching television, reading newspapers), the workplace (working at paid or voluntary jobs), and the social world (socializing with friends, neighbors, family, and home attendants). There were gender differences among informants regarding time allocation to daily activities: 87 percent of females performed activities in the private space, as compared to 56 percent of males. They were equally involved with the media (about 70 percent) and employment (about 20 percent), although among those working only the men were paid. Women tended to socialize more than males (57 percent versus 38 percent), but they spent more time than men in activities carried out in private spaces (67 percent versus 56 percent) and in the company of social connections (70 percent versus 44 percent).

Social Issues in Minority Aging: A View from *El Barrio*

Many minority and immigrant elderly have lower than average incomes (Population Bulletin 1995), making the idealized, middle-class construction of activities away from the workplace as "leisure" an inapplicable myth. Many are trapped at home and can hardly afford the consumer goods offered by businesses catering to the "graying generation." Those designing programs for these populations could profit from local-level knowledge about their daily lives.

The informants vary in their beliefs about aging and in their experiences throughout the life course: there is a "here" and a "there" (a spatial measurement of time) in addition to a "then" and a "now" (a chronological measurement of time). They also differ in their approach to the present environment where daily life is negotiated. In trying to explain their views and practices, I attempted to understand the national culture from the perspective of local-level culture. Their diverse practices clearly contest the cultural construct that labels the elderly as a homogeneously inactive sector of society. Holding on unreflectively to these cultural constructs about age without confronting them with local-level knowledge and practices of the aged contributes to the institutionalized age discrimination implemented by a society disengaged with the elderly. Learning more about the contributions and capabilities of older people as well as about how they respond in actual practice to policy drawn for their presumed benefit is a possible way to question the efficacy of societal disengagement from the old.

Despite their differences in beliefs and practices, my informants were similarly concerned about some policy-relevant social issues. For the elderly people I talked to, being old meant being concerned with one's health (the state of it and access to health care), social connections, and income. Their experience of these issues is not fragmented but intertwined in complex ways. How these issues interrelated in daily life had a lot to do with the social and physical environment. Thus, being old in *El Barrio* also meant articulating daily life within public and private spaces, one of the major themes of this book.

Anthropologists have amply documented the existence of cross-cultural variability in the ways people age and in their conceptions of the contributing factors to a good old age, one that they would have wished for themselves as they were growing up (Myerhoff and Simic 1978; Sokolowsky 1997a). Fry and colleagues attempt to sum up the variations found by a cross-cultural research study on aging by reference to site-specific characteristics:

> Have we found an answer? Is a good old age possible? If it is, what is it? Good and old are not by definition an oxymoron. In each Project AGE site, individuals were able to point out people who were having a pretty good time in their senior years. Yes, we have found answers, but not a singular one. (1997, 118)

Emiliana's view of diversity—*la edad es según la persona* [age depends on the person]—supports this view of cross- cultural diversity by theorizing the existence of intracultural diversity in ways of aging. Social gerontologists have attempted to explain diversity by arguing that, under ideal circumstances, older people would attempt to resemble who they were as younger people. In espousing exceptions to this continuity theory of aging (Atchley 1997), researchers have pointed out illhealth and disability as major constraints to the ability of an elderly person to continue the activity level that is considered important for the maintenance of one's own concept of quality of life regardless of chronological age. This study has found that an important constraint to a desired activity level for those aging in low-income urban enclaves is the perception of the public space as breeding danger to the daily activities of the aged. In the next few chapters, I will explore how external circumstances, such as access to health and social services, economic difficulties and safety concerns, constrain the ability of the elderly of low-income urban enclaves to continue their level of activity. It will be shown that the factors that account for patterns of internal variation within this population regarding level of activity relate to the social context—the social conditions under which they grow old and how these are played out in the microenvironments that contextualize daily life for the elderly. In focusing on these nonpersonal constraints to continuity theory, I will argue that we need to pay as much attention to characteristics of the social environment of the elderly—the non–culturally sensitive domains of the service structure, such as poverty or unsafe living conditions—as to individual characteristics—such as health status, strength of social networks, or income level. In the next few chapters, such individual constraints will be explored as the social context affecting continuity theory.

SEVEN

"Los Doctores No Pueden Curar Todas las Enfermedades" (Doctors Cannot Cure All Illnesses)

Illness of the Soul and of the Body

Carmen is desperate—her brother was taken by her nephew to Metropolitan Hospital this morning. We are talking at two-thirty in the afternoon and they have not called yet. Later on that evening, when I call to find out what happened, it is Antonio himself who answers the phone. He tells me his doctor took his blood pressure and drew blood but told him he had nothing. He would have wanted the doctor to touch his body, as they sometimes do, that he listen to his heart with the stethoscope. But, he did none of those things. He was told nothing about his illness. Antonio showed him the medicines he was taking, and the doctor added one bottle. He will have to find the *causa* of the ailment by himself. He thinks maybe he suffers from the nerves. That is why sometimes Antonio and Carmen talk about seeing spiritists or other non-medical curers. In the past, you could find them in *El Barrio* but they have moved to the Bronx and Brooklyn, they do not know exactly where.
—Author's diary, December 12, 1994

The informants differ from medical providers in that they make a distinction between illness and disease—between self- and medical assessment of health status. They also discriminate between illness "of the body" and "of the soul" when making health-care decisions. While from their perspective—the ethnomedical system—illness is the individual's perception of change in health status, for the biomedical system such change needs to be diagnosed by a physician with the aid of medical technology. And while the appearance of a *causa* signals the boundary between health and illness for the ethnomedical system, professional associations and research institutes validate clinical decisions regarding impairment.

A disagreement between the biomedical and the ethnomedical systems can adversely affect an individual's utilization of mainstream medical care. In this chapter I explore the interface between the ethnomedical and the biomedical systems through a cultural analysis of illness from the perspective of process (health-seeking) and context (congruence between models of impairment). I will document the process by which someone is transformed from a "person" to a "patient" in *El Barrio* before a condition becomes labeled as disease and thus treated biomedically. I developed a model of the health-seeking process as a decision-making tool—one which identifies the existence of a problem, diagnoses its cause, determines who has the ability to solve it, and explores culturally appropriate and network-validated alternatives (see Figure 7.1). Informants diagnose and treat *la causa* well before physicians do.

What does this process tell us about the biomedical health care system centered around disease? It helps understand that the way people define impairment and seek treatment for it might not coincide with the way physicians do. A comprehensive biomedical assessment of the patient is vital, of course, to the provision of quality care, but it needs to incorporate ethnomedical assessments of health status and need. In theory, there are at least five perspectives in assessing a person's health status: the clinician's, the person's, the clinician's view of the patient's view, the patient's view of the clinician's view, and—finally—the agreement or disagreement between those views (Helman 1994). How do we remain sensitive to culturally diverse populations if we do not integrate these perspectives?

The basic disagreement—indeed, the most important factor in effective communication between providers and consumers—is between the biomedical and the ethnomedical assessment of health status. Anthropologists point out that the basis of the difference is that the biomedical perspective abstracts disease from patients, whereas persons live the reality of their illness (Kleinman et al. 1978). The disease perspective focuses on data of clinical significance that have universal validity. In contrast, the perspective of individual illness, by focusing on personal experience, is

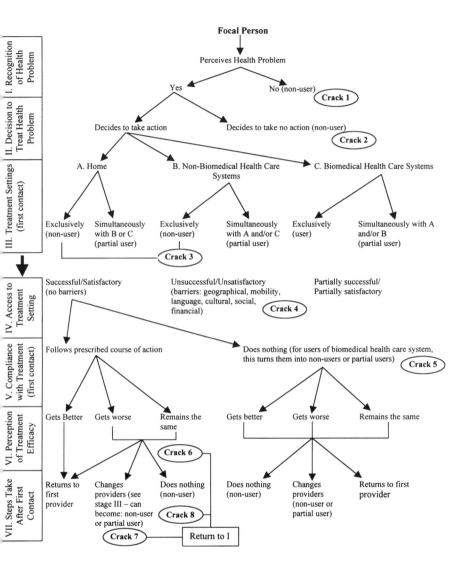

Focal Person

↓

Perceives Health Problem

I. Recognition of Health Problem

Yes ← → No (non-user) · Crack 1

II. Decision to Treat Health Problem

Decides to take action · Decides to take no action (non-user) · Crack 2

III. Treatment Settings (first contact)

A. Home · B. Non-Biomedical Health Care Systems · C. Biomedical Health Care Systems

Exclusively (non-user) · Simultaneously with B or C (partial user) · Exclusively (non-user) · Simultaneously with A and/or C (partial user) · Exclusively (user) · Simultaneously with A and/or B (partial user) · Crack 3

IV. Access to Treatment Setting

Successful/Satisfactory (no barriers) · Unsuccessful/Unsatisfactory (barriers: geographical, mobility, language, cultural, social, financial) Crack 4 · Partially successful/ Partially satisfactory

V. Compliance with Treatment (first contact)

Follows prescribed course of action · Does nothing (for users of biomedical health care system, this turns them into non-users or partial users) Crack 5

VI. Perception of Treatment Efficacy

Gets Better · Gets worse · Remains the same · Gets better · Gets worse · Remains the same · Crack 6

VII. Steps Take After First Contact

Returns to first provider · Changes providers (see stage III – can become: non-user or partial user) Crack 7 · Does nothing (non-user) · Crack 8 · Does nothing (non-user) · Changes providers (non-user or partial user) · Returns to first provider · Return to I

Figure 7.1. Hypothetical "Cracks" in the Health Behavior of East Harlem Elderly: A Biomedical Perspective. This model attempts to depict the stage in the health-seeking process as well as to identify the nonusers and partial users of biomedical care. Although this model is shown in consecutive stages, in reality some steps are taken simultaneously, especially in stage III, and bouncing from stage to stage occurs during successive contacts.

culturally relative in that experience cannot occur in a vacuum—it needs to be interpreted within a sociocultural setting.

Exploring the boundaries between the biomedical and ethnomedical systems has implications for policymaking that would enhance utilization patterns (Helman 1994). Congruence analysis of biomedical and ethnomedical assessments helps understand why some medical needs get addressed and not others and the impact this has on health care. Different cultural constructs explain the diversity and barriers that exist among different groups in their utilization patterns of mainstream medical care, often leaving medical needs unaddressed and "cracks" in a person's health-seeking process (see Figure 7.1). Thus, if utilization patterns of the biomedical system were understood both before and after people become patients, health services could better respond to actual and perceived population needs.

Emiliana

Disease and Illness

Those long nights that I spend sleepless! Those long nights! So black and somber that I do not even know how one reaches the future! Oh, my God! [*Esas largas noches! Tan negras y sombrías que ya no sé ni donde se alcanza el porvenir, ay Dios mío.*]

For Emiliana, illness means experiencing a loss of connection between the present and the future. That loss embodies the many little losses of daily life evidenced by a constant worry. Sleep is the best proof of peace and a healthy soul:

I feel a pain in my body, that assassinates my soul, because the calmer I want to be, I can't. My doctor gave me a medicine so I can sleep. I ask God that, since I have suffered so much in life, I deserve to sleep, that at least I can sleep.

Emiliana reports that, in order of seriousness, the biomedical system has diagnosed her with the following diseases: arthritis, depression (what she calls "nerves"), and vision impairment (cataracts and incipient glaucoma). Although the medical system pays more attention to arthritis, vision is Emiliana's prime concern, given its relevance to negotiating daily life: having poor vision seriously affects her life much more than the other two ailments because it increases dependence on helpers. If you do not see, you can get depressed too:

> This is the way I know who is coming, when they get close to me and stand before me. I do not know why there are times when I wake up well from here [she points to her eyes] and sometimes I do not. And I went to the doctors, and they tell me that I have nothing; that what I have, the only thing that I have is arthritis.

> The saddest thing in the world is to be short of vision. And I see you and I know it is you. But from time to time I cannot recognize anybody. Because, I do not know what is going on, some times vision is worse [*se me atrasa la vista*] and sometimes vision gets clearer.

Vision is what allows her to recognize and be acknowledged by her social surroundings. Lack of vision represents a kind of social death:

> The worst is that I am blind because if I could see I could entertain myself walking out there but I cannot tell anybody from here "let's go out" because they all have their activities [*quehaceres.*]

So eyes are far more than physical organs. In spite of the differences among arthritis, depression, and vision impairments, Emiliana experiences them as an interrelated whole—if she sees poorly, she can move about less, which affects both her emotional status, her "nerves"—since she is used to being active—and her arthritis, which is alleviated with exercise.

> Yes, I feel good . . . only vision. I get nervous when I get blinder. I cannot stay still, I have to be doing something, and I cannot go to bed early.

The elderly's lack of social visibility due to the cultural construction of activity is worsened when they suffer from poor vision. For Emiliana, seeing and being seen are opposite sides of the same coin: if you and your significant others have worked and have been "seen" by the world while in the workforce, seeing is the human right to be in the world.

> I would like to continue doing that [sewing the torn clothes]. I would ask [Saint Lucía] never to blind me, because that is the saddest thing for a

human being. Because you do not see! You do not know what you will do! You get restless, so I ask Saint Lucía that my husband never loses his vision, because he has worked so much, he has struggled all his life.

Arthritis, for which she feels there is no remedy, is made worse by an "illness of the soul," a great sorrow that affects the nervous system. For Emiliana, what made her sick of soul and worse of body was the death of her oldest daughter, whom she had followed to the United States from Puerto Rico *buscando ambiente:*

> Those muscles . . . that at night I cannot get into bed, that is from arthritis. Arthritis is a bad sickness that has no remedy. . . . She [the physician] said I had to take Tylenol twice a day.

> Arthritis is killing me. Before I started to eat, I was sitting here and I was struck by a pain [*apretones*], I thought I would not be able to eat, because arthritis is treacherous . . . and the death of my daughter, that is what I was thinking about the most.

Like arthritis, one cannot do anything about the death of a loved one but accept one's fate with resignation:

> So I tell you the truth, what was worth the most in life for me was that daughter that God took. But if it had to be [*si convenía así*], what can one do?

But, unlike arthritis, final losses diminish one's capacity to withstand changes in the availability of network members:

> I have very bad nerves. . . . I feel a sadness that makes me nervous. . . . On top of having four dead [members of the family]—that is all right because death is natural . . . but do you know what it is that I raised this son[1] . . . and this woman falls in love with my son and they left . . . and she took him [to Virginia] where he does not know anybody? Look, I spend many a sad night here thinking about that! Because one does not know who is who, right? He said he would come back right away and called from there saying he did not know when he would be back. Do you know what that is? I thought I was going crazy! Look, I tell you the truth, the death of my daughter finished me up, but it was made worse [the pain] when that boy [*muchacho*] left.

Interpreting Symptoms: *La Causa*

To understand the nature of illness, one has to fully comprehend what separates it from health, to interpret the symptoms, and to find its cause (*la causa*). Emiliana explains the latter to me:

> What is *la causa*? I will tell you what that is. Suppose I am here now, I have arthritis, right? But you have nothing, no pain, nothing, nothing, if you are fine like now when you look fine, God bless you and Christ keep you company always. All of a sudden you feel a pain in your thigh, here or there or over there on your leg, or in the toes of the feet, or in the hands, or in the head. What is that? Do you know what that is? That is the *causa*! Because now I cannot say that I have no *causa*, nor can she [the home attendant]. But you can say it because you do not feel anything. But right now, look when I wake up in bed at night even if I just go to the bathroom, I have to do like this [she demonstrates by twisting her body], otherwise I cannot get out of bed and that is the *causa* that one has and that is what *causa* means.

Some *causas* are due to age:

> They [doctors] want to operate me but I do not want to. Because you tell me, a lady at ninety-two having surgery! What can you do! [Una señora de noventa y dos años operándose, que vá a hacer!]

Other *causas* are sent by God:

> And I am not altogether blind because Jesus Christ is with me. . . . I have been a woman who had a healthy heart for everybody. Now . . . maybe God says, she has never rested, I will send her this [condition] so she rests at least some time. If not, I would be working because I am strong!

Others result from one's earlier lifestyle, either in relation to work conditions or environmental factors:

> I was told, when I was young, not to embroider *realce* at night, or take the threads off, because I was going to get blind . . . that I should not do that at night.

> Maybe it was not that [sewing at night, the cause of loss of vision]. Maybe it was that when I was a child, do you know when the sun eclipses? They

used to say that you should not look at the sun. So you want to know what I did? I looked for a mirror like this and watched it and do you know that the sun had two moons? It had a blue moon and a black moon. I watched it because I wanted to see if it was true. Yes, I watched many eclipses. The day was turned off, the sun was black and they said that the moon ate the rays of the sun. And do you want to know what I also saw? I was twenty-three or twenty-four and I saw that the night was very dark and I went to the window . . . and the sky was lit up! It made three lines, very wide. And I said: "God should guide you, I go to the sky and you go to the sea." [In Spanish, this saying rhymes: *Dios te guíe que tu guía va, yo para el cielo y tú para el mar*]. My mother said that the sky opened in three pieces. . . . I thought: "Maybe we will end now."

Buscando La Causa [Seeking for the Cause] and Barriers to Biomedical Care

Once a cause is evident, one has to do something about it. Seeking help from a physician is no guarantee of finding a *causa*:

> I have something inside the throat, I do not know where, because my throat hurts inside and up . . . sometimes it hurts there a lot, a lot! And I start coughing . . . and I feel pain inside. . . . [I] have asked for my throat to be examined and I never have anything [according to the doctors].

> They [physicians] do not find in me a cause. They only weighed me, looked at my urine, and at my blood. Then they told me that they had to give me an appointment for the eyes, but then they forgot and they did not give it to me.

One proof that physicians often do not find the cause of an illness [*no le encuentran la causa a uno*] lies in their lack of communication with the patient:

> But doctors do not say nothing to you, so I do not tell them anything either!

In addition to the inability of physicians to find the cause of the problems, there are several other barriers to accessing physician-based medical care. One is language differences between physician and patient, leading the patient to ask fewer questions:

I am seen by many doctors and none of them speaks Spanish!

Another barrier is the multiplicity of providers a patient normally consults:

I am not seen by one doctor, but by any doctor [i.e., whoever is free at the clinic].

So many years going to Mount Sinai, tomorrow they give me a male doctor, next day a woman, then a young one, then an old one, and no fixed doctor knows me. I do not like that! I went to a private doctor before. . . . When you are seen by the same person, you have confidence and explain everything.

A third barrier results when physicians fail to pay close attention to the extent to which their directions can be implemented by the patient. Often, physicians fail to prescribe treatment regimens that can be integrated into the patient's daily life schedule and social context.

You know that my son or this friend puts the cream on [at eleven or twelve at night] and I stay awake until three, with that [cream] there, with closed eyes. So I said that I will not apply it anymore, because that makes me sicker. Do you know what it is to be awake at night and with closed eyes when you have to get up to urinate? Ah! that is another thing, that I urinate a lot, I do not know why. When I cannot sleep, I feel like urinating, perhaps due to high pressure or to vision.

Prescription problems constitute a fourth barrier. Often the reason patients fail to implement physicians' directives is their experience with medicines whose secondary effects might counteract others they are taking:

I had told [my problems sleeping] to the foot doctor. He gave me small pills . . . but once I took one . . . at night . . . and next day I could not wake up, so I never took it again. Because a pill has to be for sleeping and it is logical to get up in the morning and I could not do that.

I am afraid of drugs! . . . Once I felt something in my behind and she [the physician] gave me a medicine, she said I had nothing. . . . Then I went to her two months later and she says: "I will examine your kidneys to see if you have an infection." And I told her: "How could I have infected kidneys? I have never suffered from that." She told me: "No, because the treatment I gave you could make you suffer from the kidneys." So I took the pills I had and I threw them out. Because if you have to take a medicine for something to get infected elsewhere, none is worthwhile! . . . And I know that when you get treatment for something you get sick of something else, and that is why I do not take medicines, I do not take drugs.

Finally, financial constraints associated with physician care constitute a crucial barrier to access for most of my informants:

But I do not want surgery, because afterwards they start sending you bills and I cannot pay them.

The one who made them [false teeth] told me: "I cannot fix it anymore, you need to order a new one," but now that things are so bad with Medicare . . . they are truly bad, there is no money! They [the government] say that they needed to make cuts [*que todo lo han cortado*].

Coping with *La Causa*

In the face of these constraints, how does one cope with illness when a *causa* comes up? The first strategy is to take care of oneself:

You have to take care of your body, not only with medicine. Water is medicine when you have faith. You have to take care of yourself. Look, if I were to go to the doctor each time I feel sick! Oh dear, I would have to go every moment!

Second, the person needs to make an effort to feel stronger:

I always tell everybody here: go forward [*echen pa'lante*] and live life and know how to live it and get strong because there are times that the body wants to faint. But no! We should forward life [*vamos a adelantar la vida*]. And if you feel bad with something, make an effort and say: "My God, this body is yours, and it will be here until You determine what I have to do" . . . and you get up, you walk, and you live life more peacefully, and you do not lose courage. You feel strong and light. Because I do like that here in the morning. Look, I do not sleep until dawn sometimes, and at six, I feel sleepy. So I sit in bed to pray. I say: "My God, if at night I was not sleepy, why should I feel sleepy now? The time for me to feel sleepy was at night." It is no longer time to sleep, right? So I continue to pray. It gets to be seven, I go to the bathroom, to shower immediately. When I come out, I feel very light.

Ay, daughter! I get a pain in this leg so I lie down on the other; at night, when I cannot be walking, I turn over; and, during the day I am moving so the body does not have time to feel indisposed. I want my body to be well disposed.

You have to pretend that you have nothing. That is what my grandson told me: "Mother, you look as if you had nothing!". . . You have to do like that, you cannot get afraid.

I like to keep busy [*me gusta pasar trabajo*]. You know why? So the body gets used to working and the nerves do not shrink. Otherwise, look, I should be lying down here. The day I was lying in bed, look, this bone came out, this nerve came out and, here, look, this bone popped up and the hand got swollen.

A third strategy is to "help yourself" by diagnosing your condition based on popular knowledge, and self-prescribing home remedies known from personal experience:

Sometimes when your back hurts, you stay under the shower stream. Not hot, hot, but mild, on the body. . . . This is the way I got rid of my back-ache. . . . Even if I do not wash the head, I get the shower stream here. I get rid of the headache. The arthritis is in the head . . . in a ball . . . the bone popping up. And look, I get a pain in the legs that does not let me walk. Do you want to know what I do? If I have already showered . . . I go to the bathroom, wet the towels, with mild water. . . . You should believe me, doing that I get rid of the pain. I say that my arthritis is hot.[2] Because I get rid of it with water. . . . Because if you apply something colder, it gets cured. . . . I was in so much pain a few days ago, I took a bottle of Florida water [*agua florida*][3] and I told him [her husband] to apply it on me, and with that I got rid of the pain.

[When I cannot sleep] I take camomile and eucalyptus and linden tea and, if there is, milk.

I have it [the heating pad] on and now let's see if with the heat I get bet-ter. Because if you go to the doctors they tell you to take Tylenol . . . but arthritis has no cure, girl!

A fourth strategy is to move around to get exercise, whether indoors or out:

> He [her husband] went out day before yesterday a bit. And I, if somebody would take me, I would go every day.

> Let's go to walk, to get air! Spring air that gives you health, that brilliant sun with vitamin E! I have to walk at least a bit, because [otherwise] I will get paralyzed!

> You should get out of bed, bathe, make the bed, look for ways of moving, you see? Because the person who moves around exercises the arms. . . . You fold clothes and that is exercise.

If you still cannot get better by yourself, you should attempt to get help from curers "who know." Emiliana believes *curanderismo*[4] is more effective than *espiritismo*, and she knows how do to a manual massage [*sobar*]:

> I told her [the home attendant]: "That boy, it could be that he is *empachado*,[5] bring him to me that I can massage him [*yo se lo sobo*] and I charge you nothing . . ." Yes, I know how to massage [*sobar*]. I cured a man here, who was told by the doctors there was no remedy for him, that he had stomach ulcers, and he had no ulcer. . . . You would not know how many people I have saved! A man said to me once: "I am sick, the doctor says that I have ulcers and he cannot cure them," and I told him: "Do you want to come to my house so that I examine your stomach to see if you are *empachado*?" He told me: "Look, ma'am, if you can cure me, that is a work of God, because the doctors told me I had no remedy and I went to a spiritist who told me I had a hex [*hechizo*] that somebody had put on me." I told him: "Come to my house. How much will you give me if I cure you?" "Whatever you ask me, since I am dead already," he tells me. . . . I brought him home and I touched him with the hand like this, and this, and I told him: "You are *empachado*, you have to *sobarse*, but you have to take what I tell you to." "Ah, so I will come tomorrow morning." I put him down, I put oil on his abdomen, then I started like this, then I gave him the blessing on the abdomen, down here he had a ball like a bread, fat, hard. I told him: "Touch yourself here so that you see what you have here." He tells me: "This is what the spiritists say is a hex that they cannot remove." And I tell him: "I will take it out, what they tell you about a hex

is lies." Listen, I massaged him that day, and what he had sticking there got looser. I told him: "Come day after tomorrow." After another massage, it got looser, and his tripes made a noise like this: brr, brr. . . . Then I told him: "Tomorrow . . . when you wish to go to the bathroom, make in a bowl, so that you see what you had there." I gave him the branches of *sacabuche* [a medicinal plant], garlic heads, the straw that grows behind the sowed garlic and three garlic heads, five pepper grains, and I mixed it all with two spoonfuls of cooking oil [*los troncos de las matas de sacabuche, las cabecitas de ajo molido, la pajita que tiene el ajo atrás donde está sembrado y tres granos de ajo, cinco granos de pimienta y le eché dos cucharadas de aceite de comer*]. Can you believe that the next day he felt like going to the bathroom!

You can also "help yourself" by taking natural medicines:

I am taking those pills of shark[6] that my son bought, . . . it is to make you stronger and to improve the *causas*, the body. . . . With them, you get cured of everything.

These remedies can be cheaper than prescribed medicines since their properties counteract several conditions simultaneously:

Sábila is a long plant . . . it has thorns on both sides. So you cut it here [she points to the bottom]. . . . You chop it and wash it seven times. . . . Then you drink that water even if it is bitter, every day you take some, with sugar if you wish. . . . That cleans your insides of anything bad. And if you have it in a stronger dose, it acts as a laxative. . . . That water . . . you can wash your face . . . also to grow more hair. When you put it in your face, the skin hardens. It dries up, and you get a pretty complexion. . . . That is natural, *sábila*. Do you know what *botánicas* are? There is where they sell it, sometimes at higher and sometimes at lower prices.

Knowledge about natural medicines is also transmitted through advertisements on the radio.

[In addition to *sábila*] what is also good for the hair is the potato . . . well washed. . . . You cut it and put the skin of the potato in water, you leave it from one day to the next, and next day you take it out, or as soon as you cut it, you wash your hair with that water to feed hair . . . they say that on the radio.

Do you know what they also said in the radio? . . . That when your throat hurts and is clogged, that you should take lemon and take the juice with honey and heat it up and that you put it in your throat and you get rid of hoarseness. . . . And now I will boil a bit of lemon . . . with salt to make gargles. It does not taste good but you have to look for ways to feel better. Those are natural medicines and you can get cured at home with them.

The central strategy to get better is simple: just try to overcome your limitations and continue doing what you like to do. As Emiliana puts it, "You have to look for ways to feel better." In fact, the central goal of ethnomedicine is to make the ailing person the center of attention, not the doctor. And, to feel better, it helps to both count on the help of others and to engage their assistance:

> My son came and gave me a rubbing with Bengay and some pills and now I can move the arm.

> Sometimes I feel dizzy. The *muchacho* [her grandson] prepares punches . . . before I go to sleep or in the morning.

> Night before last my son, my grandson rubbed my back, gave me medicine and applied that cream on my eyes. Last night, there was nobody and this man here [a transient guest] did it. A good person in the house is the same as family.

> So, I am here thanks to them, they take care of all my needs!

Yet belief about the instrumentality of personal relationships cannot assure that all needs will be satisfied:

> I have to make an effort to go to the post office, I have to look for somebody to take me because you see a lot of people around here [her home], but there are times [when I need something] when nobody is here.

> I have sent this girl [her granddaughter] to get me slippers like moccasins and she did not find them.

The Ethnographic Sample: Ethnomedical and Biomedical Constructs

Beliefs and Practices

Emiliana's experiences of the health-seeking process reveal categories that distinguish the biomedical and the ethnomedical belief systems. Although arthritis and poor vision are labeled with the same name by Emiliana and her health service providers, she calls depression "nerves." The two systems disagree concerning the severity of the condition. In fact, they totally disagree: for the biomedical system, arthritis is the worst ailment, while poor vision is the least serious; for the ethnomedical system, vision is the worst, while depression is the least troublesome. According to informants, the biomedical system advocates interventions—for example, medication for depression and surgery for poor vision. In contrast, for the ethnomedical model, it is crucial to find the cause of the problem. For example, Emiliana offers the following causes for her vision loss: age, God, work conditions, and environmental impacts. In fact, the ethnomedical system differs from the biomedical in diagnosis, treatment, and prognosis, and this difference affects the utilization of biomedical health systems. For example, even if the two systems might agree on the relationship between visual acuity and age, they might differ on the irreversibility of vision loss: while most informants consider that, as one should accept the consequences of aging, the biomedical system would strongly recommend surgical interventions to remedy aging problems through technology. Since informants consult with doctors at a rate similar to the larger population, their different interpretations by no means result in informants refusing surgical interventions; in fact, many have had surgery, but they are less convinced of the efficacy of the intervention and tend to be less satisfied with the results than other population groups.

It comes as no surprise, therefore, that the two systems also differ regarding the action to be taken. For the ethnomedical system, identifying a health problem does not preclude consultation with a medical provider. Moreover, for the ethnomedical system, health problems are interrelated and thus should be diagnosed and treated simultaneously. Misdiagnosis—what for the ethnomedical system entails the provider's inaccuracy in finding the "cause" of the ailment, and which results in barriers to consumer access to the biomedical system—is attributed to language differences during the consultation, the multiplicity of providers assigned to a case, dichotomizing the patient from the person who implements treatment in daily life, the failure to communicate interactive side effects of prescribed drugs, and the inability of the health care system to finance the totality of prescribed actions. In fact, the biomedical system's central strategy to get a patient better is to utilize more resources within the system itself, in sharp contrast to the ethnomedical system, for which the appearance of a "cause" signals the onset of personal strategies intended to overcome the misfortune within.

In fact, from the informants' perspective, faith determines the simultaneous or successive utilization of health care systems. Dominga explains how health care decisions result from personal experience:

> You go first to the doctor. If the doctor does not do anything, you go to the spiritist. If the spiritist is good, he tells you what you have. The doctor gives you medicine, the spiritist gives you baths and *despojos*. Baths with *botánica* plants. Many people go to the spiritist and now they are into *santería*. . . . The *santeros* today are more than that, they look for money. Nowadays a *santero* comes to your house and tells you to *hacer el santo*.[7] And they tell you how much it is to *hacerse el santo*. It is over $4,000.
>
> You go to one or the other depending on what the result is. Because there are material and spiritual *causas*. If it is material, you always go to the doctor, but if it is no good, I change. I go to the spiritist if it is spiritual, if my body aches and the doctor finds nothing wrong. I go to at least two doctors and [I conclude] it is spiritual. For example, headaches, body aches, but also for luck.
>
> I have *facultades* [but] since my husband died I cannot [use them] because I need to concentrate. *Tener facultades* means that you can see in the water, you can see the water spirits. You can see in the sea. People are not appreciative, you do charity and then they say you do not help them anymore. People go from one to the other. One is born with *facultades* and you see the saints converse with you. I see my husband in my dreams and awake. One sees the dead. For psychiatrists, it is a problem of nerves, that makes me angry [*para los psiquiatras, son problemas de nervios, me dá coraje*]. People suffer more from nerves and head and body. Psychiatrists are for mental illness, for crazies [i.e., it is more common for people to suffer from these ailments than from a mental illness].

To what extent are the experiences of other informants similar or different from Emiliana's? Their cultural construction of the health-seeking process is similar in three respects. Although biomedical and ethnomedical assessments of health status differed, their patterns of utilization were similar: everybody in the sample went to doctors; virtually everybody used multiple systems of care—popular, folk, and mainstream medical; and, finally, rather than choosing one system over the other, all systems were used simultaneously. Thus, informants did not seem to compare the effectiveness of one system over another and to develop priorities based on such a judgment—at least not in a manner that would predict their utilization patterns of the mainstream medical system.

The cultural explanation for this pattern is based on two related beliefs. One belief is embodied in the phrase *"Hay que buscar la causa"* [Find the cause of the ailment]. This means that in health-seeking, it is important never to stop looking for what caused one to be ill. Thus, in going to any provider, including a doctor, one is cured effectively if one feels better immediately. If that does not happen—a sign that the cause was not found—one continues to consult any or all systems because the goal is to "find the cause" so that the appropriate solution can be implemented. This explains why many informants report that doctors do not cure.

The other belief is embodied in the phrase *"Hay que ayudarse con lo que se puede"* [You have to help yourself with whatever you can]. This means that, once the cause for the ailment has been found, you implement the appropriate curing strategy, which does not preclude continuing cures from other systems of care. This is understandable since the goal is to get better and human agency is required.

Understanding the interplay between biomedical and ethnomedical cultural constructions of appropriate utilization of health care services is important to provide effective treatment. Medical providers define appropriate utilization on the basis of outcome, such as attending primary care clinics on a regular basis rather than solely the emergency room when sick. From the ethnomedical perspective, however, the input of the patient and her network in the decision-making process bears a direct relationship to the outcome. Thus, appropriate utilization means using various providers, both within the biomedical system (for example, hospital-based physicians, private physicians, pharmacists) and the ethnomedical system (for example, healers and home remedies), depending on what the patient and her network consider more effective in responding to symptoms at a particular time in the health-seeking process. I call this health-seeking pattern "pragmatic syncretism" because it subsumes all possible strategies in the cultural repertoire of everyday health practices, basically, they use whatever works. In fact, all informants display patterns of syncretism in their use of both ethnomedical and biomedical systems of health care.

How can one explain pragmatic syncretism? A biomedical explanation would interpret medical pluralism as inappropriate utilization of the biomedical system. Resorting to folk and popular medicine, however, occurs usually after the biomedical system has not proven satisfactory in finding the cause for the ailment. Alternatively, a cultural explanation relates medical pluralism to the fact that this population, indigenous to Latin America, carries belief systems and health practices over to the host society. This explanation does not account for the fact that decision-making in health care for this population is not an either-or choice. In fact, informants rarely choose one way of dealing with their health problem to the exclusion of others. Rather, they choose from a wide range of treatment alternatives and select whichever is most effective. Thus, I propose a preventive explanation to account for pragmatic syncretism, as a version of medical pluralism. Notions of health and disease are tied to fatalism, within which disease is but one of many possible manifestations of bad luck. The informants' response to misfortune can be viewed as a means of exerting control over their lives. Thus, in using several options at once, they are more likely to offset misfortune, of which disease is but one manifestation.

How does the experience of the other informants differ from Emiliana's regarding their regularity of use of medical care? Although everybody uses physicians, some use physicians regularly and some use them only when they consider themselves to be sick. This could result in differences in the type of care one receives: those who have medical needs and access to care regularly obtain preventive medical care. This distinction is relevant not only for theoretical reasons but also for its policy implications. Thus, regardless of this population's perceptions of its supply options, there are some who will have their medical needs met while others will not. This is particularly important for ailments that benefit from medical treatment and/or medical follow-up. The obvious policy implications of this finding are in the areas of medical management, primary care outreach, community interventions, and health education programs. If the medical provider can be sensitized to the fact that its clients are shopping around for systems capable of telling them clearly what is wrong with their health—that is, if the provider could understand its own and the patient's explanatory systems, their communication during the consultation might be more successful in terms of predicting compliance with treatment. If the ethnomedical system could be understood in relationship to the biomedical system, rather than in opposition to it, health education interventions could integrate the local knowledge base and reach audiences more effectively.

Ethnomedical and Biomedical Needs

The informants explain their patterns of utilization in terms of whether or not their perceived needs are being met by the biomedical care system. Petra provides instances of problems with the biomedical system encountered by the elderly at the center where she volunteers:

> Even if there are available services, it is so complicated to get services. . . . To get a benefit, if you have some income, you do not qualify. . . . Elderly who live alone have problems [accessing the system] . . . that is why we find elderly three or four days after their death. There is always a loophole in the regulations, a person who does not want to help and see to your needs.

> Another thing is that they have to wait too long until they are seen. You can get sick one thousand times until you are given an appointment. If you go to the emergency [room], you wait all day. People leave. Either you do not wait to be seen [*no se atiende*] or you go to a private doctor.

> [Other problems with physicians are that] they make one wait, they do not explain, they take people for granted . . . like guinea pigs. They think they have to tell us nothing, especially Puerto Ricans. When we get in, the doctor is already writing. People from other nationalities are given explanations. They [the doctors] complain about compliance and say they [the elderly] do not go [to them], but people go and they are not well taken care of [*la gente vá pero no los atienden bien*]. It is not fair

that if I go to Metropolitan [Hospital] because I am sick they give me an appointment for three or four months later. In that time, I can develop a very bad sickness!

This is the part of the system that I think is not working. I ask, the doctor should not wait for me to ask [i.e., the doctor should ask questions as soon as the patient walks in]. They give you medicines and do not explain. I took two or three pills, and *ví que no hacían nada* [realized they did nothing] and threw them out.

With my Medicare card, I need to pay seven to fifteen dollars. They get your money first and then Medicare returns some of it. We have to meet a deductible of seventy-five dollars but in the clinics they continue charging you even if you covered the deductible and they return nothing.

Since informants feel their needs cannot be appropriately addressed exclusively by use of the professional medical care system, they rely on combined strategies of care, particularly the use of home remedies [*remedios caseros*].

My problem is health. The only things I do about that is to take medicines, use *remedios caseros*, and continue to have faith and have God within me, go to church.

—Matilde

If my doctor is not there [if I have a bad case of the flu], I take home remedies: ginger with milk and butter or eucalyptus tea with lemon. The best is yellow apple and bouillon cubes. Also orange juice. It is very important to have a clean intestine. Doctors tell you to take Milk of Magnesia, but I buy *Magnesia Bisurada*, which comes in a little box from Puerto Rico. It comes with mint and it gets rid of your germs. The doctor knows this and thinks it is fine.

—Petra

The only thing good for *catarro* [cold] is *té de gengibre* [ginger tea], a root that you scrape a bit of and you get in *los chinos* [Korean groceries in the area]. I do not like to take medicine.

—Augustina

What doctors give does not work [*no le dan resultado lo que dan los médicos*]. First day it does you good, if you do not take it the second day, you feel the same. So if I am going to feel the same, why take it? Sometimes herbs [*yerbas*] have better results [*hacen mejor*].

—Aurelia

The use of *remedios caseros*, which can be obtained in a variety of stores in *El Barrio* (including specialized herbal stores or *botánicas*), brought over from Puerto Rico, or planted in backyards, is based on practical knowledge about properties and a popular culture to protect consumers:

I made him [her brother] teas of the leaves of *aguacate* [avocado] which is good for the *bronquios* [bronchus]. . . . They sent it from Puerto Rico. Many people do that because they have no faith in *botánicas* [in *El Barrio*] for some products. Camomile, linden teas, I buy at the *botánica*. Another is eucalyptus with ginger and green apple. That cannot harm him.

—Carmen

Flor de Jericó is good for baths. There is a man down there who plants it. He gives me herbs of *pazote* and mint good for the stomach to put in the bath. The Mexicans also use *pazote* for soups. It is medicinal. Puerto Ricans use it for baths, they boil it and put it in pots. They sell it in *botánicas* for a lot of money, but this man plants it in the courtyard and gives it to all of us [*lo reparte*].

—Antonio

To feed the lungs and the *bronquios*, take McCoy pills, a *tónico* [tonic] you get in the pharmacy, one of the most ancient home remedies. If you feel weak, take malt extract with cod [liver] oil [*aceite de hígado de bacalao*]. Mother took that, not the *porquerías* [trash] they give you today, and she lived ninety three years. She got rid of headache[s] putting coffee on her head [*se colaba café en la frente para que baje bien*].

—Dora

For colds, take anything, like a tea of *sávila* [aloe vera], that you buy at a *botánica* or a tea with bee's honey.

—Luz María

You can also get *genjibre* [ginger] in a *botánica*, but you should not buy anything in a *botánica* without a prescription from somebody who recommends it. For example, in this case I know about *té de genjibre* being good because my mother took it.

—Augustina

I go to Paco's *botánica* for all kinds of herbs to make tea with: *naranja* [orange leaves], *yerba buena, curia, eucalyptus, jarabe de Tolu, jarabe de Altea, jarabe de goma.* I boil all those herbs in a tea and it's good for asthma. I also take the seven *jarabes* for asthma. Another thing that is good is *aceite de huevo* [egg oil]. You whip an egg very well and then let liquid pour out, you drink with it with bee's honey. The herbs with *jarabe* [syrup] you make a tea with. The egg oil you drink separately, it's good for *flema de pecho* [phlegm in the chest]. These [remedies] have nothing to do with doctors [i.e., doctors need not be told because they can do you no harm].

—María

For those who are dissatisfied with biomedical care dispensed at hospitals and clinics, a common strategy is to consult with private physicians. A *doctor privado* is a physician in the biomedical system who sees patients in his own storefront office in of *El Barrio*, as compared to physicians who see patients in offices located within one of the major hospitals in the area (Mount Sinai, Metropolitan, North General).

I got sick with the flu [*la monga*]. I had it bad for several days. I had to stay in bed for three days. I went to the private physician I always go to. I could go to the hospital doctors who accept Medicare but I prefer one who charges for the consultation because then you are treated well. When they get Medicare they give you something cheap so they get reimbursed. I want to get something that cures me quickly, not the little pills they give you at hospitals. This doctor gives me a set of four shots, two each week, and he charges me twenty-five dollars per shot, but I get strong right away. The most important thing is to get cured [*la cosa es que lo curen a uno*].

—Florentino

After Julia and I waited three hours to be seen at a hospital clinic, she voiced her dissatisfaction with the biomedical system shared by many others thus:

I go to a private physician because here [at the hospital] they do not care, nothing, here you can die. Private physicians are more interested in you. [*Aquí no se interesan, nada, aquí se puede morir uno. Los privados se interesan más.*]

Other informants echoed this sentiment:

I like private doctors because they tell me things [talk to me].
—Dominga

I felt a terrible pain when I was mopping the floor and I went to see a private physician who is old, and I respect him because . . . he does not give you drugs, he gives you medicines. Many give you drugs that leave you asleep [make you drowsy] like the *tecatos* [drug addicts]. Medicine cures you.
—María

My private doctor takes care of me. He does not accept Medicaid so I pay him little by little. Some doctors do not accept Medicaid because they had trouble getting paid.
—Julia

A private physician listens to you.
—Pura

I give him [her brother] camomile tea [he suffers from *los nervios*, a nervous condition]. Who knows if the cough is not also from the nerves? If it does not get cured, he goes to a private doctor who gives him a shot and in three or four days he is cured. But he mostly goes to his doctor at Metropolitan [Hospital].
—Carmen

In the informants' personal experience, private physicians are valued over hospital doctors because they provide immediate responses to patients' needs and pay attention to their diagnostic tool—*buscar la causa*. A private physician in *El Barrio* confirms their interpretation:

We [the biomedical system] create a specialized and sophisticated medicine that does not solve problems immediately.

Congruence between Ethnomedical and Biomedical Models of Impairment

The biomedical view of a health condition as a diagnosed disease is different from the ethnomedical perception of illness, which interrelates maladies of the body and of the soul. The biomedical understanding of patients excludes the patients' knowledge about illness and impairment, their practices during the health-seeking process, their experience of constraints in accessing professional medical health care, and the strategies they find useful to prevent and cope with sickness.

The case of one informant provides an illustrative example of the practical implications of these different belief systems. Luz María, who only consulted physicians for emergencies, was taken to a hospital by neighbors when they recognized an alarming behavioral change: she refused to eat, rest, bathe, and perform other activities of daily life. Hospital personnel found a series of chronic conditions, unrelated to her concerns, for which she could be treated at the institution. The psychiatrist found her mildly delusional due to her being severely dehydrated and malnourished. Yet, when it became clear that she did not suffer from any disease that legitimized her occupying a bed, arrangements were made to discharge her. Luz María, however, suffered from illness, not disease: she believed she had been "crossed over" *(le hicieron un maleficio,* she was bewitched) by a neighbor whom she believed desired her death in order to occupy her apartment. Every time the neighbor came to visit, Luz María thought she brought bugs with her. Ceasing to carry out her daily activities was the means that Luz María thought most effective to counteract the maleficent effects of the bugs. Hospital discharge did not address her health needs.

Luz María, like many informants, dichotomizes illnesses "of the body" and "of the soul":

> The doctors cannot cure all illnesses. There are illnesses of the soul in addition to illnesses of the body.
>
> —Aurelia

> They [those who suffer from illnesses of the soul] are sick of body and soul. They have remorse in their soul, [guilt] of the heart [*remordimientos del corazón*], something one has done to someone, or something that has been done to you.
>
> —María

> There are many things . . . how can I explain it? . . . things that affect the heart. Illnesses of the soul are like remorse, something you repent from having done or something that was done to you. Maybe I did something wrong. You know, the elderly are stupid and do not realize what they are

doing. Somebody did something to me but I keep it to myself and only God will know my secret when I die. I have a heavy luggage in my heart [I am heavy hearted, *tengo una maleta aquí en el corazón*].

—Luz María

Yet the biomedical professional can only treat illnesses of the body; illnesses of the soul need to be addressed by spiritual providers or by tapping one's inner resources:

You go to the priest for spiritual problems, and to the doctor for material problems. When you are depressed, you need to seek God first and then everything follows. But also diabetes depresses you. The priest told me to pray to God to recuperate my calmness.

—Armando

On the basis of this belief system, Armando follows instructions from the physician and the priest, as well as taking teas—such as orange and cinnamon—that help him fall asleep. He uses the medical and non-medical systems regularly: he has a medical appointment every three months; has a home attendant four hours a day; and uses social services and nutrition programs at a senior citizen center that he attends almost daily.

Different health belief systems also affect the assessment of impairment by the biomedical and the ethnomedical systems and, consequently, the identification of a health problem that needs to be addressed. An analysis of congruence of biomedical and ethnomedical models of impairment shows significant levels of disagreement (see Figure 7.2) and no congruence between the ethnomedical and the biomedical assessments of functional, cognitive, emotional, and physical health.[8] This has important practical implications. When there was congruence between biomedical and ethnomedical assessments, informants consulted with biomedical personnel for their conditions. For example, a sixty-eight-year-old patient, who was found to be mildly impaired clinically, expressed concern over one health problem—asthma—for which he sought the attention of physicians only when it worsened. Similarly, a severely medically impaired eighty-year-old woman who realistically worried over her health had a full-time home attendant. When there was no congruence, the informants were very distrustful of consulting physicians. A severely biomedically impaired eighty-seven-year-old man was

Biomedical Model

	Mild ($n_M=28$)	Severe ($n_S=11$)
Mild ($n_M=23$)	21	2
Severe ($n_S=16$)	7	

I. Functional Assessment

Agree 30 (77%)
Disagree 9 (23%)

	Mild ($n_M=27$)	Severe ($n_S=12$)
Mild ($n_M=23$)	17	6
Severe ($n_S=16$)	10	

II. Cognitive Assessment

Agree 23 (59%)
Disagree 16 (41%)

	Mild ($n_M=25$)	Severe ($n_S=14$)
Mild ($n_M=23$)	16	
Severe ($n_S=16$)	9	7

III. Depression Assessment

Agree 23 (59%)
Disagree 16 (41%)

	Mild ($n_M=15$)	Severe ($n_S=24$)
Mild ($n_M=23$)	11	12
Severe ($n_S=16$)	4	12

IV. Physical Assessment

Agree 23 (59%)
Disagree 16 (41%)

Ethnomedical Model (row axis label)

$$n_M + n_S = N$$

Figure 7.2. Congruence of Biomedical and Ethnomedical Models of Impairment (N = 39). Adapted from Freidenberg, J. N., and I. Jiménez Velásquez, 1992, Assessing Impairment among Hispanic Elderly: Biomedical and Ethnomedical Perspectives, *Clinical Gerntologist II (3,4):* 131–44.

unable to live independently but viewed himself as only mildly impaired. He was concerned mostly about "life worries," which, in his view, physicians could not address because:

> they ask you a lot of questions and they do nothing. You waste your time. I want the doctor to tell me what I have, not to ask me. They just told me last time that I should stay calm *[que lo cogiera suave]* and return for another appointment. They only give you another appointment because they get paid for it.
>
> —Julio

Finally, a sixty-one-year-old man, whose clinical impairment was found to be minimal, perceived himself as severely sick and, although he consulted a physician with regularity, felt his health needs were unaddressed, particularly his feeling of despair, which "sticks to you to such an extent that you look at the clinic to alleviate the feeling, you go to a doctor to get medicine."

The utilization of the biomedical health care system is affected by differences between the provider and the consumer's assessment of impairment, or by the constraints experienced by consumers in accessing medical facilities, such as distance, transportation, or financing the cost of care, exceeding the benefits they perceive obtaining from such care:

> I have difficulty going so far. [Yet] the doctor scolds me if I do not take the tests.
>
> —Rosario

> What am I going to do if I do not have Medicaid and I have to go to the hospital?
>
> —Aurelia

Conversing over photographs of other elderly in *El Barrio*, Dora provided information useful to understanding the interrelationships between health status and income:

> Nowadays the hospitals have become more aggressive to get insurance payments. . . . When the elderly have to go they get anguished if they do not have Medicaid. The social worker [the woman in the photo] is probably telling her not to worry, that she will try to solve her problem.

This is a project. This man is talking to a social worker. He is comfortable in his room. He is telling her that he is worried because if he has to go to the hospital, he will have to pay medicines and will be left without enough money to pay his apartment [rent].

Many elderly have home attendants who take care of them but they have to struggle a lot to get them.

What are the policy implications of a lack of congruence between the ethnomedical and biomedical models of impairment? A lack of fit between the cultural and the clinical assessments indicates that health needs, identified by either system or both, might be left unaddressed by either the medical (doctors, nurses, and other medical-related personnel) or the nonmedical (home care attendants, social and nutrition service providers) health care sectors.

Utilization Patterns and Planning Medical Care Services

Medical anthropologists have been concerned with the impact of the hegemonic biomedical model on people's health (Menéndez 1987; Lindenbaun and Lock 1993; Schepper-Hughes 1992; Singer and Baer 1995; Baer, Singer, and Susser 1997). If health is considered a right (Navarro 1994; Susser 1993), then addressing the hiatus between the biomedical and the ethomedical models becomes even more relevant to formulating a national prevention agenda (U.S. Department of Health and Human Services 1991). The lack of congruence between the ethnomedical and biomedical models can result in major obstacles to accessing biomedical services that people have the right to use. Public health officials should understand the practical implications of this discrepancy. As Figure 7.1 shows, in the path of becoming a patient a person may encounter up to eight "cracks" in accessing the biomedical system. When this lack of fit is examined with reference to the assessment of health status, as in Figure 7.2, it becomes clear that the misuse or underuse of the biomedical service structure can affect both the provision of medical services and the health of consumers.

Planning of medical care services at the local level is based either on data gathered about the health concerns of consumers identified by provider organizations or on consumer belief systems and practices.

The fit between provider- and consumer-defined health concerns is usually unaddressed. The data presented here have shown that the lack of congruence in defining needs can result in a failure to address consumer-defined medical needs. Based on an understanding of providers from the perspective of consumer culture, the following recommendations are offered:

Education of Biomedical Providers. Since the population distinguishes between illness and disease, service providers should be trained to elicit and treat both (Kleinman 1995).

Health status and impairment assessments do not predict utilization; rather, utilization patterns are related to beliefs and barriers to access. There is often a gap between the biomedical and the ethnomedical assessment of health and disability that needs to be addressed if access to health care is to be improved. Either a condition is not thought to be problematic by one model (problems of congruence), or there are hindrances to solving the problem, including barriers to access such as financial resources, insurance coverage, and, as we shall see in the following chapter, weak social networks.

Training Consumers to Address Population Needs. Needs can be defined by the biomedical and/or the ethnomedical system. These definitions may or may not coincide, and the needs may or may not be addressed. Although policy cannot realistically address every population concern, an equitable health care system should provide citizens with access to biomedical interventions that are devised to enhance quality of life. An example of a health concern of many elderly Puerto Ricans that the medical system can address efficiently and effectively is vision problems, such as cataracts, which can be corrected by surgery. Yet the majority of those affected refrain from seeking help because they believe that vision loss results from aging (and thus is irreversible and incapable of correction) or because they are overwhelmed by barriers to access.

Applying Anthropological Knowledge about Local Systems. Yoder asks: "How can we apply local knowledge of health problems and practices to enhancing utilization of biomedical services? And to design more appropriate public health interventions? How can local knowledge be made relevant?" (1997, 131). Anthropologists can respond to this challenge by translating their understanding of ethnomedical systems to health planners. The study presented here has identified eight "cracks" in the health-seeking process when a patient is lost to the biomedical system. Through comparisons of the biomedical and ethnomedical systems, this study found significant disagreements in four measurements of health status. These findings can be used to plan specific interventions so that access problems are reduced. Narrowing local and provider perspectives of need would contribute to addressing locally defined needs that the biomedical system is equipped to address.

EIGHT

"Usted Sabe Lo Triste Que Es Eso? No Tener Quien Vele por Uno?" (Do You Know How Sad That Is? Not Having Someone Watch Out There for You?)

Connections and Illness of the Soul

I visit Emiliana often (mostly alone, although I have taken my elderly mother and aunt). We spend time together in her home, where we exchange food, gifts, stories about men and children, cooking recipes and tell each other the story of our lives. When I visit with Emiliana, I am also visiting with her network in action: people come in and out of her house—real and fictive kin, neighbors, friends, home attendants—. . . asking for her *bendición* while Radio WADO paints the world in Spanish. Emiliana tells me that it is important to have people coming and going, that silence is no good.

—Author's Diary, March 16, 1995

The health-seeking process, described in the previous chapter, cannot be understood from a policy perspective if we focus only on the individual as decision-maker. To predict utilization patterns of the biomedical care system, we need to pay attention to the characteristics of social networks. Since we can intervene in the "cracks" of the health-seeking process, we should also be able to intervene on social networks to enhance addressing medical needs.

A positive relationship between networks and health has been well documented, both for general populations (Hammer 1983; Auslander and Litwin 1991; Mor-Barak, Miller, and Syme 1991; Abraido-Lanza,

Guier, and Revenson 1996; Antonucci 1995) and for elderly Latinos (Barsa 1997; Tran et al. 1996; Angel and Angel 1992). In this chapter, I explore how three network variables—size, frequency of contact, and reciprocity—might influence addressing medical needs and utilizing the biomedical health care system.

Although network size decreases with age (Fischer 1982), reducing the number of connections does not necessarily imply social isolation (Palinkas, Wingard, and Barret-Connor 1990). What is different for the elderly, however, is that health needs increase with aging, so diminishing the frequency of interaction with social contacts can make individuals more vulnerable. For low-income populations, reciprocal exchanges of goods and services through social networks may become the main economic system available to cope with these changes (Stack 1974; Lomnitz 1977; Groger 1992).

Giving and Receiving: Emiliana's Being in the World

The Meaning of Personal Connections

Listening closely to Emiliana's voice helps us understand the mechanism by which social networks relate to health and illness. As different from feeling alone, experiencing loneliness means lacking "someone out there." Emiliana considers herself lucky to have constant company:

> So we are never, never, never alone. I thank the Lord! Thanks to the Lord that we are not so alone! Because when he [her live-in grandson] is not here, the boy his brother is here, or his sister who is grown up already.

Because Emiliana understands the value of being connected, she uses her *bendición*[1] to alleviate the suffering of those in complete solitude:

> I feel for all those people who are unhappy in life, who do not have a remembrance of a mother and who do not have anybody to give them the blessing, but I give it to everybody, I bless all those people who lack education, prayer, food, and who are suffering for the absence of their relatives and their parents, which is the greatest [absence] there is.

She believes is that illnesses of the body and of the soul—although interrelated—can be differentiated. If illnesses of the body can result from a variety of *causas,* for which one goes to a specific provider, illnesses of the soul always are a symptom of a breakdown in social relationships. Emiliana admits being depressed after the many recent deaths in her family, especially because she was unable to be with other family members of the deceased, since *"la pena compartida es más llevadera"* [shared unhappiness is less burdensome].

> I feel *causa* and I do not feel *causa,* because I sometimes have dizziness spells and I do not sleep. But I do not look for a cure, because being unable to sleep comes from the worries a person has. And in these days [recently] I had four deaths in the family. That [is enough to] give me worry, is it not true? I do not blame [try to cure] only the depression one has, because one gets depressed with those *causas.* Because if you could at least go to the place where you are needed, when even your gaze is needed, one would not feel so depressed. If one could face the relative who is suffering that pain [of the loss], you console yourself. Aha, the relatives the deceased has left. One would not feel so depressed, right? . . . Because everybody has their depressions and everybody has the same pain, and one comforts the other. . . . It is not possible that my family is there [in Puerto Rico], and that I am here, that three [members of her family in Puerto Rico] have died already and that I have not been able to go. And you love the family a lot, but there are some you love more . . . because I raised a boy at home that was my brother and my son . . . and he died and I could not go to see him when he was sick. I could not go! Even if he called me, he named me aloud [*Llamándome a voces*]! That is the greatest pain I have in my soul, that I could not go see them, first because of my husband's sickness, then because of my daughter's sickness.

While not having personal relationships carries the highest risk of contracting illness, even those who can count on them can get sick if these relationships change drastically. The worst is termination of the relationship by death.

> Because, solitude is bad, right? [*Que mala es la soledad, verdad?*] The loss of a loved one . . . [even if you know that] God has to take one person or another anyway, you can only think on your loved one. But then you think that it has to be like that, because God sends you on loan for a while [*Uno viene de prestado aquí*]. I have a sorrow in my soul that you cannot begin to imagine . . . from October to December, I lost five relatives. I lost a brother, a sister, a brother-in-law that I raised at home, so to speak, and I

lost a cousin, and I lost my beloved daughter, a treasure. . . . Two of my sisters are in critical condition there [in Puerto Rico].

Nothing on earth can replace the loss of one's child:

> I give thanks to the Providence. . . . I tell you: happiness is to have your children turn out good, that you do not have to suffer on behalf of your children. But there is no greater suffering than when your own child dies.

If a person has behaved improperly to the deceased, as in the case of the ex-husband of her daughter who had recently died, sickness can strike too:

> So he came here one day after her death and started to talk and saw her portrait, got closer and he had tears in his eyes. I told him: "Do not take her death seriously that everything has passed already. . . . And everything is forgiven. . . ." Can you believe that night he fell seriously sick and is still sick? Since she died, he is sick.

In contrast, a person who is connected and gives of herself, so that she feels needed, has a better chance of being healthy, because the existence of such connections helps a person take care of herself:

> I was sad [when my sister died], but I was sadder with the one who died in October, my brother. We got married and finished raising him. And I will never stop grieving, but I feel very satisfied that I was very good to him, that is the most important thing in life, to behave well towards people.

> And so has been my life, I have done many things that were not good, for me, to save others. I help all those I can help. . . . One has to compromise in life to be able to live it for others too. . . . Because you have a great pain inside . . . that could end your life . . . but you reflect . . . that you can be needed . . . by those around you . . . and [even feeling] that cruel pain that is assassinating one's life, you remember that and the suffering stops for a moment, because you say: "There are my grandchildren, . . . my children, . . . my sisters, and I am needed. . . . My husband, he is old, he has nobody to be for him . . . and I, pain or no pain, am chosen to be at his side. . . . Because if I cannot help him with my hands, I can help him with my mouth if I tell him what he has to do or what

they have to do to him. . . ." You know that one has to have a person who takes care of you . . . and that is worth a lot . . . [even if] you . . . have a great sadness.

Relationships with Connections: Family and Nonfamily

Emiliana stresses the difference between feeling needed and feeling taken care of. She felt needed by her natural children, grandchildren, and the stepchildren she raised:

I have raised three children and three grandchildren at home. . . . This one [Alan] is living with us. . . . Then there is one called Emily and one called Lilian, I raised them. One lives on 116[th Street] and the other lives on 102[nd Street] and First Avenue I have raised many children, girl. I have raised many children who are not related to me [*que no son nada mío*]. I thank the Lord and the Virgin who gave me the strength to raise them and help them all, because their mother left them, and I raised them and another one who had a mother but did not want to stay with her and returned here.

And her family in Puerto Rico make her feel that her presence is very welcome:

And the family in Puerto Rico that does not let me live [*que no me deja vivir*] calling me. Every day they call me . . . my sisters, and the nieces and nephews always call me . . . always, always. Those from there are well-off, everybody studied well, they are professionals. I have a niece who comes because she has a daughter that lives around here. Thank God that they have never forgotten me, now with my pain they came to see me and they always called. They love me very much. I was good to all of them.

We were six siblings, but among those six, my family has always felt very close to me and [was] always looking for me and worrying about me. . . . When they called me from Puerto Rico and I went you would not believe how [attentive] that family was to me . . .

[When her sister died in Puerto Rico] I called there and asked God to help me and give me love, fortitude, to be able to talk to them. When I called there, they were in the funeral home [*funeraria*]. Everybody wanted to talk to me at the same time. I spoke to all of them! They told me: "Ay, aunt, you know, that you were the one who toiled with me [*Usted era la que pasaba los trabajos conmigo*]. I always remember, God give you health, because you gave us life and helped our mother to raise us.". . . And that one [another sister] in the picture [pointing to a framed photograph] has been sick for the past four years and God has not taken her, because she tells God that she wants to see me before she dies.

Among the four [deceased relatives], I loved my brother the most, because he was my son, my brother and everything, like the one here [grandson]. . . . He did not stop buying me things and he always gave me presents when I lived in Puerto Rico . . . love is the boss [*El cariño es el que más manda*]! Because you see a person whom you know loves you but you do not feel the warmth . . . that you can feel with another person. . . . That [kind of] love that lights your soul, because somebody can love you but not like that, and I did not go to see him.

Puerto Rico is not the only place from which Emiliana gets calls:

I have calls from Puerto Rico, I have calls from New Jersey, I have calls from over there in Connecticut, I have calls from Florida, I have calls from one relative who lives in El Salvador, who many times cancels the call if I am not in. [Turning to the granddaughter who is on the phone]: "Leave, leave the telephone alone because they cannot call. . . ." Well, this afternoon I have been expecting [a call], I have been sitting here, to see if someone calls.

But only very few family members make her feel that they both need her and are willing to take care of her on a daily basis. She certainly acknowledges the companionship of her husband:

But you need a husband for everything, . . . he has to see to the needs of the mistress of the house. . . . You know that the twentieth of this month it will be sixty-seven years that we are married?

But nobody made her feel better taken care of than her older daughter:

Look, you have the children, you love them the same, but it is not the same, because that one [her oldest daughter, who died] was the treasure of this house and of all the family. She oversaw everything here, she took us wherever; she saw to what was needed in the house, she took care of taking us when we had to go someplace. She said herself: "I will look for the car to take you." Do you know what the morning sun is in the house? I have a son too, who is also a treasure because he does not let us suffer. But he lives far from here, he lives in the Bronx, he is married, has a wife. Every time he comes around here, he is very nice, but he is never like that daughter, you know? That daughter, when she did not come during the day, she came at midnight and she would say to me: "Mami, come Mami, put this on; look, Mami, this pretty thing that I brought you, look how pretty." I was at the doctor's, I was at any place, and I had just arrived and she would call from wherever she was, she would come . . . and she always was different from the others. I tell you that you teach the children, but some learn what you teach them and others do not.

Nonfamily connections can also provide services varying from running errands (as in the case of Frank, a transitory guest), to housekeeping (like the home attendant who cooks for both her and her husband, who is on a special diet), to tending to her spiritual needs (like the church mates who come to minister to her).

I cannot go to church, because I cannot go up the stairs. Today two ladies that I know from the church that I used to go to came here. They always come here and they give me the communion. I am very satisfied because they were my fellows from church and they always visit me and that brings me much happiness. . . . I have many remembrances of those visits . . . they are part of my past life. . . . They gave me the communion in the name of Jesus Christ that is for the good of my soul and theirs and everybody around me. They come from Santa Cecilia and from Los Angeles, the one on Third Avenue . . . the brother . . . of the church from over there . . . came to wish me happy Mother's Day and talk a bit and give me the communion. . . . From the churches they know me.

Since her disability, Emiliana cannot be as socially active as before:

She [her younger daughter who now lives with her] does not visit anybody. I do not visit anybody either. I had some neighbors here but they moved and now I have nobody.

Yet nonfamily connections can be severed. Thus, unlike blood relatives, nonfamily connections need to be reinforced through periodic personal contact. Due to her impairments Emiliana is constrained in her

daily activities and depends on others to take her visiting or to the courtyard downstairs as often as she would wish.

> And so many people came to me [when she went to the courtyard in her
> wheelchair]! Look, I went downstairs and they did not leave me alone!

The Value of Connections: The Supply Side

Connections, like resources, give and take. They give personal care, take
care of housekeeping chores, run errands, visit, call, show gratitude for
past care, escort on trips, and bring food and presents. As Emiliana puts
it: "*Ellos se desvelan por mí*" [they lose sleep over me]. It is usually expected that family members supply most needed resources.

> This one [pointing to her grandson] was born here, he has stayed here
> with us, and here he is. He is the one who is in charge of us at night. That
> boy [*muchacho*] is like the key to this house.

> You should see, how they [the family] come and fill up the house! And
> look, the grandchildren, the great-grandchildren, and the great-great
> grandchildren, everybody addresses me as *mamá*, and Jovino as *papá*. . . .
> They all ask us for the blessing, they come to see us.

> This house was full of people on Saturday. . . . They brought the presents
> and the flowers and the food, all the family, the majority of them. [It was
> Mother's Day.]

Emiliana makes a distinction between her deceased daughter—who
would give her everything she had, as Emiliana did with her own
mother—and her husband.

> That one, ay my God, I ask God that this pain [for her loss] disappears, be-
> cause I remember my daughter day and night, because she was very close
> to me, very close, very sentimental, she was always with me, she would not
> stop coming to me, always. Look, if she could not come during the day,
> she came at night, always, I tell you. Because she said the only person that
> loved me was her, she always said that. My mother had died, my mother
> died many years ago. . . . I brought her here, she lived here for one year,
> my mother. That is the treasure of one's soul, the mother and the children.
> The husband no, husbands are mean.

Husbands are only needed if they are good to the women:

And while one lives you have hope to find somebody good. And if you do not, a woman alone can go wherever she wants, to make money.

He has been mean to me as well. But I do not pay attention . . . and it seems God has helped me to carry the cross. . . . That one [her husband] has had about twenty women! Nobody puts up with that, right? Because I would ask God to give me courage and help me. But the woman who is hard-working does not need a husband. He was false with me but since he was like that, I did not pay attention. If he came back home, fine, and if not, fine too. When he would arrive I would be sewing, because I hired myself as a seamstress [*yo me alquilaba para coser*]. Right here where I am sitting now, right here I would be sewing by dawn. But I did not need him because I was entertained with work and when you are working you do not let anything bother you. You start a job and you go crazy until you finish and would like nobody to come close, nobody to talk to you until you finish the job. Is it not true? I entertained myself like that, sewing.

It is better to be alone than in bad company. And yet . . . last night I was not feeling well . . . and this morning he woke up and he prepared an egg and a coffee for me. . . . He is almost blind. And he suffers [*está malo*] from the legs. He rubs my back and he combs my braids . . . and he goes to the kitchen and he fixes punch. And feeling as he does, he comes and he helps me. And he warms Lipton soup, if I need a bouillon, if I feel something here, in the womb [*como que es la matriz*], and I tell him to boil garlic with a bit of water and a cracked egg inside, he also knows how to do it, yes!

Nonfamily connections can never fully replace family:

This man [a transitory guest] is also here always, but it is not the same. But be as it may . . . if I have to wash the feet to cure them, he applies the medicine. If there is need for a tea, he fixes it for me, even if my son is here too, he does it as well. She [the home attendant] leaves the food, this man gives me the food, warms it up and gives it to us. Before I go to bed, he gives me the crackers, the milk or the coffee, whatever I want.

Naturally, not all connections are good for a person, as shown by the incident that Emiliana narrates about her daughter Vidalina's marriage. Emiliana's next door neighbor, who had became very friendly with the couple, started flirting with the husband, who eventually ran away with her. Since then, Vidalina would attempt to have the neighbor open up the door of her apartment every time she visited her mother. When she succeeded, she grabbed the neighbor by the hair and threatened to kill her. Emiliana faults the husband for his behavior, but not Vidalina whom she considered rightfully teaching the neighbor that friendships should not be abused.

The Cost of Connections: The Demand Side

Like any other commodity, giving—whether to family or nonfamily—has its costs. Emiliana puts herself out for her connections: she visits, does favors, gives money, offers advice, provides company, offers food, and takes care of the sick and even the dead.

Emiliana gave without calculation to her mother, even after her death. According to Emiliana, her mother called her three times to announce her death, so she had time to prepare her shroud [*mortaja*]:

One day she told me, there in Puerto Rico: "When I die, I want the *mortaja* in white, because I married dressed in black." Because when you had *luto* [were in mourning] you married in black. So I told her: "You come to the store with me to see what color you want. I will buy it for you." [When she got sick] she told me: "Mmm, do not leave it here, because the girls will like the fabric and will start making suits for themselves so the fabric will be finished." I [Emiliana laughs at this point in the story] asked her: "So what do you want me to do, take it?" "Take it and keep it there [in New York] and I will announce when I am about to die, I will call you three times." Listen, that is the way it was: the night before New Year's Eve at night, I am in bed when I hear her saying: "Miliaaana," she spoke *ladino*, she sang very pretty, "Miliaaana!" Look! I heard those three voices clearly. I sat in bed and told Jovito: "Jovito, I heard a voice like mother's!" He told me: "Girl [*muchacha*], you are dreaming!" "No," I said, I was awake when she called me three times, it must be that she got worse." . . . At dawn I went to my daughter's and told her what I had felt. She tells me: "Mother, could it be that you were dreaming?" I told her: "No, I heard my mother calling me clearly, it was her who called me," I would tell her. "Eh, mother it could be that you were dreaming. Did father hear her calls?" "No, father did not hear them." As she started fixing lunch, . . . my brother . . . Santiago . . . comes: "Mother, they are calling for you [*mandado a buscar*] from Puerto Rico right away." I told him: "What happened?" [He said] "That mother died last night." I told him: "Really?" And I was at my daughter's and here on 114th [Street] was the fabric, so I told him: "Go fetch me the fabric, bring it here so I sew her dress here." My daughter went to the bank, to phone this one [her husband] who was at work while I started cutting the fabric. I sewed it exactly as she wanted it, like this, so that only her face could be seen, I sewed a long sleeve, I stuck it in a box and right there I sent for my sister in Queens. By the afternoon they got us the tickets and we left for Puerto Rico. When I got there they did not want to open her coffin [*destapar la caja*]. I told them: "You have to open it because this was a *promesa* [a promise] that I made to her. You have to uncover her because I will put this suit on her. I had offered it to her and she wanted it." Listen, you should have seen her, she looked like a bride when I dressed her! Yes, they even took photos and everything. And to think that they were about to bury her!

Emiliana also offered herself totally to her daughter as she was dying:

My daughter told me: "Mother, I am going to die, but I am sorry to leave you because you will have to suffer. I will ask God that you do not suffer because you were a good mother.". . . And I told her: "Ah God, let me tell you something to give you resignation and to take you on a good road to heaven: since you are going to die, do not be afraid and forgive everybody who has hurt you and forgive all those who have offended you and ask God forgiveness for all the evil and all the good you have done, so you take the road of clarity and do not suffer because you are dying. Give yourself to God in body and soul and ask forgiveness of Jesus Christ who is all powerful [*El que todo lo puede*]. He knows everything and He can do everything." But thank God I am satisfied because even if I was dying [i.e., dying inside because of her daughter's death], I went to her house to take care of her, to be with her and stroke her [*pasarle la mano*] and to do anything I could do for her, like rub her with towels with alcohol. And to hold her hands and help her move around [*pasarle el brazo*]. To touch her face, comb her hair. And every time she asked me for something I would get it for her little by little [because she herself had difficulty moving around]. And I spent three days at her house, until they took her to the hospital and I came here. After that I told her that I could not go take care of her, because a man had taken me piggyback upstairs because they lived on a seventh-floor walk-up. So she told me that she would come here. She came here, she stayed here. She stayed here a few days, a week, they took her to the hospital and after she returned, she lasted here another eight days.

But she is also very responsive to other close family members in need, whether in New York or in Puerto Rico:

Last Sunday I went far to see my nephew, my grandson. . . .

Yesterday I went to see Evelyn, because I go anywhere even if I have pain! As long as I can walk, because nobody was there to help her, she was crying, I stayed a bit and told her: "I have to leave soon because it is mother's day and my children are coming to see me."

I have had many good behaviors [*buen comportamiento*] with all my family. They know very well that I was a mother to the older ones and mother to the younger ones. Because I have nothing . . . cannot have anything [on earth], but I think that in heaven I have earned the glory [*me he ganado la gloria*] . . . I don't know . . . because I helped my siblings, my mother, my father.

Reciprocity: Emiliana's Social Contract

One type of giving is what anthropologists call *reciprocity*, which involves giving with no expectation of return, at least not in kind. The act of giving becomes a metaphor for making a presence in a connected world:

That is the way our parents taught us and that is the way I will die. I give anything to anybody. I have nothing here [on earth], I only have what I can buy, yet if somebody comes here with a need, I give him what I have here. I sewed in the past and if my sister would tell me, "That suit is pretty, if you would lend it to me, I would use it," I would ask her: "Do you like it?" And if she would say, "Yes, I like it, it is pretty," I would tell her: "Take it, it is for you, I will sew another one." That is the way I was with my sisters . . . that is why they are now dying calling me [*llamándome a voces*]. But since my husband has that *causa* [an ailment] of the heart, I do not dare leave him alone.

Since giving is costly, exchanging "favors," even if not of the same value, makes good sense to both parties. Another type of exchange is when one expects to balance out giving and receiving.

[When the home attendant does not come] the girl [*muchacha*, referring to her granddaughter] cooks, does housework. . . . [Today] she cooked lunch, cleaned the kitchen. . . .

That is logical, that somebody comes always, because you know, I have five loved ones who died . . . since November. . . . That is why it is very necessary that people come and go, that way you entertain yourself. . . . Ay, my God, Saintly Father, I hope it will always be like that! That I stay calm here because sometimes you have a strong thought and somebody suddenly comes and you get happy and that [bad thought] disappears from your mind. . . . At night, when nobody is there, you lose your sleep. . . . We are lucky that there is always somebody here, so . . . , when somebody comes to the house, your [bad] thoughts, your sadness . . . go away . . . and you get on with other things.

This leaves those who never give to Emiliana in a negative position. When a grandson's girlfriend asked her for money, Emiliana explained the reason for her refusal:

No, even if I had the money I would not give it to her. Do you want to know why? Because she never comes here. I am in such a situation now that I need anything, even from the dogs [*que hasta necesito de los perros*]!

What does it take to qualify as an appropriate connection for Emiliana? What are the expectations? *"Doña Emiliana, usted me dijo que me iba a enseñar como reconocer si una persona es buena"* [Mrs. Emiliana, you told me you would teach me how to recognize if a person is good], I said, to which she responded:

It is the duty of a person, no matter where she goes in . . . to greet. . . . And right there, we demonstrate the education a person has. Because a person that does not show up at the door with that phrase is not well educated. Because if it is small children, you forgive them because it could be they have not been taught or that they do not want to do what they were taught. But to my children I have taught that they say "good morning" or *"buenos días"* or whatever, you understand? Because it is good for the person. . . . Because I am a poor woman but I know how to behave towards any person. . . . When [her grandson's girlfriend] went straight to his room [without greeting her], I said [to myself]: "Mm, there is no education here [*aquí no hay cultura*]."

You have to be fair with people and know how to treat them . . . even if you do not know how to read and write. You talk with good manners to grandchildren and they respect. . . . the people living here or visiting here.

The Ethnographic Sample

How does Emiliana's way of being in the world resonate with the experiences of the others who talked to me? There was consensus among informants that having connections made a person feel that she or he had a place in the world, and being connected was associated with positive health outcomes. Yet, despite these similarities, macrostructural factors—particularly those related to housing, social organization, and the legal structure—affect the availability of connections, especially for daily interaction.

The political economy of housing for low-income people affects the living arrangements of households. Although there are a wide range of personal experiences that diverge from Emiliana's, no one in the study population was found to be totally isolated: saying one lives alone is far from saying one lives unconnected. I observed various types of household arrangements that disputed census data, according to which 39 percent of the elderly in East Harlem live alone. Eight informants who originally told me that they lived alone did not live alone. Rather, often consanguineal, affinal, and fictive kin slept, cooked, shared meals, and used facilities for laundering or washing at their residence.

For example, eighty-nine-year-old María reports living alone yet opens up her apartment to her social network composed primarily of fictive relatives with whom she exchanges services: her deceased godson's daughter sleeps over to keep her company; his widow does her own laundry there; and his male children, who have recently painted María's apartment, often share her rice pot and the leftovers from her free meal from "Meals on Wheels." On most weekdays, María eats lunch at her goddaughter's apartment nearby. The Housing Authority's social worker is aware of the discrepancy between María's household arrangement and meeting the official definition of "living alone" to qualify for housing subsidies for the low-income elderly. The social worker, who does not have the heart to report her, interprets María's situation as exploitation rather than exchange and often reprimands María for acting against her own interests: she predicts eviction when this exchange strategy is found out.

Social class also influences network availability. Social network members sharing socioeconomic status have the potential for more frequent interaction. Julia, for example, is proud of her only son whose upward mobility took him out of *El Barrio* to live in Westchester. Although he calls weekly and visits twice a month, Marta rarely sees her daughter-in-law and two college-educated granddaughters. Social class adds distance to geography.

Finally, the legal structure invests only family members with the power to represent the person to access health and social services. Yet, for most informants, a mix of family and nonfamily connections are available. Luz María, for example, has daily interaction with her neighbor and weekly interaction with her goddaughter, who does her shopping. Yet neither of these connections enjoys a legal mandate to act on her behalf should she experience a need. Even though he has daughters and a home attendant to take care of him, Félix feels the person "who checks over him" is a younger friend who lives a few blocks away and has a key to his apartment so that he can come unannounced should Félix not call.

Thus, connections who "care" or "give a hand," particularly to the homebound elderly, are not restricted to family members. Even family members may not take proper care of their kin. Worse still, they could add more problems by demanding care at a time when they should help the older person:

> They [the elderly] feel alone, sometimes they have family but they feel alone. I know a lady with two children, one [of whom] has health problems due to drugs. She is so thin, thinking all day and all night about her son.
>
> —Monchito

> Sometimes they are sad because they have housing problems, because they cannot pay their expenses. Sometimes the mothers suffer from the vices of the children, the children are given money to start peddling drugs. The worse problems are family problems.
>
> —Pura

If informants perceive being cut off from their families because of either geographical distance from "home" or changed social customs, what other types of companionship have become important? For some, companionship is provided by neighbors and friends, most of whom are also elderly. In response to photos of other elderly, informants said:

Living alone in a small tenement room. (Photo by Edmundo Morales)

This man is waiting for a visit. He says nobody comes anymore and that he might be alone but he hopes someone would come to see him.

—Dora

The daughters never visit him or take him out.

—Elsie

A neighborhood visit. (Photo by Edmundo Morales)

She is sick but she is happy because she has visitors. The sick feel happy when they have visitors.

—Telesforo

Maybe the other person is her home attendant. . . . Some elderly have home attendants who take care of them but they have to struggle a lot to get them. They get so fond of them that they treat them like family.

—Telesforo

For others, companionship is provided by home care attendants who provide more attention than the elderly receive from their own children, who, contrary to expectations, continue to need their parents' care as adults:

> We talk about anything . . . the home attendant takes good care of me.
> —Matilde

> I now have help and she keeps me company, as if she were family.
> —Elsie

Life with family. (Photo by Judith Freidenberg)

Pets as companion. (Photo by Edmundo Morales)

For still others, pets, particularly dogs, are the equivalent of human company. For those living alone, pets are humanized since they often constitute the only company.

Some elderly have dogs, I imagine they live alone . . . so that they can have company.

—Armando

They are like her children; they are her company. She would fight if somebody wanted to take them away from her, it is the only company she has. . . . She has no family close to her.

—Dora

This woman is happy because she has animals. I had a dog that died when he swallowed a piece of glass. I spent a lot of money [to cure it]. When it died, I cried a lot.

—Aurelia

All the elderly [who live alone] have dogs so that they have somebody to talk to if they are alone and have problems. Maybe it is because they get bored: I have seen elderly women talking alone to their dogs. They talk to them like if they were persons! I do not have problems with loneliness. I would never do that, I try to entertain myself.

—Antonio

To have animals helps because you pass the time.

—Carmen

Animals are good to you.

—Julia

In contrast to human connections, access to pets' companionship and reciprocity is predictable: they respond to love, give love back, watch out for you, and entertain you.

Yes, I would [recommend the elderly to have animals] because one finds oneself so alone, so alone, that at night you need somebody or something to look after you. And an animal is the most essential being there is . . . because an animal smells if something or somebody is coming to your house. . . . They smell even from far away. . . . I talk to them, I play with them, I tell them what they have to do.

—Marta

Without such companionship or other strategies to overcome loneliness, these elderly people believe they are at risk of falling into excessive worry and reminiscing about the past, of "thinking too much."

The absence of connections, or having connections that worry or upset a person's ego, causes "illnesses of the soul"—unhappiness. Some informants spoke of loneliness among the most troublesome.

They [the elderly] are unhappy. They think all the time about what they were in the past and what they have become. They are alone and feel lonely.

—Monchito

Sometimes it is good to be alone and sometimes it is not, because loneliness makes you have bad thoughts.

—Florentino

They are sick of body and soul. They have remorse of the heart, something one has done or something that has been done to one.

—Aurelia

Social Networks and Health Care Policy

What can we learn when we move from individual cases to a network perspective? Can we understand the experiential awareness of a link between connections and health status within the context of the existing provision of health and social care services? When the informants were interviewed systematically to analyze the relationships between their social networks and their health needs and behavior,[2] it was found that their networks of social contacts affected the utilization of the medical system and their likelihood of addressing medical needs. Thus, those informants with stronger networks[3] had fewer medical needs, or had their needs met, while informants exhibiting weaker networks had more unmet medical needs and used the medical system more rarely and irregularly. A third of the sample, who did not have their medical needs addressed, were found to be medically more needy and to be more irregular users of the medical system.

Another important finding was that about half listed only relatives among their daily contacts, and that those for whom relatives were the only source of daily contact tended to have weak networks. Networks that included non-relatives in daily care are increasing in number, size, and composition, in terms of relationship as well as age, including neighbors, home attendants, church members, and friends. Living arrangements reflect current demographic trends (while the total population of East Harlem has decreased, the proportion under eighteen and over sixty-five has increased) and the increasing inequality between these two age groups regarding access to housing turns doubling-up with the elderly into a strategy used by the younger generations to avoid homelessness.

What is the applicability of research findings to addressing the medical needs and improving the access of a geographically defined population to the provision of health care in their immediate area? An illustrative example may be useful. An informant in this study was admitted to the hospital when she was at the limit of her functional capacity. She was treated, yet could not be released when medically appropriate because arrangements for home-care services were problematic. Although she did in fact have a rather large network, she had no close family, and no connections that discharge planners deemed suitable to act as emergency backup. Thus, she was simply "parked" in the hospital for several months after she was medically able to leave. Better information may be needed for such patients about specific network members, their frequency of contact with the person, their connections with each other, and about the constraints these potential caregivers experience that might place obstacles to more frequent contact with the frail elderly. Yet non-kin connections are generally not recognized as decision-makers for a patient, unless they are legally appointed guardians. Official policies use a much narrower definition of kin than does the study population, for whom the broad notion of "kinship" includes ritual kin, some church "brothers and sisters", unofficial stepchildren, and so on.

These analyses have two policy implications: one is to consider network members that are available, regardless of kinship, as legal representatives for the patient. Another policy is to increase the daily contact among network members of those medically needy with weak social networks. Recognizing and strengthening their actual networks would reduce unnecessary institutionalization of the frail elderly. These policies might not only upgrade the quality of life for these individuals but also prove cost-effective to the biomedical care system.

Health and Networks: Ethnographic Findings and Policy Implications

Ethnographic Findings

1. There are two types of illness: of the body and of the soul. The worst illness of the soul is solitude.

2. Unlike Emiliana's, many families are not together today, but they were in the past. Without companionship or other means of combating loneliness, these elderly people believe they are at risk of falling into excessive worry and reminiscing about the past, of "thinking too much"—

all illnesses of the soul. Children either do not take care of their parents or, worse still, often continue to need their parents' care as adults, contrary to the elders' expectations. Other ways of being/feeling cut off from families is either geographical distance from "home" or changed social customs.

3. Since there are more women than men among the elderly due to higher male mortality rates, networks are smaller among men, reversing a pattern for the middle years.

4. In order to prevent or cure "illness of the soul," it is important to connect to significant others and to lead an active life.

5. Connections are not only with people but can include pets.

6. Connections with people are not only with family: home attendants, neighbors, and friends play an important role. Yet many of these are also elderly and frail, and have transportation problems.

7. Connections with people are not only with the living but could include the supernatural—for example, images of saints, altars, or just praying to God.

8. Connections need not be face to face. For some, like Emiliana, families are extended, together, and supportive, even if not all members are geographically proximal. For those who have relatives close by, there is a lot of visiting. For those who do not, including those who live far, the telephone is the glue that connects. Thus, telephone is crucial to bring elderly out of isolation.

9. Connections relate to addressing medical needs.

10. Not all connections are good. Networks are important mediators of health status but one should not assume that their sheer existence necessarily results in positive effects for the individual. The elderly are not only receivers, they are also givers. Kinship ties and extended family commitments require fulfilling certain obligations voluntarily, or being involuntarily pressed to contribute to younger generations, including sharing personal resources.

Policy Implications

While research on social support has begun to inform clinical applications in gerontological service provision for the individual, more needs to be done in the area of network interventions.

First, networks not only help the individual feel supported but are also instrumental in addressing medical needs. Thus, networks are not only important to the elderly individual but also to the biomedical service structure interested in predicting under what circumstances planned services will be utilized. Providing local knowledge about networks to program planners might contribute to increase utilization rates of such services as senior citizen centers.

Second, most of the attention paid to networks of the elderly goes to the family. Antonucci (1990) argues that family members are responsible for the provision of personal care while friends are the locus of emotional support. If tested on larger samples, the finding that the elderly in low-income urban enclaves might have more extensive daily contact with nonfamily network members, as traditionally defined, is important to dispute the service delivery system's assumption of family availability. The findings reported here show that the factors responsible for the ability of personal networks and the service structure to address needs, the extent to which these two service systems overlap, and the areas in which neither is available are still poorly understood. For example, foodstuffs could be brought home to an elderly person still able to cook for herself but unable to negotiate the public space where these are obtained.

In conclusion, the boundaries between the service structure and the network system need to be further explored, and the extent to which each addresses perceived needs has to be mapped, to identify neglected populations who are left with neither. Particularly in planning local community health and social services, we need to figure out the available network structure in assessing not only the need for services such as meals, information, referral services, homemaker services, senior citizen centers, to name but a few, but also whether and to what extent those needs are being addressed. Most "cracks" in the service structure are filled up by community-built support structures that are fragile from the start—helpers are also elderly and often frail themselves. There are potential risks in the ability of these networks to provide daily assistance; as Sokolovsky (1997a, 272) aptly puts it, there are limits in the informal supports of low-income urban elderly.

Moreover, community health and social services presume the ability to recruit unpaid volunteers to service the needs of vulnerable populations. Informants have a clear sense of the cost of services provided—

even when good will provides a moral basis to social exchange—and pay for personal care either in money or in reciprocal services. Government-financed programs should look into paying community helpers either by the hour or for the expenses they incur when involved in helping out. Reimbursement for transportation and telephone costs, for example, would enhance caregivers' ability to provide help. We might entertain the possibility of funding existing caregivers and not assume that services provided by networks should be free of cost.

Funding for the Older Americans Act, which provides the infrastructure to attract funding from the federal and state government as well as philanthropic organizations, should be monitored for its scope in targeting the additional services to an increasing yet aging population within the context of existing daily practices of service. Since funding for the Act has not kept pace with demographic conditions and service needs, most of its services have been reaching low-income elders as individuals. These data support the validity of identifying the elderly's networks and funding them for the services they are already providing.

NINE

"Estamos Pobres de Dinero Pero Somos Todos Ricos" (We Are Poor in Money, But We Are All Rich)

Coping with Economic Constraints in Daily Life

> Many questions come to mind as I, a professional from a mid-dle-class neighborhood in the same city, walk the streets of East Harlem and converse with its people inside homes and in public spaces. How to explain why people are poor but find meaning in their lives? How to make sense of the apparent contradiction between being, as Emiliana puts it, "poor yet rich"? How to unveil their consciousness of social class? How is poverty construed at the local level? Can their understanding illuminate ours and be factored in the national debate on the many wars we have waged against poverty?
> —Author's diary, September 11, 1994

One of the recurrent themes in my conversations with informants was the extent of their poverty, and particularly how their income was insufficient to cover their expenses. The political economy of their displacement (Centro de Estudios Puertorriqueños 1979; Torres 1988; Morales and Bonilla 1993) was a vivid presence throughout their career trajectories, both while still in Puerto Rico and since they outmigrated. The structural characteristics of the labor market they confronted in the United States—among others, low pay, little job security, high firm turnover—accounts for the economic constraints they faced during their working years. But it was their lack of knowledge of citizens' rights—such as employers' mandatory contribution to Social Security, pension plans, and union benefits—under labor legislation that made them easy prey for exploitative employers during the years spent in the labor force.

The work conditions they faced not only adversely marked their working years but also dramatically increased their risks of economic marginalization as they retired from the workforce. As the largest Latino contingent in New York City, Puerto Ricans have experienced limited upward mobility since their massive migration in the 1950s and have not reaped substantial benefits from work to sustain their old age.

What was the economic impact on their retirement years of the historical circumstances that affected their working years? Although direct observation of their life conditions as well as population data corroborated their assertions of poverty, I often and repeatedly wondered: How did they actually "make it"? How was income distributed among their many needs? What were the discrepancies, if any, between actual and perceived poverty? In this chapter I, first present a conceptual framework to understand how poverty affects daily life in the inner city. Then, I interpret research findings on the informants' social construction of poverty within the framework of ethnographically derived budget schedules where reported income and expenditures are compared. I use a needs assessment of the study population to make policy recommendations that might enhance their current ability to address needs and access entitlements.

Being Elderly in *El Barrio*: The Social Construction of Poverty

The persistent, and increasing, inequalities among segments of the population question the ability of existing public policies to deal with poverty as a social issue. Latino elderly living in low-income urban enclaves are four times a minority: they are Latino, they are old, they are poor, and they live in a deteriorating environment.[1] A view from *El Barrio* of income problems and alternative solutions can contribute to understanding elderly Latino poverty.

Growing old in the United States carries economic risks. In 1992, 12.9 percent of the elderly were below the poverty threshold and 23.6 percent were below 150 percent of the poverty threshold (U.S. Bureau of the Census 1996). Personal income declines by one-third to one-half as an individual ages. One reason for income decline is retirement from the workforce: most industries do not employ persons above a certain age. Another reason for income decline lies in the types of occupations persons held: it is not the same to retire as a physician as it is a restaurant busboy since these occupations have access to different opportunities to save and invest for retirement during the working years. A third reason for income decline is the unequal attention paid to workers' rights: to use the same example, the physician is sought by investment agents on tax-deductible savings, pension plans, and so on, and is protected by strong professional associations. The busboy often ignores the range of employer's contractual obligations to workers and the government, and often is unaware of his entitlement to postretirement benefits—or he knows about them, but feels powerless to confront inequities in later life for fear of losing his present job. Attentive to what he has heard about union racketeering, he often rejects union membership for fear of exploitation, and thus finds himself with no pension benefits when they are most needed. Often, he translates language barriers into a lack of power, equating his limited knowledge of English with lack of citizens' rights. That this situation applies as much to undocumented migrants as it does to Puerto Ricans, who are in fact American citizens, evidences that perceived powerlessness is constructed in the interstices between state and civil society.

How does poverty affect the informants? As this labor force entered the New York labor market in this century, with a sharp demographic increase after World War II, they had the following characteristics that would translate into deficits in old age. First, a large proportion of their previous labor force participation had occurred in a different country and, in the case of men, in a different industry. Second, many received no social security benefits (i.e., income from employment) when they retired because employers had failed to report their earnings during their working years. Third, their employment rarely provided for job-related retirement pensions: thus, many received no pension benefits either because their jobs were not unionized or because they refused to join unions during their working years.

As a consequence, when the elderly of *El Barrio* retired from the workforce, they were left not only with inadequate incomes but also with greater percentage declines after retirement than the general population. Their life course experiences with work account for three income deficits upon retirement. First, everybody entered the New York labor force upon migration. Since a large proportion arrived in New York during midlife, their contribution years to the state to be computed as retirement funds later in life was shortened. Second, since social security income is based on income earned and they held low-wage jobs, their social security is less since their income was less to begin with. Third, their sources of income from retirement from the workforce are restricted to state contributions. Thus, their personal income in old age suffers an even larger percentage decrease because somebody with a pension gets 60 percent of his or her preretirement income, but somebody without a pension gets nothing. Thus, these elderly Puerto Rican not only count on inadequate income, as compared to other populations, but also get less work benefits as they retire. The percentage of declining personal income with retirement is thus larger than for people with worker benefits.

In addition to changing with age, income declines significantly among women and minorities in comparison to men and Whites (24 percent of Hispanic elderly were poor in 1997, and women doubled men). By the time Hispanic women reach age seventy-five, their poverty rate is above 50 percent (Atchley 1997).

Poverty also relates to health. A greater proportion of income is allocated to defray out-of-pocket health care costs as people grow older, yet Hispanics have been found to have less access to health insurance than other groups, thus severely compromising their health care and long-term alternatives (Markides and Miranda 1997; Angel and Angel 1997). A national survey conducted on the elderly living alone (Commonwealth Fund Commission 1989) depicted not only a poor population but a population in poor health and with restricted access to medical care and entitlements such as Medicaid and Supplementary Security Income (SSI). Even when benefits are available, many elderly poor do not apply to obtain them. The health of poor Hispanics has been of concern to practitioners (*JAMA* 1991), researchers (Markides et al. 1997; Brink 1992), and policy analysts (Sotomayor and García 1993), yet the study of the health status and health needs of aged Hispanics is in its infancy in comparison to the study of younger populations (Markides and Mindel 1987; Markides and Miranda 1997). In health, as in wealth, Puerto Ricans have fared worse than other Latin American populations: they exhibited greater mortality and morbidity differentials and reported a higher prevalence of disability (Arellano 1990; Hazuda and Espino 1997).

Poverty and neighborhood location are also thought to be factors that retard Hispanic access to the utilization of service delivery systems (Ginzberg 1991). How does this image of Latino elderly relate to the current debate on inner-city poverty? The conceptualization and policy implications of the underclass construct has been the subject of much controversial debate in U.S. scholarly and policy circles (Jencks and Petersen 1991; Annals of the American Academy of Political and Social Science 1989; Wilson 1997; Massey and Denton 1993) and has included Latinos in U.S. *barrios* (Tienda 1989; Moore and Pinder-hughes 1993). As per the major indicators of underclass status—absolute income, residential segregation, and persistent poverty—the elderly in East Harlem constitute an underclass, although there are differences from street to street (Williams and Kornblum 1995)—yet we know little about this age group.

Longitudinal analyses of economic conditions for Latinos demonstrate a steady erosion of Puerto Rican income relative to that of other populations, resulting in a clear increase in poverty rates (Bean and Tienda 1987; Carnoy, Daley, and Ojeda 1990). Being Puerto Rican in New York City adds a fifth minority status, since the dramatic increases in poverty rates in the 1980s (Community Service Society 1987) and 1990s (Morales and Bonilla 1993) have exacerbated Hispanic wage inequality (Meléndez 1996).

Persistent poverty throughout the lifecourse becomes aggravated in later life, particularly for those with restricted access to private pensions. Informants' low wages generate low Social Security benefits, even if they remained employed nearly all their adult lives. However, many poor people encounter no drastic change in their level of living. In fact, with SSI, Food Stamps, and low-rent housing for elders, "some lifelong poor find that their situation in old age actually improves, although it is hardly a standard they would choose" (Atchley 1997, 350).

The poverty debate tends to theorize about class and ethnicity by prioritizing expert-derived poverty indicators, primarily rendered as economic measures expressed quantitatively as outcome data. Less attention is paid to understanding poverty at the micro-level and to how poor people construe the impact of poverty on daily life. This inattention to poverty as process results in important gaps in understanding how poverty affects daily life for specific populations, such as the aged

Latino in East Harlem. First, the conceptualization of poverty as outcome minimizes the historical perspective on poverty throughout the life course of the population under analysis, minimizing the impact of preretirement labor market experiences on postretirement financial equity. Second, an exclusive emphasis on a macro-perspective of poverty reduces our understanding of the impact of poverty on daily life, especially the extent to which activities of daily living constrain individual's access to resources within the immediate environment. Third, poverty studies tend to focus on sources of income, paying little or no attention to the way specific populations distribute expenses—in particular, how the social context is relevant to the allocation of scarce resources. As a result, initiatives for poverty alleviation usually recommend income allocation based on policymakers' categorization of needs, often underplaying specific populations' assessment of the extent to which perceived needs are addressed. Poverty data collected on income alone have important implications for policy design since they minimize the ability to predict the impact of unaddressed perceived needs on the well-being of the population, based on indicators such as their ability to address medical needs or to access entitlements.

This chapter frames the question of poverty alleviation on the assumption that to translate knowledge into action to address population needs, we need information on specific populations' sources of income and distribution of expenses within the micro-level of daily life in the immediate neighborhood. To elicit people's view of poverty it was necessary to work with them on their categorization of income and expenses. First, I assumed that both the source and the distribution of personal income were relevant to drawing an economic profile of this population that could be instrumental in making policy recommendations. Then, I collected information on the sources of personal income and on the distribution of expenses by means of a budget schedule. The schedule was generated by participant observation and interviewing and validated by the study participants before it was incorporated into a survey of the ethnographic sample that profiled their life circumstances during the month prior to interviews. I compared data obtained by ethnography and survey, and analyzed expenses related to addressing predicted versus perceived needs.

The analysis revealed, first, that the study population was poor in absolute terms: monthly reported individual incomes ranged from a low of $81 to a high of $1,133 ($972 to $13,596 annually, averaging $6,000 or less, the official poverty line in 1991). Second, they were poor in situational terms (i.e., they lived in a low-income urban enclave). At the time this study was initiated in the late 1980s, census data indicated that 31 percent of the Latinos of East Harlem had incomes below the poverty level. Third, like the general population, they faced diminishing resources as they aged.

How do the elderly Puerto Ricans in *El Barrio* survive on limited incomes? What is the role of social networks in expenditure distribution at the household level? How does expense distribution impact on the satisfaction of perceived needs?

"Estamos Pobres de Dinero": The Meaning of Emiliana's Wealth

The Origin of Wealth: Economic Strategies
in a Social Context

Emiliana reported that her income was not enough to cover present expenses because she could not accumulate savings while she was in the workforce:

> When I worked here in the factories they would fire you if you said you were not given papers . . . because they did not want to pay to get us Social Security. That is why I get his [her husband's]. Do you know how much I should have? Five thousand dollars in earnings! And I only have $3,500 because this man [the factory owner] did not put us down and took our money. He would not allow us to punch our cards nor gave us the money [that he should have given the government], only our salary, not in an envelope, nor with a receipt, nothing.

> I have to buy many more medicines than they give me . . . in the hospital. It [what I get] is not enough money, but I buy them even if I cannot eat Fridays. Do you think money stretches for everything? I also help my granddaughter and this man here, and we do not suffer because each morning we breakfast on crackers and coffee with milk . . . and God gives us His blessing and we have more than enough, and we dress and shod ourselves [*nos vestimos y calzamos*].

Emiliana would often observe that a person who has more than he or she needs does not necessarily do well. When I asked her to explain, she discussed economic strategies in a social context:

Yes, I will explain to you how it is, I have many ways of explaining it to you. Because we are all poor, and we are all rich. Because the person that has wealth in money, that is not wealth. Wealth is a happiness that God sends to you. . . . There are times . . . I don't know whether this happens to you. . . . Wait, I will tell you. . . . Yesterday was a day when I didn't have a cent [*no tenía un chavo*]. . . . Well, today I have thirty dollars and I have not worked for them! That means that one has faith in Christ and that what you have sowed in the past . . . it isn't that you sowed it for that reason, it is another person that comes to help you even if you do not ask for it. Do you understand? Sometimes you stay awake for a nickel which you do not have or which you have but cannot spend. Momentarily, somebody comes and says: "Here, have ten *pesos* in case you need them." In a little while, somebody else comes and tells you: "Look, have these ten *pesos* in case you want to buy milk." And that is what I am trying to tell you. That is why a person is sometimes badly off, sometimes worse, and sometimes does well. Because what you have here on this earth is what God gives you to reap. You might not believe me, we are poor, but it is poverty of money, because in happiness we are wealthy.

The Distribution of Wealth: Households as Food and Housing Co-ops

Money is spent on food for oneself but also to honor social relationships:

Go to the stove so you see how . . . here we cook to leave [extra] food, so whoever wants it can eat it. No [it is not thrown away], you need to cook food in case somebody comes by the house and there is nothing to give him, you just prepare and give him [the heated food]. Do you know what it is for a family member or a friend of yours to come and there is nothing to give him [to eat]?

It is a priority to provide a social contact with food or housing:

Last year I had my stepson [*hijo de crianza*] with two daughters and a wife living here; I also had my stepdaughter . . . living in this same apartment. The manager found out. I would tell them not to go into the street too much because people like to watch out and tell, and people get bothered. But being children they would always go out. So the manager was told that I had the house full of boarders. But they did not have a job nor welfare. So the manager comes and tells us: "Ah, there they are telling me that you have the house full of people and that is forbidden. We have to know that and we did not know it." So I told him: "Yes, sir, it is true, I have the house full of people. I have my family here. . . . I have a good heart for myself and for the world because they do not have another place and have no work. And they have no home because they had to give up their house because they had no work, but I have them here and I will not allow them to sleep in the street." So he tells me: "No, it is forbidden and they could call you from court downtown and . . ." "You are wrong, you know why? Because here there is no discrimination, because if you were out there without a home, in the street [*rodando*] and I did you the favor of having you here, and I would give you food, the government could not object. . . . You must excuse me, but I can go to court, even to Supreme Court I would go if I have to, and tell them all this, they would not tell me to [have them] leave this house. What they would tell me is that when my family finds jobs they can leave. And you should tell me that too."

Look, now I have here a nephew, who sleeps on the couch, on that other couch sleeps another one, and I feel so happy! Because if I get up at night and I am pacing around the living room, I am happy and I pray for them so God protects them and helps them.

Emiliana sees herself as a giver regardless of her economic situation, a self-image that has a tremendous impact on her dignity and self-respect and makes her central in her personal network:

You would not believe how kind my family was to me . . . because I was always like a mother to all of them, and I have helped them in everything, in everything I have helped them. Not because I am rich, but in whatever I could help them, I would help them. And I do not pay attention to whether I have money but if someone tells me he is needy, like if they tell me they need fifty-nine *pesos* and if I have them, I say: "Here they are." And I have been like that with the family and with almost anyone, and thanks I give to God that I am still here. I have never denied anything to my family or anyone, and they have always seen me as the mother of the oldest and the youngest, do you understand?

Intergenerational Transfers of Resources

The value Emiliana places on the role of giver relates to her awareness of the increasing importance of social networks as systems of resource exchange throughout the life course:

> I pay what I can pay and he [her grandson] pays what he can pay. We have just paid the rent, the telephone, what is left over is to eat, dress [buy clothing], buy shoes, buy medicines out there. Because I buy a lot of medicine here, I buy . . . in the drugstore . . . well, alcohol, soap, Tylenol, for the home. But now there are a lot of people here. For Christmas, I told them: "Anyone thinking of giving me a Mother's Day gift, I tell you, I prefer the money." This one gave me ten dollars, Miyin gave me twenty dollars and brought a present and flowers, her husband gave me ten dollars, the home attendant gave me ten dollars, well they gave me a lot of money! . . . Up to now, I have lacked nothing. Do not worry, that God does not make a hungry mouth. [*Dios no hace una boca sin pan*].

Giving enhances the predictability of being socially recognized during lifetime and compensated in the afterlife:

> Look, if I have nothing to give you from what I am about to eat or drink, do not think that I will sit here to eat. Never! Here, if I am given anything, I should be given half, and half should be given to that who is next to me. If there is nothing for the other person, I do not want to eat. I was born like that and will die like that, you know? Because I suffer the hunger of the other and my own.

> Since I have nothing . . . I cannot have anything, but I believe that in heaven I have earned my glory . . . because I helped my siblings, my mother, my father.

Just as there are people who are prepared to give, there are those who take away, not only strangers but also family members or friends of the family who come to the house:

> Since I do not see, people take away things, they have taken away so many things! Some of those who come here.

> You should learn! Men are like that! They wait until one spends the last cent. And it should not be like that because say I have my daughter who

needs a *peso*, then I have to have it to give it to her, because she has nobody, only her mother, isn't this true? But he [her father] does not say that! No. Because things are like that. One cannot talk, but that is how things are. Men live off women [*vividores*].[2]

Do other study participants also experience nonpecuniary wealth in a social context? How do they understand the meaning of poverty, both their own and that of others?

Perceptions of Poverty in Daily Life: Views from the Ethnographic Sample

There are at least three different, and often contradictory, means of arriving at calculations of poverty. One, based on governmental sources of information, calculates a figure on the basis of known income and predicted expenses. A second method to calculate poverty is to draw on people's calculations of reported income and expenses. While reported income sometimes differs from real income, it is interesting to note that actual expenses always differ from estimated ones. A third method, which is proposed here, is to look into both sources of information so that we can compare and contrast policymakers' knowledge of income and estimated expenses to what people define as needs to be met and how they address them.

Unlike the statistical calculations of state bodies, experienced poverty results from people's inability or difficulty in addressing locally defined needs, which might or might not coincide with state-defined needs. Given the potential lack of congruence and the fact that populations orchestrate their own ways of addressing what they perceive as needs, with or without state funding, uncovering population-defined needs is relevant to assessing the extent to which public policy programs truly succeed in addressing poverty. Since population-defined needs are not acknowledged publicly, two potential biases in information can arise: people allocate resources to activities without acknowledging them as needs, and thus fail to balance expenses against income. Conversely, researchers tend to collect information solely on state-defined needs.

What are the sources of personal income? How are expenses distributed? How much of personal income goes into covering basic needs?

How can basic needs be defined? What is the best way to get information on reported and unreported income and expenses?

Data on both sources of income and distribution of expenses were elicited from the study participants in the course of ethnographic field-work. Their experience of the impact of poverty in daily life was obtained in conversations about what they considered to be "the things in life that are good to have" and in understanding how they ordered their priorities. This exercise provided information for an ethnographic classification of needs into actual and perceived. Actual needs were considered to be rent, utilities, food, and health care. The "food" category included both that purchased for home consumption—including food bought with the specific purpose of establishing and consolidating social connections—or for consumption away from home, for example, if one was hungry and purchased a meal during an unexpectedly long wait at a hospital. The "health care" category included information on all out-of-pocket costs—most informants are covered by Medicare and Medicaid—of purchases made at pharmacies, drugstores, and *botánicas*, which they deemed instrumental to maintain or upgrade health status.

A survey conducted to validate the ethnographic information had remarkably similar results, confirming the validity of the information and dispelling the probability of measurement error. As is well known by econometrists, it is more difficult to obtain exact information on expenses than on income in any population: most people have faulty recollections of their expenses, especially those incurred in cash. Additionally, the study population perceived me, and the interviewers I hired, as staff of the Medical Center, and thus might have had reservations about entrusting us with such private information, for fear of being reported and losing existing benefits. As a matter of fact, some informants flatly refused to provide information on budgets, while others were distrustful of my verbal promise of confidentiality, even after they signed a consent form and often asked me to refrain from taking notes on some of the information they provided. Thus, I resorted to photographs of people in *El Barrio* to stimulate informants to reflect on the needs they had disclosed through verbal prompts during the ethnographic and survey phases of the study. This method made them more comfortable, as they objectified their own circumstances within the context of those of others.

The Budget: Reported Income and Expense Categories

Budget ethnographies show that reported income often does not square with reported expenses, as in the case of Juan:

Total Monthly Income: $333
  Social Security $265
  Welfare $68
  No Supplemental Social Security Income and no Food Stamps ["I used to receive SSI from Social Security but no longer since they give you very little and sometimes you have to go downtown to report. It is not worth it."]

Total Monthly Expenses: $776
  Rent $225
  Electricity $53
  Telephone $59 ["I use it a lot for emergencies"]
  Food $240 ["I spend $7/$8 daily at the Chinese takeout"]
  Laundry $20 ["Take clothes five times a week"]
  Cleaners $30 ["They charge $8 for 4 pants"]
  Transportation $70 ["I pay $6 for a taxi to the hospital"]
  Haircut $2 ["I get a haircut every three months"]
  Other: $35 ["I pay $35 a month for my VCR"]
        $42 ["for cable"]

Juan covers the difference of $443 through earnings in the informal economy, in this case watching out for gambling operations, an occupation that can bring in as much as two hundred dollars in cash in a good day.

María can barely subsist on a budget where reporting excludes the many resource exchanges that take place within a social network:

Total Monthly Income: $400
  Social Security $400
  Pensions $0 ["I did not get union benefits"]

Total Monthly Expenses: $404.17
  Rent $275
  Electricity $50

Telephone $0 ["I do not have a telephone"]

Life Insurance $14.17 ["I am paying since 1955 for the box to bury me so my family does not have to ask for the money [*para que no tengan que pedir*]"

Laundry $0 ["I do not have to pay for laundry because I have a washing machine."]

Health Care ["I do not have to pay for the doctor because I have Medicaid"]

Food ["I cannot remember. For two weeks I just had rice; I buy for myself and my dogs; when I run out, Marta— neighbor—gives me some and I sew for her. I often eat at my stepdaughter around the corner when I help her with home child care."]

Transportation $5 ["I am always on foot but if I need to get to the hospital I pay a taxi, I do not like to be late."]

Church $10 ["To St. Paul Church so that they give a mass in my name when I die."]

Clothing $50 ["This month I bought fabric for bed covers which was $7 the yard and then I have a lot left over to make clothing."]

If we could include an estimated food expense in this budget, the $4.17 difference between income and expenses would certainly be much higher. Certainly, this method of calculating budgets does not account for what is really going on in her life.

Subtracting expenses from income, as the analyses presented above eloquently show, does not explain how the study participants make a living at the present time or why their budgets should not reflect their past contributions. Confusing benefits with assistance, the study participants often take pride in their long-term work trajectory and on their personal ability to earn a livelihood:

> I have not been feeling well because I cannot do anything and I do not like to ask. I have been in the country for sixty-four years and I have never been on welfare. . . . I do not like to accept charity: I did not come to this country to get relief [welfare]. I came to work. The day after I came down from the *Ponce* [the ship that brought her] I already had work.
>
> —Luz María

They are all fully aware of how the inadequacy of income to cover basic needs affected daily life, and especially constrained their ability to afford health care and housing:

> I feel dizzy . . . because I do not eat right. I only have $105 left and it went mostly on electricity and gas. I cannot afford much food, a chicken quarter is three dollars.
>
> —María

The impact of poverty was better articulated when reacting to the photographs of others:

> Here you see a man who needs a hearing aid . . . he is touching his ear. . . . He lives in a nice room but is worried because he has just heard that the rent will be raised. . . . He needs to get medicine and his check is not enough. . . . The rents are raised every year, when it is not every month. . . . [the elderly person] needs to move . . . gets thrown out to the street.
>
> —Dora, on a photo of Felix

> Here you see a social worker asking something of an old woman who adores animals, they are like her children, they are her company, she would fight if somebody wanted to take them away from her, they are the only company she has. . . . She lives with what she gets, is humble but at peace yet poor. She has no family close to her. She is not sick but thoughtful. The social worker is from welfare. She is telling her about her poverty, about her diminishing check, she is being asked about Medicare and Medicaid. She probably asks the social worker how can she live without sufficient money. Maybe she lives on social security, maybe on SSI, but her income is not enough to survive. Nowadays the hospitals have become more aggressive to get insurance payments . . . when the elderly have to go they get anguished if they do not have Medicaid. The social worker is probably telling her not to worry, that she will try to solve her problem.
>
> —Dora, on a photo of María

A few, like Armando, are satisfied with their income and health benefits:

> I have not done badly. At least I have two checks and if I get sick I go to the Veterans Hospital.

In absolute terms, informants are keenly aware that income does not keep pace with expenses. Most would agree with Dora, who reflects that finding *ambiente*[3] did not lead to economic sustainability:

> Many people think that because you live in New York, you have more money and live like a king, but I say this is not true: we live in misery, worse, because often the check that one gets, like I get a check each month, is not enough [*no me alcanza para nada*].

There are also needs that would not enter into the projections of a public policymaker. Taking a view from the expense side, these are perceived financial obligations—such as personal relationships, entertainment, charitable contributions, life insurance, and out-of-pocket medical expenses—that allow for a reconceptualization of income needs.

The first need to be budgeted is the social context. Social networks need to be fed. The aphorism "man does not live by bread alone" really fits a world view that values social connections as much as material well-being in assessing the quality of life. Thus, income is perceived in its financial and social connotations: it motivated migration in the past, and serves to fund "the good things in life": food, housing, and significant others to enjoy them with. Monchito was shown a photograph of Luz María sitting at a table with a radio, crackers, and coffee mugs (see p. 169). Next to her is her friend and helper Aurelia. Luz María's walker is visible in front of her chair, showing she has no locomotion without it. Monchito said:

> This lady lives alone, I think. . . . She has problems with her legs or her hips, but she is happy because she has a roof, food, and there is always a visitor.

Looking at the same photograph, Florentino said:

> She is happy, amused, satisfied to be alive.

In addition to feeding them, informants often pay their network members. Informants reported having to cover a variety of needs that arise from their life circumstances, as defined by the cultural context, and thus are not covered by state programs geared to addressing basic needs such as food, shelter, or medical care. An informal economy has developed to address such needs through neighborhood-based social connections. For example, it is common to hire connections as chaperons for errands, although they are sometimes paid in services. Luz María, for example, gives money regularly to two helpers who bring her the weekly shopping:

> I give thirty dollars to Alicia [a stepdaughter who comes Sunday with the weekly shopping] and twenty dollars to Aurelia [a neighbor who helps out].

In a world of social connections that give but also take from people, where there is trust and distrust, where friends and relatives can also steal from people, the issue of doing for the other without interest is doubly valued:

> Here people are untrue [*falsa*]. She [Aurelia] is sincere. She buys, cooks, pays the rent, takes me with the walker, I do not give her money. But from time to time I do because she only has a pension. Aurelia takes me to cash my checks. Aurelia takes me and does not charge me. She is a healthy person. We do not have monkey business [by this she refers to another woman whom she said came to help out and ended up stealing from her].
>
> —Luz María

Although this reciprocal exchange network addresses their needs, the system has disadvantages: since helpers have their own problems, their service is unreliable. If somebody is sick, for example, emergency arrangements need to be made, as Luz María explained:

> Alicia [her elderly stepdaughter who brings the weekly shopping] did not come, she is sick. She did not bring the *compra* [the food shopping]. Her son could not bring it. She will come tomorrow to bring it to me. Aurelia brought [food], she came.
>
> I pay my sister-in-law weekly to cook food for me.
>
> —Juan

Entertainment also needs to be budgeted. Informants allocate scarce resources for gambling on an individual basis, but also collectively raise funds for group outings. Bingo is played at many senior citizen centers, not only to pass the time but also to raise funds for outings:

Yesterday I spent the day at Pomona, a recreation park in New Jersey, with the money the bingo group had collected. People pay twenty-five cents a game and that money is given to the director for these retreats. The money the city gives is not enough for that.

—Petra

Don . . . comes by frequently to sell me a *numerito*.[4]

—Luz María

Informants also contribute money to organized religion, and charitable organizations, or to fund activities related to their spiritual beliefs:

In Puerto Rico my mother would take me to a spiritist and they would do good work and not charge for it. Nowadays you go to one of them and they ask you a lot of money to do you a small job [*para hacerte un trabajito*]. They do not do it for charity as in the past, when you gave whatever you had and if you had nothing, they even gave you chickens or other good things to eat."

—Juan

The candle [in the altar] is always lit, day and night. You buy them at *botánicas* like the statuettes.

—Juan

Informants complain of spending money on out-of-pocket health care expenses; they believe the state should provide free health coverage and automatic retirement benefits. They illustrate how, even when they are aware of existing services and programs, they often experience restrained access to entitlements due to a lack of appropriate information about their rights:

Government is not fair. If one has worked, they give one Medicare. Medicaid is for those who have not worked. For Medicare you need to have worked and only pay 20 percent of doctors and hospitals. But it should be free.

—Dominga

The [orthopedic] sock costs eighty dollars. We will see how much I get back from Medicare. In the past there was no limit. Now there are limits for everything.

—Julia

I asked the social worker who came last week [about Medicaid] and she did not tell me anything. My daughter called and said she was told I had Medicaid but I was not told.

—Felix

I am after a doctor who prescribes liquid medicine and a shot. A doctor on 106th Street, a private doctor. I have not been able to go yet because I was waiting to receive a sum of money.

—Carmen

I do not wait . . . when I feel an attack [he suffers from asthma] coming, I walk or take a taxi and rush to the hospital.

—Juan

The private doctor takes good care of me. He does not take Medicaid so I pay him little by little. I owe him four or five hundred dollars. There are many doctors who do not take Medicaid because they have trouble getting paid. . . . I will always have my teeth made, they cost six hundred—in Mount Sinai they would take two years to make—I started going to a private dentist in the Bronx, 186th and Prospect. My son helps me little by little.

—Julia

I could have gotten [health] benefits from the union, Local 25, but I refused to learn English so I lost them because I was dumb [*por boba los perdí*] and I lost my work contract [i.e., she no longer has proof of employment to redress the situation].

—María

Influential contacts and political participation are believed to help in accessing entitlements:

I was one of the first persons to get Social Security. I gave my vote to Roosevelt, I am involved in politics.

—Dora

The state is not ready to help. In Puerto Rico they know me and we would have addressed the same need. We would have gone to the person who has influence [*Nos vamos al que cogió la sartén por el mango.*] But here one does not know anybody.

—Monchito

But neither strategy helps when benefits are discontinued by the state:

> We elderly people used to get a supplement for heat [about $100-$200] and they called me from the office to tell me they had abolished it [*lo tumbaron*].
>
> —Julia

Informants believe they should be entitled to free burial services to rid their network members of the preoccupation of disposing of their bodies after death. What they call "death insurance" is an extra expense that they pay local collectors who are dubiously accountable to network members upon the incumbent's passing. Moreover, saving money for this need often prevents them from obtaining important services during their lifetime:

> I was not given a home attendant although I am an invalid because I refused to let them know about the money in the bank. Silvia, my stepdaughter, knows because it is destined to bury me. I will go to St. Roman in the Bronx where my mother and first husband are. In the cemetery where my second husband is, there is no more room. I bought the land for all three there by myself.
>
> —Luz María

The informants' offspring are often unemployed or underemployed, and they often resort to parents who rely on an assured check a month. Although requests are not always honored, these intergenerational transfers place the elderly in the ironic position of being, comparatively speaking, self-sufficient:

> When Josefa's children need money, they go ask her. My son comes to ask, but I do not give him money. I tell him: "What I have is for me alone."
>
> —Dominga

Other expenses reported include commissions charged by stores to cash their checks. Losing money over their inability to dispute bills and tipping government employees for fear of losing their services.

> The travel agency charges me four dollars for cashing the check."
>
> —Julia

The home attendants are paid too little and sometimes they leave. You have to give them fifty cents weekly, but I give them a full dollar.

—Luz María

They overcharge me and I do not know how to deal with the bills. I do not call because I do not speak English. I do not ask for help here [in the United States], I do not know why. Unless there is somebody I can trust [she equates trust with speaking Spanish] . . . I do not speak English.

—Julia

How do the study participants finance the needs that are not covered by their reported income? To raise additional income to pay for other needs, such as out-of-pocket medical expenses, they resort to employment in the informal economy, like Juan; self-employment in the household, like Telesforo; reciprocal exchanges of resources, like María; and other strategies, such as asking for gifts in cash, like Emiliana:

Hallo [he tells me when I walk in]. No, I did not go out. I was repairing televisions that I find in the street and then I sell well.

—Telesforo

I cannot live on that money, so I have been earning extra money by working for a gambling place where I have to tell if the police are coming. I make a hundred dollars a day.

—Juan

A more common strategy, however, is to engage in systems of exchange of personal resources, which includes generating enough credit to borrow money as needed.

I am fine without money. I do not have enough for the telephone and cable. I need to get money from my friends. Whoever lends me money knows that I am very responsible and I would give it back.

—Julia

I sew for Julia, she gives me cooked food.

—María

Every month I give her [his ex-wife] twenty-five dollars to help her. When I do not have money, she gives money to me. I just took her some expensive shrimp.

—Telesforo

Personal Income, Expenditures, and Social Networks

Like other low-income older people, the informants receive their incomes mainly from government-sponsored programs such as Social Security and Supplemental Security Income (see Figure 9.1). In addition, a considerable proportion of informants reported income from Food Stamps. Only about a fifth enjoyed income from having joined unions while they were part of the labor force. Income from private pensions was negligible.

An analysis of income and expenditures shows that for some among the study population, income was insufficient to provide for basic needs. For example, about 25 percent reported spending more than 40 percent of their total income on rent (see Figure 9.2).

These results revealed variability in the cultural construction of both need and deprivation. Despite the public image of homogeneity, this is a heterogeneous population: there was a wide spectrum in the reported availability of income that could be used for actual and perceived expenses. Also, while some informants were quick to notice that they had no money left over, thus making reference to absolute deprivation, others tended to compare their income availability to that of others whom they perceived as being worse off than themselves.

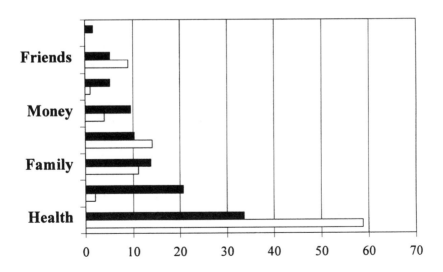

Figure 9.1. Diverse Sources of Income (N = 43)

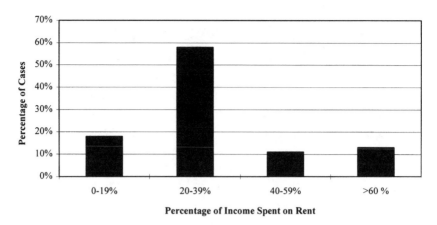

Figure 9.2. Income Spent on Rent

The informants dichotomized expense items such as food, shelter, and health care as usable by an individual or by a network of connections. Food, for example, exceeds the notion of adequate nutrition to include a public relations strategy to entice social connections to repeat their visits. Thus, food is not only consumed as a survival strategy but also to nurture a network that would provide a safety net during crisis situations. This explains why there was always food when I came by, even unexpectedly, and why informants cooked above and beyond the number of people expected for a meal, even if leftovers were discarded or given to the homeless. In addition, many among the disabled elderly paid extra money to connections for the service of buying and bringing food. Finally, visitors often brought food when they stopped by. Given all these different sources and uses of food in a household, it is hardly surprising that study participants had difficulty recalling exactly how much money they spend on food. Although nutritious meals are available for only a few cents at senior citizen centers, only about half the males and 17 percent of the females among the nondisabled in the study eat there.

Shelter is presumably an easier item to recall than food since people pay the same rent every month. But even for those who reported living alone, shelter was often shared with family and friends, on either a permanent or a transient basis. Although the proportion of total income spent by the elder on shelter is fixed, the use of space is not: members of the younger generations, related by blood or fictive ties, often stay over when they find themselves too crowded where they live or when they come for visits from Puerto Rico. Others would stay over temporarily when encountering a problem (e.g., a grandson who was threatened by a gang at his high school was taken out of public view for a month), or stay permanently in a mutually convenient arrangement (e.g., to stay with the elder at night). In such situations, the elderly get personal care and the younger people get free rooming. It is important to notice that in this respect, the elderly are relatively better off than the younger generations in spite of their restricted incomes: not only do they receive a steady income from government subsidies, but they also benefit from entitlements restricted to the aged, such as Title VIII housing reductions. The sharing of shelter also has important implications for the working poor: many more would be homeless if they did not have access to elders' residences.

Planning for health care financing, based on prediction of biomedically defined costs, overlooks the population-specific allocation of significant proportions of total income to ethnomedically defined health care needs, given that health care insurance fails to meet health expenses that they consider instrumental to well-being. Their medical care costs include fees for private physicians, self-help aids with physical or spiritual illnesses, and "death insurance" to address their preoccupation with disposing of their bodily remains.[5] But there are other costs that relate to their ability to sustain the strong networks necessary to address medical needs, such as telephone use, contributions to philanthropic associations and churches, or support of social connections undergoing personal troubles. In addition, many informants, in fact, contribute to mail campaigns on behalf of hungry children. In sum, the income intended for the elderly covers needs that are ignored by policymakers, including an important social cost: a hungry unemployed younger population.

Policy Recommendations

1. As reported during ethnographic interviews, median income was about five hundred dollars a month. This population is, therefore, in need of additional resources to be able to make a living in New York City in absolute terms. Sources of income need to be both diversified and expanded: for example, the healthy elderly could be paid to take

care of so-called latchkey youngsters (children who come home to an empty household).

2. Both relatives and nonrelatives are included in exchange systems based on reciprocal giving and receiving. More care should be taken by social service providers in eliciting information about the people who provide care for the elderly, whether they are family or not, and in estimating their real availability to make daily contact with the person. Similarly, a system should be set up that pays those network members according to their provision of services to help cover their out-of-pocket expenses.

3. There are many programs set up for the elderly on the basis of entitlement assumptions, and yet little comparative information is gathered about the extent of their knowledge about these entitlements or the constraints some individuals might experience in accessing such entitlements. For example, in my study population, only a few of the healthy elderly used senior citizen centers for entertainment and congregate meals. A topic of inquiry is to find out the reasons for the small demand for nutrition services at senior citizen centers. More research should be conducted on other alternative modalities for dispensing nutrition services. Informants cooked and ate at home, or had meals brought to the house, independently of mobility status,[6] and acquired foodstuffs at reduced prices by joining in cooperatives, among many other ways of obtaining food. Programs should be designed on the basis of current eating patterns at the household level.

4. Although taking a household versus an individual perspective does not alter the cost of rent for the elderly, we do not have information on the contribution of other household members to rent or other expenses. Studies that monitor who contributes what in households need to be undertaken. From my observations, the elderly put up the rent, but younger household members contribute with goods or services.

5. Telephone communication was central in providing instrumental and emotional social support to this urban elderly population, particularly to those living alone. In fact, only one of the 46 informants did not have a telephone at home. Programs to help defray the telephone costs of the elderly, similar to those set up for heating during the winter months, for example, would be crucial for their well-being.

6. Some expenses are also destined, as income transfers or sharing of resources, for younger family members. Programs should identify these

family members and support them, rather than providing resources to the elderly without acknowledging that these will be shared in intergenerational transfers.

7. Often, the informants and their relatives have limited knowledge about the services that are available to them or do not know how to obtain such services. Better public education campaigns should be designed for that purpose. These campaigns should not construe state services as state charity (the study participants' notion of welfare), but rather as a right earned through a lifetime of hard work.

The finding that in this apparently homogeneous population there is diversity in terms of the distribution of household expenses suggests that population-specific needs assessments should be sensitive to uncovering the fit between actual and perceived needs within the context of the existing service structure. Programs based on the elderly's actual allocation of resources could reduce costs to the state, the major source of the study population's income, while making the well-being of the aging poor an objective of society. In sum, to translate poverty research into the development of policy alternatives geared to designing action programs that address the equitable distribution of societal resources, to follow Williams' (1992) challenge, I suggested a population, rather than an individual, approach to (1) collecting economic profiles of the elderly; (2) providing equal attention to expenses and income; (3) assessing needs at the micro-level; (4) understanding how poverty affects daily practice; and (5) designing interventions in the household economy that take a network and life-course approach to need identification.

PART IV

Policy Ethnography of Aging

in *El Barrio*

I went back to *El Barrio* today. I had asked Susana to read a chapter and she said I should come over, that she had some comments. And like every time I go back to my friends in *El Barrio*—not as an anthropologist—there is food: sautéed steak, vegetables, rice, white beans and of course plantains. When I protested, Susana said she was the one who had an *antojo* [a desire] to eat white beans today. While we chatted in the kitchen about her upcoming eye surgery, I watched her fry plantains. (Here is the recipe for *tostones*: take a green plantain, *un plátano verde*, and cut it lengthwise in thick pieces. Fry in very hot cooking oil until tender. Place pieces separately in the peel and crush them gently. Then put them back in the pan and fry them slowly until golden.) We ate slowly, talking about us, about life, and about politics. She wanted to know my opinion about what a local politician had said about Puerto Ricans coming in the forties: that they came as sheep, looking for welfare. I said in many other words what I am conveying in this book: that people are just people, and thus different from one another. She showed me her comments on the chapter, made suggestions, told me Emiliana was right on target. We talked about her own writing and my possible help in publishing her last novel. We parted with kisses and hugs and good wishes.

Walking back to my bus, I reflected on the street scenes that enveloped me as I walked to her home. I had not been back since Christmas, when I came to visit with Emiliana's family for the first time since she passed away. There is also death in the streets of *El Barrio*. In the physical and human decay: garbage on the sidewalks, rubbish inside vacant lots, boarded up buildings, signs of prostitution, blatant evidences of drug addiction. And yet there is enthusiasm for life and vital signs of mission and purpose: people flood the streets with children and lovers, loud music that makes one participate willing or not is coming out of stores (there is also a singing contest in a blocked side street), and from a party going on at a *casita*[1] where they invite me to enter when I stop my march out of curiosity. Spanish is spoken everywhere, in many tongues (the man who sells me the flowers I take to Susana is Mexican). A delicious smell escapes from my favorite restaurant for *mofongo*.[2] And there are the elderly, going about life as usual, making a clear statement that they hold on to life as a right, like everyone else. Some play dominoes on tables in the sidewalk of Sabater grocery and, as usual, bystanders watch attentively. Some take care of children in an open lot. Some sit around a table dressed with a Puerto Rican flag and ask me to sign a petition to free political prisoners. The woman who hands me the pen sighs as she comments that they have been pleading for their release for over fifteen years. And some, like Susana, are indoors but thinking about their lives and their own place in the world. How do they hold on to life?

—Author's diary, July 27, 1997

Part III attempted to understand the issues affecting the elderly of *El Barrio* from a policy perspective with the goal of exploring the congruence among existing policies, the provision of health and social services at the local level, and people's needs. Part IV invites the informants to the forefront, by attempting to understand how they articulate the problems they perceive and reflect on alternative solutions.

For these elderly, daily life acquires meaning within the context of *El Barrio*, a social space where they feel they belong. Part IV addresses life and death in *El Barrio* from the perspective of survivors who show that people have developed their own resources to cope with economic as well as personal, emotional, and spiritual needs. They identify both the constraints and the joys of life in *El Barrio*, and suggest solutions to government. They add an important voice to the policy debate and suggest that the government, private service agencies, and the public in general should acknowledge their ability to survive in a low-income urban enclave while holding onto personal relationships and deriving security from spiritual beliefs. Learning how they go about their lives and how they cope may challenge existing policies about human problems and designs to solve them, based only on the experience of the outside expert. Learning how local residents define their needs and listening to their suggestions for solving problems can provide the policy analysts with important information for designing policies that address the needs of specific populations, rather than generic types. Learning how they go about their everyday lives might also teach us about what is considered essential—and what is not—to a life contextualized by a specific space. In sum, learning about how these elderly go about their lives need not be used as an argument to convince government that these people, despite the odds against them, can manage. Local knowledge on the impact of existing policies could help narrow the hiatus between the program-planner view and the vision from *El Barrio* and contribute to actions that make sense to this population. I argue that such local knowledge should be elicited from the population rather than intermediaries such as community organizers.

TEN

El Barrio: A Metaphor for Social Issues in New York City

Confusing me with a prostitute on the way to Emiliana today, a man followed me asking: "How much, how much?" I
bumped into other people staggering as if intoxicated with
drugs. Then, there were children's screams of delight in the
yard of her building. As I pushed Emiliana's wheelchair on the
way to cashing her check and going shopping, we passed people settling into domino games on the sidewalks or just hanging out in the streets, to have a better view of the life that un-
folds in the great theater that are the streets of East Harlem.
—Author's diary, August 13, 1994

How does living in a low-income urban enclave relate to the way a person utilizes space? What are the interrelationships between public and
private space? To answer these questions, this chapter examines perceptions of public space from a historical and comparative perspective to understand how informants contrast "streets as public entertainment" versus "streets as constraint." It explores the impact of perceptions of public and private space on the notions of "trust" versus "distrust." The
informants suggest that, although public and private space are physically
separate, they should not provide a different sense of comfort. Thus, a
person should be able to trust the neighborhood, to feel ownership of
the used space, and to feel comfortable in the living space, whether inside or outside the home.

Perceptions of Public Space: The Streets

The neighborhood—El Barrio—deeply affects the lives of the Puerto
Rican elderly who live within its confines, in both positive and negative

Playing dominoes in the sidewalks. (Photo by Judith Freidenberg)

ways. Informants made constant references to worrisome concerns about the streets of *El Barrio*, such as the poor condition of housing, homelessness, crime, drug addiction, and lack of public services. Yet they were also enthusiastic about having a place in the world where they were known and thus felt safe. They discussed the importance of sharing entertainment in the public space and the enjoyment of hanging out in the streets; of listening to music coming out of the stores; of basking in the noise of the streets of *El Barrio*, or of looking at the outdoors from indoors.

El Barrio: Better or Worse? Views of Two Generations

Whenever conversations that assessed the present situation came up, Emiliana, like most informants, compared the present conditions in *El Barrio* to the past. She contended that in the past employment was available, so there was less street crime and less violence, since most conflicts were over ethnic territorial claims. Were these perceptions related to age at migration? Let us hear two generations of the Moreno family discuss the issues:

Sixto [Emiliana's son]: When we came from Puerto Rico, there were Italians and Irish, a few Puerto Ricans. We boys ran after them to over there [he points towards the East River] and they [Italians and Irish] ran after us to over here [this conversation is taking place on Lexington and 112th], and there were fights around Second Avenue . . . the Italians were afraid of the Hispanics.

Emiliana: That is, they [the Italians] tried to make them [the Hispanics] afraid. . . . It was there at 114th and Madison. . . . He knew how to fight! He threw him [a bully] to the floor and hit him hard and he never abused anybody anymore, he did not come back! Because you have to teach boys to defend themselves. I told him: "If they provoke you into a fight [*si te buscan pelea*], do not allow them to hit you, fight!" And you did not have to tell him, he was courageous [*guapo*]!

Sixto: But [those times] are over. In the past, they fought with fists for an hour, for a bit and then they drank and made friends, without going too far. But not now, now they come back with a gun and they kill you!

Emiliana: You are not allowed to have a gun, but all the bandits in the streets carry guns, hidden. Can't you see that all over they are killing people out there?

Sixto: But if you live here, you find it is the same [i.e., things have not changed that much] because everybody knows you.

Emiliana: We have been living here for forty years in this house and nothing has happened to any of us.

Sixto: But if you are not from here, it is worse.

Thus, although a resident is still better protected than an outsider, the increase and the progressively violent nature of crime have changed *El Barrio* for the worse. According to two generations of the Moreno family, the causes of the deterioration of quality of life in the neighborhood relate to the pervasiveness of drug addiction across generations, to the leniency of the legal system in combating drug commercialization, and to yet unaddressed problems of adolescence, such as teen-age pregnancies and juvenile delinquency.

Emiliana: Drugs have harmed youth and some mothers who do not know how to resist . . . take drugs and forget the children.

Sixto: What is harming the whole city is the laws . . . which are too soft for people. . . . Well, the one who is bad needs to be eliminated because . . . Here what is also happening is that there are many families that start very young, fourteen- and fifteen-year-olds, to have children and then they do not know how to raise them: when they get to be twelve or fourteen they are bandits!

Jovino [Emiliana's husband]: This city is rotten. Here everything is abuse. People kill each other. Even the kids do not behave today [*no cogen orden hoy en día*]. This is lost [*Esto está perdido*]. You ask me if it was always like that? No, it has been like this for the last twenty years. It is drugs, drugs. When I came to this country, the drugs were not known.

How, specifically, do these problems affect daily life? Emiliana provides examples of what she likes and does not like about where she lives. Facing the courtyard of her project building, which she can barely see, she points out, in the same breath, the ups and downs of living there. She likes being known: stopping to chat with the many people who greet her, sitting in the downstairs patio, hearing the sounds and smells of *El Barrio*, basking in its sun "full of vitamin C."

But she also feels she is under multiple jeopardy: the perception of crime in the streets is multiplied manifold by the fear of crime instigated by the media, by neighbors' gossip about building vandalism, and by her own sense of physical vulnerability. Crime is one of the many domains where the boundary between public and private blurs, where safety can be located both within and outside, rendering a person socially visible and invisible at the same time. The service structure fails to understand how crime can affect what could be minor chores, like the ability of an elderly person to cash a check:

> They [Social Security Administration] brought the check [to my building] and the mailbox was broken and they asked me to go [get it at the post office] so I have to ask someone to go to the post office, to 110th Street with me.

What are the reasons for these problems? What is causing crime? The most important factor is the lack of structured after-school activities for children:

> Because at four or at three o'clock they are dismissed from the schools. The children laying down at the house and there is no work for them! The government does not care [*busca la perdición*]! That is why there is so many people killing and stealing. The child should be taught to work, as

in the past, since childhood, to earn a living working and to learn the honor a person needs. Yes, my daughter, there in Puerto Rico, everybody worked before, but now, neither there nor here [do people work].

Another important factor, which also contrasts with the past, is the lack of employment opportunities for young people in the local area:

> *Emiliana:* Here [in this house] there are several youngsters [*muchachos*] without work. . . . In the past there were all kinds of work here, and now there is nothing. Things are bad, very bad, if children cannot learn to work or anything. They are not taught!
>
> *Judith:* And why do you think that government would not care?
>
> *Emiliana:* It is not that government is interested in sending anybody to do sad things, but you tell me now: there is a youngster who is twenty, or sixteen, or seventeen years old, who looks for a job and does not find it, goes [again] to look for a job and does not find it, goes [again] to look for a job and does not find it. He goes to enroll in a school and because he has no money he is not wanted either. What does the government expect of him and what do parents expect of him? You tell me!

There is also a lack of educational opportunities to keep unemployed youth busy or to upgrade their skills so they can better compete in the labor market:

> What is a father hoping for? The father expects his son can study or at least can find a job. But if there is no work and no study because he does not have the money, the thousands of *pesos* they charge to give him college [education]! You tell me, what can that child give you? He goes to the street and falls in love, gets a woman out there pregnant, makes a child, he does not work, she does not work, ha, because that is what is expected of him. Because boys at fifteen like women and women like men, that is God's law . . . because that is what we know since the world is the world, you know? And that is because they do not give him work or a school to study, to become something. . . . Well, no. Here the one who has money studies and the one who has a godfather [*padrinaje*, somebody who can help] who says: "Look, I will bring this one and we will do something for this one." But if he does not have that, he has nothing.

Government programs, reasons Emiliana, ignore the relationship between youth idleness and the risk of antisocial behavior. Because pro-

gram planners are often uninformed of local conditions, they cannot assess the impact of the economy on people's daily lives across the life span:

> And here there are such bad things happening that you would not believe,
> that the government would not believe, because the government does not
> know what is happening here. There are a million children and youngsters
> who have no work. Those with bad thoughts are in prison, the others are
> in their house or in the house of a friend, or they go to the mailbox to see
> if there is mail. . . . That is what this life is. . . . There is no work! They go
> to another agency and they fill another application, hmm? Sit to wait, there
> is no work! And that is life. . . . So some of them do not want [to continue
> looking for work].

Given these life conditions, how do people manage to earn an income?
Three ways are identified: getting a paying job, getting on welfare, or
getting an education to increase future chances of landing a paying job.
The latter path is very uncertain, as Emiliana's daughter's case illustrates:

> My daughter, she studied, she is a secretary and did not find work.
> Being a secretary she did not find it! So I told her: "Well, if you want,
> go to welfare." "*Mami*, but I did not study to go to welfare." I told her:
> "No, you go, you never know, maybe you get there and they call you,
> you tell them that you are not there to get help, but to get work . . . so
> you do not have to live off the help of the government." Because I came
> to this country and I worked even with my nails [*hasta con las uñas*] but
> I have not gone to welfare ever. That is the way I raised my children and
> my grandchildren, nobody here went to welfare. So she went and could
> not get in because that place was full. Two or three days later she came
> back and they gave it to her; they told her to go to a place to see if there
> was work, and she did not get it. They told her that she had to call later.
> So she took notes, see? That she could not find work anywhere. And I
> told her: "Do not call any more, go there, get on line, and see."
> "*Mama*, she told me, I will not get in line, because when your turn
> comes, it gives you too much pain, because welfare is full, full, so full
> nobody can fit in and the people there [the employees] do not rush to
> take care of you. . . ." But they took care of her, they told her to go
> downtown to look at a job. So she told them: "I cannot go because my
> savings are spent and I have no money to go." So they gave her the
> money to go and come back, and this way she went and came back from
> places until she found a job around here. Little by little, it took some

time, but she got it. She works with the nuns, in a house that was built with welfare [money] and is like a clinic, to house women who have nowhere to live until they find a job. She works as police [she means security guard]. She has to register the newcomers, make sure they have sheets, everything, towels, so she sleeps there. Every day the women have to go out to look for a job. And they have to be back before 10 P.M. They give them a room and when they get a job, they look for a place to live. . . . It is a large house! And it is full! Some of them come with children, and they [the staff] look after their children [while the women go out to look for a job] and they give them clothing.

In addition to facing diminishing opportunities in the labor market, Puerto Ricans also suffer from the discriminatory attitudes of service agencies:

> And there are people there [at the agencies] who ask them: "Where did you come from?" And when they answer that they came from Puerto Rico, they are told: "This is what you came for, to do as if you looked for a job [in order] to get on welfare." They would dismiss them [*los despachaban*] without anything.

Puerto Ricans also feel that they face a discriminatory judiciary system, even when they might have only erred once. According to Emiliana, not everybody who is in prison is guilty. She offers the case of her grandson as an example:

> Look, they took him to prison, due to a whim of a detective who hates him . . . and he would not release him . . . and they wanted to pay people to say he had done something [*querían buscar gente alquilada para que dijeran que él había hecho algo*]. Can you believe how shameless is justice? But I told him: "If tomorrow there are no changes, you sue the city . . ."

Streets as Entertainment/Streets as Constraints

So what are the delights and the problems of living in *El Barrio* for Emiliana's cohort? Obviously, the answer to this question depends on both the inner resources of the informants and the external circumstances affecting their lives. People spoke of the streets as public entertainment, where they enjoyed games, music, sanctuaries, and just hanging out; at the same time, they spoke of the constraints the streets placed on daily life due to issues of housing, crime, safety, and public services.

Most people enjoy *El Barrio* as a place with soul: the lively streets, the games played on sidewalks, the stores that cater to their tastes, the spaces that engage their spirit. The games—dominos, bingo, *bolita*, and Lotto (the state lottery)—turn the streets into public entertainment, whether they are played out in the streets or inside institutions such as churches or senior citizen centers.

> The game of dominos is important for everybody including the Puerto Rican family man. It is good to play after you have worked all day.
>
> —A domino player interviewed on the sidewalk

> The happiest time for us here [in *El Barrio*] is when we can have a beer and play dominoes. . . . We play every day . . . for entertainment. To keep the mind busy with something.
>
> —Another domino player

> I always go to play domino on 103rd Street. Now that I am sick I cannot go. . . . That [not being able to play] affected me a lot.
>
> —Felix

Many constraints affect informants' involvement in these leisure activities. Some of the constraints are personal, such as sickness; others stem from neighborhood ecology, such as street crime, which affects the attendance of players but also often forces some of the facilities to close down.

> Sometimes to play helps. I used to play bingo at the church one block away. But now the priests closed it because they said they did not have funds. It was my only entertainment. . . . There is also bingo on 116th Street but I am afraid [to go] because they took my purse on my way there once.
>
> —Rosario

> Yesterday evening I went to play bingo. I am afraid but I go with eyes all around me.
>
> —Dominga

Other constraints stem from national culture, such as the public-sector regulations that make some games, such as *bolita*, illegal:

It [*bolita*] is forbidden because there is [it competes with] Lotto. I play Lotto three times a week, *bolita* every day. I spend fifteen dollars a week on lotto and thirty to forty dollars a week in *bolita*. Many elderly play.
—Florentino

Cívico [her friend] came and I gave him coffee and food because he is not responsible and spends all his money in the *bolita*.
—Luz María

Music, imbuing public space with the profane, exudes from almost all corners with a message of survival:

Latin music is like a soul, it is like a tradition, it is like an expression, it is like a relief for us. We Hispanics need music because it gives us life, it gives us energy, it gives us strength, it gives us more enthusiasm to continue on the struggle for daily existence, which is so hard!
—A musician who used to play in Felix's band, as we got together to honor Felix's memory in a club

On the other hand, public sanctuaries are a reminder that public space also contains the sacred:

This is a sanctuary to the Virgen del Carmen. The church has her image, but this is a relic [*reliquia*] that people on the block celebrate among themselves. The Virgin is there all year round but they parade her in July.
—Dominga, referring to a handmade altar on 117th Street

I give to that altar. You can light candles, too. They offer mass and take the Virgin in procession. She is in the street because she appeared there saying that she wants her church to be built there.
—Juan

But the best is just hanging out in the streets:

I know him [his best friend] for ten to twelve years. I met him in the group [that hangs out in the street] and we remained like brothers because he takes care of this [the apartment] when I go to the hospital. We all know each other, we are all brothers. There is a center on 101st between Lexington and Park and I go there to get the sun [*me siento a coger el sol*]. It is a private organization. Everybody sits there, it is not a senior citizen center, it is for everybody but there are more elderly. Everybody knows each other. I have lived here [in *El Barrio*] for almost forty-two years but I always go there.

—Felix

What is not good in the streets of *El Barrio*? What turns such lively streets into personal constraints? Four social issues in *El Barrio* adversely affect the informants' daily lives: deteriorated housing, crime, lack of safety, and inappropriate public services.

In order to understand the specific aspects of housing that affect people's lives, I engaged the informants in talking about other people like themselves and thus, through them, about themselves. They classify the

A street scene. (Photo by Edmundo Morales)

types of housing available to the elderly, in order of preference, as projects, tenements, and hotels. Although they lived in projects or tenements, it was common to hear that "the majority of the buildings of *El Barrio* are projects." Projects are where "mostly Blacks live," "for people with low incomes," "for people on Title VIII," or "for people who had no homes."

> In *El Barrio* all the housing is projects that they make for people who have no home . . . they rent under Title VIII.
>
> —Rosario

Compared to other choices, however, projects are considered the best place to live, in terms of architecture and maintenance:

> This man [looking at photo] is . . . in a project, it looks pretty. I do not know because I have not lived in projects. . . . It looks better than here [where I live].
>
> —María

Tenements are older buildings consisting of one or a few floors, owned by the city or by private individuals, which are not well maintained. This general state of disrepair, caused by lack of maintenance by the landlord, does not give tenants incentives to improve the building's condition. While Emiliana cited the case of her granddaughter, whose complaints were left unheeded, others believe that tenants are often destructive:

> There are so many old buildings that the city could renovate and yet they are given to people who destroy them and there is no law that can stop them.
>
> —Telesforo

> There are also buildings with one or two floors. Some buildings are private, others are owned by the city, many are for people with low income. Some are for the elderly.
>
> —Pura

The tenements are alike in terms of disrepair so moving from one to the other does not change one's own living condition:

I have a basement apartment overlooking the backyard. I think I should apply for housing but I do not know where to fill the forms. [The landlord] grew up with my kids so he helped me out and gave me this apartment. I used to live on 110th Street but the landlord had abandoned the building and there was no steam, nothing, so I had to leave.

—Juan

Considered the worst possible place to live, hotels offer "furnished rooms for single people."

The hotels are full of people who have nowhere to go.

—Rosario

Most single men live in hotels that rent furnished rooms on Lexington. They charge twelve dollars a week for a bed and a chair; if you want a stove, it costs thirty or forty dollars. They all share a bathroom.

—Florentino

The informants were aware of social issues embedded within the theme of housing. While their own living conditions were of great concern, so were issues arising from the general lack of good housing stock in the area, such as the flight of many Latino-owned businesses due to rising rents, and homelessness. The distinction between providing housing and affording shelter was often pointed out. If housing is to address human needs, it should be provided at an affordable cost, consist of appropriate space for long stays indoors, and be designed to make the inhabitant feel safe. Yet the informants referred often to problems beyond their control, such as difficulty in meeting housing costs; lack of maintenance; being forced into spaces too limited to conduct normal activities of daily life or to have hired help, such as home attendants; and unsafe shelter.

This man lives in a room. Many elderly who live alone live in one room. How can these people live in a single room? You cannot move anywhere in a single room!

—Pura

Many elderly have to put bars in their windows for fear of somebody coming in.

—Juan

Why do you write all this down? If it would serve for something, but they don't do anything for you. I am tired of telling Tony [the superintendent] and the [management] office to give me a small apartment facing the street because they do not fix my apartment: water falls down, it is next to the boiler, I am tired of facing the backyard. It has to face the street but not too high because I suffer from *la presión* [high blood pressure]. But nobody helps me, they don't come to fix. Call the city, you say? What's the point? Nobody will come anyway!

—Juan

Housing conditions were related to issues confronted by the larger society. The informants were particularly concerned that the city did not build sufficient housing; that the housing bureaucracy was itself a barrier to accessing appropriate housing; that there was no public effort to renovate existing housing for the elderly; and that the gentrification process in the city was adversely affecting *El Barrio* housing stock, as owners of vacant lots speculated about the future of real estate in the city.

She lives well, has a good life. Many do not because they are denied housing. Sometimes they apply for it, they are told to come back the following day and the person they have to see is not there.

—Monchito

Many windows are boarded up [*tapiadas*]. They do not fix them so that people move elsewhere; then they fix them, and they rent at a higher price. The city housing is going up: an elderly person can be asked to pay up to five hundred dollars a month, even if it is a city project. . . . they raise the rents every year, sometimes every month. . . . The elderly cannot afford this, so they keep moving, they throw them out. . . . nobody knows where *El Barrio* will end [*Adonde vá a ir a parar El Barrio*].

—Dora

Only one of the informants had no housing—due, in his view, to his unease with obtaining entitlements because of his lack of knowledge of English. He alternated between a shack he had built on a yard next to the *botánica* where he worked and his daughter's city-owned appartment on a "nice Italian block." With this exception, none of the study informants were concerned about having shelter over their heads, or about their ability to pay for housing.

La Marqueta under the elevated train. (Photo by Edmundo Morales)

If residential housing conditions affect the individual's life conditions, availability of commercial real estate affect the economic vitality of the neighborhood. Deteriorating housing conditions, restricted public safety, and raising rents result in rapid business turnover in *El Barrio*, replicating the ethnic succession of earlier times. For example, only Mexican and Korean merchants, the new wave of immigrants, can afford to rent in the newly opened section of *La Marqueta*.

There are businesses under the elevated. *La Marqueta* is almost destroyed because they charge too much and previous tenants cannot afford the rent.

—Dora

| 221 |

On the other hand, insufficient housing translates into homelessness for many:

> In *El Barrio* there are many people without housing; the majority is living on the street.
>
> —Dora

> A lot of housing has been built, but the people with no housing continue to be without housing.
>
> —Monchito

The theme of homelessness was discussed by the informants as both a housing issue and a social issue. The homeless are visible in *El Barrio* in public spaces such as vacant lots, parking lots, or basements:

> There are people who do not have a place to live; they sleep in a car and cover themselves with cardboard. The police do not do anything. Some people go to live in a vacant lot [*yarda*]: a building is destroyed by fire and the empty lot is invaded over the weekend and they build on it. If they come to evacuate them, they say they have nowhere to live and so they leave them [alone]. Those with less ability [*los que tienen menos habilidad*] get into the cars or in the basements. You have to call the police to get them out but they come back.
>
> —Monchito

The homeless are thought to resist evacuation strategies orchestrated by either the police or intolerant residents. Many sleep indoors, clustering in basements or entrance halls, and some building superintendents even allow them to stay temporarily.

Homelessness is thought to be related to an apathetic government that does not build enough living units. Homelessness is also discussed as a part of the ecology of *El Barrio* that affects both the living conditions and safety of the elderly. The informants refer to the permanency of the problem and their own powerlessness to address a structural problem.

> There are empty buildings because they are burnt and they remove the windows. One does not know whether it is getting better or not because they [the politicians] talk and make comments [about the problem] but then do nothing [*ellos dicen y comentan pero después a la hora no hacen*

nada]. There are a lot of people without housing sleeping in the street. And in winter they get into the basement, they break my padlocks and they get inside to sleep. I have to call the police. What is one to do? When I find them there, I tell them: "Stay here but do not break anything." If they behave, I allow them [to stay] because I feel sorry for them, but it does not help, because you leave two or three in and twenty come and this does not help because one [of them] lights a cigarette and they put the building on fire.

—Telesforo

Twice already the bums have broken the [building] lock to sleep warm inside yet there is no heat in the lobby.

—Rosario

Concern for crime, both indoors and outdoors, runs second to housing, although it is perceived as closely related to housing:

On Sunday, they were cleaning blood on the floor [at the entrance of her building]. . . . they had shot somebody [*le habían pegado tiros a uno*]. . . . Things are very bad here, you can't go out, people steal from one another.

—Dominga

My check got robbed. I think it was the super who comes sometimes to say he has no money or he is hungry.

—Julia

On this floor, there was an Italian man who went to the garbage. A man pushed him and robbed him.

—Luz María

The elderly feel threatened in public and private space. When in the streets, they are pushed around by the young, and often mugged. It is not surprising that many go out only when necessary:

You do not dare [go out], you have to lock yourself up. Youth is different nowadays, there are drugs outside.

—María

I do not use a purse . . . I take [money] in my pockets.

—Augustina

Around here they assault [*le dan golpe*] the elderly when they have money and they break the mailboxes [to take checks out] so I arrange to have them pay the bank and I take money orders. When I pay my rent my oldest godchild accompanies me to the bank and I bring the money in my bosom.

—María

I am very nervous. I was attacked two years ago [inside the building]. [Because of bad vision and crime] I am concerned to go out alone because I am afraid to fall and not know where I am.

—Felicita

Projects should be especially avoided:

I do not go out. I am afraid of the projects, I am afraid of the elevator, they hold it [*lo aguantan*], and they kill you up there or in the basement. They must be on drugs.

—María

In those projects there are many robberies at night. You cannot go out. I went once to a lady's who sells *piraguas* to change her lock because they entered thinking she had *chavos* [money]. At night, one should not walk on the sidewalk because delinquents can beat you up [*le pueden dar un cantazo a uno*].

—Felix

I wish I could move [from a housing project for the elderly] because here a lot of things have happened. I was mugged [*me asaltaron*] in the elevator with a knife. There have been many muggings. That door [the front door] is very bad and a lot of people have vices. Since I suffer from the nerves, all that affects me.

—Antonio

Some days are especially dangerous:

The most dangerous days are from the first to the third [of the month] because that is when the checks from SSI [Supplementary Security Income] and SS [Social Security] arrive and the pensions, and they mug [the elderly] as they come out of the cashier.

—Aurelia

Many outside spaces should be avoided, for example, parking lots:

This is a parking lot where they keep stolen cars and break them up [*los desmantelan*]. People sleep there, people on crack, with a bad life [*de mal vivir*].

—Dora

Safety, a third concern in their daily lives, linked their deteriorating environment to their own vulnerability. *El Barrio* is unsafe because "there are drugs, crimes, the children have no structure, the youth is lost."

I do not like to go out, there is much danger. One does not know who is who.

—Aurelia

Drug addiction is linked in the informants' minds to the increase in homelessness and crime, which is of paramount concern, for it circumscribes their already restricted lives:

This is a yard [*una yarda*] where there is a little house. Nobody lives there, the drug addicts [*tecatos*] do that. They get in to make drug addict business [*negocio de tecato*]. That is why the police are tearing them down all [*las están tumbando a todas*], because they have found drug addicts there.

—Florentino

In this building there are people who sell drugs, on the second, eighteenth, and twentieth floor. One of them is an older couple, the others are young disabled persons. I am afraid to go out to throw the garbage in case they come by the stairs.

—Aurelia

Drug addiction affects the family and thus destroys the fabric of social life:

Sometimes the mothers suffer from the vices of the children. The children are given money to start peddling drugs. The worse problems are family problems.

—Pura

My oldest daughter got killed. She went out with a friend to a dance and was found dead in a yard. I have had bad experiences in this country. I have a son who is thirty-four, went to the Navy, studied but became a drug addict [*se hizo tecato*]. I do not see him any more.

—Felix

The elderly feel like easy prey, whether in the streets or inside their buildings:

They get the elderly because they cannot run.

—Florentino

My daughters tell me that after 6 P.M., I should not open the door. From 6 P.M. on everybody locks themselves up in their apartments here [a housing project for the elderly].

—Matilde

This feeling causes helplessness, which breeds hopelessness, since they report that nothing can be done about the situation:

The elderly are not safe. . . . In the streets, another segment of the population takes over.

—A private physician

Informants were also concerned about the lack of services in public housing, such as heating and garbage collection:

I have a heater because I am cold. . . . I spend forty-two dollars a month in electricity.

—Julia

I have arthritis. . . . I need the heater, it is worse with humidity.

—Matilde

Everybody throws food in the backyard [behind her apartment].

—Rosario

There is too much garbage. People are careless and the city does not pick up often. That creates a fly haven.

—María

The culprits were identified as careless people and the Sanitation Department, which does not pick garbage up often enough. (Even when they do, their job is left half done, since the number of sanitation workers has diminished, and those who remain are paid less than in the past.)

The four social issues of concern to the study population—deteriorated housing, crime, lack of safety, and inappropriate public services—spill from life outdoors to indoors and instill fear and hopelessness in daily life. To counteract this fear and embrace private space with a sense of safety and trust, the informants strive for inner peace and hope through the practice of spirituality.

Perceptions of Private Space

In *El Barrio*, it is hard to draw the boundary between the outside and the inside. One day I took my fictive aunt Isabel, a seamstress whom I thought could help Emiliana continue doing manual work despite her poor vision, to an afternoon of *arroz y habichuelas* and conversation at Emiliana's. While introducing Isabel to *El Barrio*, I reflected on the blurry boundaries there between the outside and the inside. As we walked up Lexington, two elderly women sat on a sofa left on the sidewalk as garbage. As we went upstairs, dozens of family photographs glared at us from the frame of a large painting of the Triborough Bridge. The familiar is both outside and inside in *El Barrio*. Let us now enter the homes.

—Author's diary, July 1, 1996

"Faith Is Foremost": Household Practitioners of Spirituality

According to Emiliana, hope and faith in God bring a person what is truly needed: not wealth, but health and inner peace:

If you call God, you have God within you. One cannot ask for wealth, one cannot ask for things that cannot be, but one can get many things one asks for. God taught me to live life in peace and to take care of myself too.

It is the ability to master inner peace that encourages respect from others:

Happiness means living in peace and having everyone holding you in high esteem [*que todo el mundo lo aprecie a uno*].

| 227 |

Violence and disrespect should be counteracted with nonviolence and respect:

> Listen to me, here [in *El Barrio*] there is a lot, a lot of bad manners [*mala educación*], people in the street use foul language [*habla muy mal*]. But you have to pretend that you do not hear them.

Emiliana has found many other mechanisms that help her attain inner peace: reciting poetry, singing, and lighting candles and praying:

> I used to do [improvise] poetry and love rhymes for girls to say to their boyfriends.

> I sang so much in the past! I sang a lot at church, here in Santa Cecilia and La Milagrosa. On 77th and Seventh Avenue, there was another church where I also sang a lot, and here in Santa Cecilia and in María de los Angeles which is on 113th and Second or Third [Avenue].

> When I am in bed and cannot fall asleep I make up songs [*saco canciones en la cama*]. I also think in poetry [*Yo pienso en verso, también*]. I continue to learn poetry, since one is never old to learn.

> *Judith:* And that candle that you light for your daughter, what is it for?
> *Emiliana:* The candle is dedicated to the divine spirit so her road . . . to go up to heaven . . . is illuminated, so she can see her road open and clear, remove the darkness of sin and can go up to the Glory.

> Yes, I pray every little while. There are times that I pray the rosary three times, and it is now on the table because I am not praying now. Christ helps if you ask with faith. Faith is what counts. But without faith, there is nothing.

> The rosary . . . is the support of the earth, removes war and brings us peace. You take it and you pray with it. You ask God for peace in the world, for peace for the nonbelievers in God or anything, to have God light your way, to give you peace, strength, and sacred knowledge in the name of Jesus Christ. You ask it [for all these things].

> *Judith:* And you, how many times do you pray it?
> *Emiliana:* Me? Every time that I can. . . . You should always say prayers, day and night. Anywhere you go and from wherever you come. They

are short. They help . . . if your opponent is intent in harming you.
. . . With God everything, and without God nothing [*Que con Dios todo, y sin Dios nada*] . . . Do you know what are the rosaries? . . . I will teach you. . . . Do you know how to say Our Father?
Judith: No.
Emiliana: Not even *Salve Ave María* [Hail Mary]?
Judith: No, I am not religious.
Emiliana: You have no religion? Don't worry, I will teach you.

The Social and Civic Roles of Hope

Trusting the Private Space

Spirituality is the strongest response to the "greatest loneliness," which is defined as lack of hope. The informants rely on at least three ways to buttress hope, alone or in combination: organized religion, household artifacts, and self-knowledge.

Organized religion is important not only because it helps the informants carry on with their beliefs, but also because it is a way of connecting socially, addressing loneliness or getting a sense of self:

> Now Aurelia [a guest] is leaving and I will remain alone again. I have to resign myself. I go to Good Neighbor, with Reverend Matos. It is poor but it is spiritual. My son comes Mondays, Wednesdays, and Fridays to see me. I go to bed with confidence in the Lord, but I ask Him that if he has to take me, that I would not be found after several days. My son has the key. And a church brother lives in the back and when he does not see the light he calls me. That is all I have.
>
> —Julia

> I go to bed with the conviction that God is with me. I do not have fear. I pray to God and I feel safe. We have no safety nowadays, the church brothers give me support.
>
> —Matilde

Organized religion can be practiced at special religious sites or at home. Many disabled get religious services delivered at home. Emiliana, for example, brought three "praying women" [*rezadoras*] from Santa Cecilia to conduct a home prayer two years after her daughter Vidalina passed away. Luz María gets a statuette of the Virgin at home for a week—it is passed from apartment to apartment. Church brothers and sisters, from any religion, read at each other's homes:

> Flor and Rocio, mother and daughter who were neighbors at Los Tres Unidos, came by to read the Bible, especially the texts that encourage one to be patient since Jehovah provides for everything one needs help in. They come from Jehovah's Witnesses.
>
> —Pura

Common visitors in Julia's house are the evangelical brothers, who often call when I am there. Similarly, if Elsie fails to show up at church, her church sisters and brothers always call her. They call Matilde every two days, even though Elsie, whom she can see from the window, and David, her son who lives upstairs, check on her every day.

The future can be predetermined and hidden from human knowledge, as in the more traditional mainstream faiths; or, specialists can be sought to intervene through spiritual activities in the quest for knowledge about one's future, as in *espiritismo* and *santería:*

> I believe in God [I am Catholic] but I also believe in the spirits because Jesus Christ comes from the spirits. There is this woman in the neighborhood who invites me to a *centro*, but I do not have the money for the train and anyway I am afraid to leave at night.
>
> —María

> *Santeros* only work for the money. But I go. Yesterday I went to a *santero* party in a big clubhouse on 115th between Park and Madison. They gave free food and drink, they did demonstrations of getting spirits out of people. I respect everybody but only believe in Catholicism.
>
> —Juan

People might also connect to religion by other means, like joining organizations based on the Bible, although they do not necessarily need to be connected to religious activities:

> I belong to the Society of Saint Rosary [la Sociedad de Santo Rosario], which is for women. They meet downstairs, they give you breakfast, every month. We talk about the church, about God. Sometimes they organize trips. Yesterday there was a trip to New Jersey.
>
> —Augustina

The many facets of a botánica. (Photo by Judith Freidenberg)

I went to a meeting of the Logia Hispano Americana de Oro, which has a house on 116th where the bottom floor is rented to an Italian club—it is like a fraternity, they do good things for members and for others. It is like a charity, it is a lot of work.

—Petra

I am *ofdela* [a Masonic lodge] for over fifty years. We pray to the two testaments, we have rites that we have to repeat each time, we have to keep secrets. When we have a meeting, we have to dress in white. We cannot talk about politics or religion. It is like a club, like a sorority, we are based in the Bible, we are the daughters of Ruth.

—Susana

The private space of the household is sacred, and the boundary with the public space is signaled clearly through greetings or specialized objects. People come and go at Emiliana's house—real and fictive relatives, friends, neighbors, home attendants—and everybody asks for her blessing [*"la bendición, mamá"*].

The main purpose of the household spiritual artifacts is to protect

Spiritual artifacts borrowed from two collaborators for display at the *Growing Old in Spanish Harlem* exhibit at the Museum of the City of New York. (Photo by Judith Freidenberg)

people. Spiritual objects are mostly bought at *botánicas*, which sell palliatives for both material and spiritual conditions. The medicinal plants can also be obtained at health centers, *bodegas*, brought over from Puerto Rico, or planted in the backyard.

While the public space contains myriad reminders of spirituality—including *botánicas*, religious icons in many stores, storefront churches—some homes also contain altars of various sizes. One such home is Juan's. I once appeared at Juan's at 9 A.M., as we had agreed, but Juan was not outside where I often found him. I saw Tony (the super) cleaning the sidewalk and asked him to open up the front door for me. Juan, whose buzzer was broken so he could not hear me, was downstairs in his apartment. This was the second time I had been to his very small studio apartment—the first time the management company was fixing it because there was water coming down the pipes. This time he invited me in and offered me a broken chair. On the far end, he had made an altar in the closet space, where he had artfully organized: Santa Bárbara in the center, Saint Lazarus (both, he told me, are saints of the ill), a smaller statue, and two *conguitos* (black saints that bring good luck). He told me that the candle was lit, day and night, and that he bought the candles and the statuettes at the *botánicas*. There was water in a large bowl that was destined for all the saints. There was also an American Indian, a wooden statuette, on top of the refrigerator. "Why do you put up the statues?" I asked. He answered: "To repel the bad spirits, to throw out the malevolent influences [*Para alejar a los espíritus malos, para echar para afuera las influencias maléficas*]. I have the Indian, the Catholic saints, and the congos because it is good to have a bit of everything [*un poco de todo*].

Felix, who lives at street level, has made an altar around a statuette of Saint Lazarus:

To cure yourself, if you invest/put faith, you cure yourself; it is [the faith], like with everything else.

For Susana, a sense of place and security is provided by her altar:

Amid all the objects I have in my house, I have a small altar . . . made up of statues of religious saints, such as San Martín de Porres, and the Virgin of Miracles. . . . I keep them because they belonged to my mother, who died twenty-five years ago. . . . She would pray on behalf of humanity first, then for her own family, and lastly for herself. . . . Since the absence of my mother, my saints are my spiritual keepers.

Some people develop a strong affection for *respaldos*, objects invested with spiritual meaning that protect one from the bad spirits.

It is my devotion to light a candle to the Sacred Heart of Jesus so grants me what I ask, especially health. The candle can be bought in the *bodega* on 116th. Then there is also San Alejo, a saint that prevents bad things from entering the house. Then there is Saint Bárbara, to help in everything that one asks and also to remove bad thoughts from people. And there is the Virgin, there she is with the child Jesus. In the kitchen I have the Virgen del Carmen, to ask for my health. There is the crucifix, the Very Holy Virgin, mother of the Lord Jesus Christ, the Virgin of Guadalupe, . . . they are my *respaldos* [they back me up]: I ask them for health and protection and they take care of me. One needs to have faith, then you ask them [*les pide a ellos*] and they take care of you. I have a very strong faith in God. But I always ask the Sacred Heart. The Indian is for good luck. The glass of water gathers all bad things, bad thoughts or bad things which could be coming. You change the water every seven or nine days. I place one next to the door, another one under the bed. It is to repel the bad spirits. It is better if it is holy water. Also there is a glass of holy water and the rind of a lemon in a small plate. Everything for the same [purpose].

—Antonio

People have statuettes around the house to remind them of the spiritual realm and to broker for them. Otherwise, according to María, who shows me a statuette in her bedroom, you run the risk of not having your prayers heard:

San Martín de Porres. One asks Him for a miracle but it is God that grants things to you. So you ask Him [the saint] so Daddy God [*Papa Dios*] listens to you.

Similarly, Angela keeps San Martín de Porres "in my bedroom, to protect me. He is black."

For Dominga, protection is granted by a crown of palms hanging above the entrance door:

They give it on Palm Sunday at church and one hangs it to have protective spirits, to turn evil away.

She also keeps a statuette of Yemayá, the Virgin of the Sea:

She comes out of the water. They [*santeros*] put out food for her, dance to her. I do nothing. I light her a candle. The *santeros* give her a party. I used to go. Now I don't because I can't—my toes have been cut. I also go to mass at church. For the *santero* party you need to stay standing up and conduct the services. It is very complicated. The *santeros* pray to her, dance to her with the *congas*, they make her offerings, they distribute food to people. I have *facultades* [power of doing a thing] that I had worked with charity but that I do not practice now. They charge you, that is a business [*eso es un negocio*]. If God has given you a *facultad*, it is so you help your brother [*su prójimo*] and not so you cheat [*defraudar*] a poor person so they then buy themselves a house and a car. I have many friends who are *santeras* and they are all doing well. In the spiritist center you only need to pay a *peseta*, the same as in church. When you go to the *santero*, you go to their homes. I used to go to the spiritist center but I no longer do. There used to be a few but they have all been torn down. . . . I stay home, I do not go, I put out my things here [*yo aquí pongo mis cosas*].

Convincing me to go to her bedroom, which has pictures of Christ and saints everywhere, Luz María points to "San Miguel Arcángel. With his sword he destroys all the enemies that come to your house. I place him at the door just in case."

Most informants light candles, but there is a sense that this is a private activity that should not be shared. Julio, for example, got angry when I asked about candles on the side table and told me: "That is a sacred thing for a person, that one has for oneself [*eso es una cosa sagrada de una persona, eso lo tiene uno para uno*]."

A third way to buttress hope is to develop self-knowledge, considered the ultimate spirituality, which results from seeking "God within you" through activities one enjoys. God is what determines life, and so to please God one has to take care of one's life. Seeking within encourages faith, which can be nurtured through various strategies, such as reciting poetry, singing, praying, or helping others:

I dance *merengue* in bed, happy that everybody loves me very much. When you have faith you are satisfied. It is bad when you yearn [*el que tiene fé es conforme, malo es el que aspira*].

—Juana

Sometimes I feel sad, it is Satanás [the devil] who talks to me, but I show him I have God: I pray, I sing a hymn, and I feel happy.

—Julia

You are told: "Pick up he who has fallen and guard yourself of your contrary" ["*Levanta al caído y cuídate del contrario*"], to do good for others, to give, and to feel God inside you.

—María

Ultimately, faith is trust. Faith can be trust in a human being, a supernatural being, or a special spiritual connection:

Isabel [her daughter] is like my mother, my father, my husband, and my daughter, my feet and my hands. . . . Isabel pays my bills, cashes my check. I have trust in her, after God [I trust] her.

—Angela

I stay alone, with God, the Virgin, and the Sacred Heart. At night, I am in good company with God.

—Angela

I go to the spiritist because she helps me spiritually, she gives me strength [*me alienta*].

—María

Distrusting the Private Space: The Violence Within

Where is it worse? Inside or out? Even if informants lock themselves inside for protection from the outside, sometimes they are also afraid and distrustful when inside. Thus, locking oneself indoors is no insurance of safety.

Monchito, who takes a daily walk, illustrates vehemently the incertitude experienced in deciding whether violence is outdoors or indoors:

A religious man was robbed at home. The super here [a house for the aged] takes money from drug addicts for not reporting their breaking the door locks.

The elderly feel vulnerable and distrustful inside their buildings:

When you are old and sick, everybody turns against you [*Cuando usted está viejo y enfermo, todos se le tiran en contra*]. A lady from [another apartment] stole from me. She said she was coming to help. There is a lady in [a different apartment] who also stole from me.

—Luz María

Gloria is my acquaintance, almost nobody is your friend, Mice are friends of cheese, the best friend sells you out nowadays [*Es conocida, amigo no es casi nadie de uno, amigo es un ratón del queso, el mejor amigo hoy lo vende a uno*].

—María

I have no friends, I do not trust anybody. Friends one had in the past when one was raised at home and did not leave one's hometown [*pueblo*]. Now everything is for money. A good friend is a *peso* in the pocket.

—Juan

Although spirituality as practice strengthens moral character to withstand a hard life, nobody would invoke its power to change external circumstances. According to Emiliana, God might have the power to provide health and peace and happiness but cannot offer wealth. Thus, spirituality becomes a metaphor for the ability to survive for many who, despite their material situation, have not given up on themselves.

Domains of Environmental Concern

El Barrio is a metaphor for social issues in New York City. The personal concerns voiced here affect people in other city neighborhoods. Understanding the specific impact they have on the study populations' daily lives might contribute to clarifying these social issues in the larger society.

This elderly population believes that four domains in the environment of *El Barrio* increase their vulnerability: housing, crime, safety, and public services, in that order. They also believe that these domains affect how they use both the public and the private space, and that they are interrelated. The net effect is, often, that these domains are perceived together and that the boundaries between the public and the private blur. For example, housing maintenance affects safety indoors and outdoors. Crime affects public safety—some are discouraged from playing games outdoors—but it also affects the sense of trust in the private space. The most visible signs of the elderly's fears are broken mailboxes in public projects and bars in tenement windows. In turn, safety, which they believe has worsened as a consequence of deteriorating housing and drug addiction, affects daily life both indoors (where the elderly are fearful of muggings in corridors and elevators) and outdoors (where they report being harassed by the homeless and drug addicts, and are especially fearful of the young who might mug them on payday). These concerns breed hopelessness, which they counteract by the sense of security provided by spiritual practices, where public and private spheres also overlap.

Policy Implications of Neighborhood Trust

Residing in a low-income urban enclave impacts space utilization, both public and private, in specific ways. Although there are differences between the way public and private spaces are used, what is similar is that some aspects of space make people feel safe and secure and some do not. These research findings help draw some conclusions with important policy implications: (1) that it is more important to look into what constitutes a neighborhood for this population than for others; (2) that neighborhoods should be imbued with a familiarity that suggests safety; and (3) that aspects of safe neighborhoods might reproduce preferred home environments. How much informants can trust their immediate neighborhood predicts their definition of need and their utilization of space, which in turn predict their utilization of local services.

Conceptualizing Microneighborhoods as Units of Study. Within East Harlem, a low-income urban enclave, there is a smaller space—*El Barrio*—where informants bond to artifacts of spirituality and connect socially through public activity. And, within *El Barrio,* informants tend to utilize an even smaller public space that rarely exceeds a ten-block radius. This microcommunity is the space that is used: focusing on its study, rather than on the individuals residing there, can be rewarding to policy planners interested in assessing the community impact of service interventions.

Like other human populations that spend a great amount of time in a restricted space, the study population has formed emotional attachments to their physical surroundings. These feelings are internalized and are expressed in myriad forms: from playing dominoes in the street to venerating altars in the home. People can be better understood in the context of their immediate surroundings.

Perception of Crime and Space Utilization. The perception seems to be that crime is more prevalent than what is reported at local police precincts. For the elderly who feel vulnerable to attack, fear of crime has a greater impact on the planning of daily activities than its actual occurrence. Planners interested in predicting the widest possible range of activities for the elderly should take this feeling into account, regardless of the statistical significance of crime reports.

Safe Neighborhoods. Building on the target population's definition of safety, as opposed to the program planner's assessments, might lead to cost-effective policy decisions. It is, for example, well known that senior citizen services are not utilized at full capacity, and yet the elderly yearn to have access to public spaces where they can spend their time without feeling harassed.

Playing dominoes on the sidewalks, praying to altars at home, basking under the sun listening to Latin music, entering a *botánica* in search of a *respaldo*—these are some of the many ways in which the people whom I befriended struggle with the fear in their lives. The use of public and private space allows us to understand a particular set of people and the mechanisms they use to become rooted in the larger society. Thus, in order to understand the patterns of utilization of neighborhood services, we need to devise better ways of understanding the section of the neighborhood that is actively being used. And, conversely, understanding this physical space from a population perspective will translate into understanding the people who reside within its parameters. These findings can translate into more cost-effective policy decision-making.

ELEVEN

"Nadie Sabe Donde Va a Parar El Barrio" (Nobody Knows Where *El Barrio* Will End Up)

Local-Level Policy-Making

My last visit to *El Barrio* before this book was completed was over lunch at Millín's, Emiliana's daughter, who had moved in to take care of her parents, now both deceased. I have been fed so often that this time I bring lunch for a group of women who have actively collaborated in the writing of this book, in many more ways than they may be aware of. Three generations are there: older Petra, Dora and Susana, middle-aged Millín and two young women—Millín's daughter and daughter-in-law. For four hours, we eat, talk, pose for photographs, laugh, tell stories, voice concerns about *El Barrio*, and about what can be done to address them. As Susana walks me to the bus stop and on the way home, I am left with the distinct feeling that we have engaged in policy conversations.

—Author's diary, August 28, 1997

Policymakers and analysts, including social scientists, identify population problems and suggest possible solutions, some of which might be translated into action. While anthropologists have contributed to this process by analyzing policies' impact on specific populations (Wulff and Fiske 1989; Freidenberg 1995; Williams 1988; Stack 1974; Leibow 1967; De Havenon 1990; Agar 1973; Hamid 1996; Jones 1976; Waterston 1993), they have elicited information from informants without allowing them to collaborate in generating new knowledge or questioning existing knowledge about their needs.

As the previous chapter made clear, informants prioritized social issues chronic to life in low-income urban enclaves (e.g., housing conditions, increases in crime and the drug trade, youth unemployment) over categorical issues affecting the individual (e.g., the state of their health, social networks, or income). This chapter explores the extent to which various policy consultation methods—ethnographic interview, survey, public forums, audiences' reactions to visual and oral testimonies—contributed to translating the study population's personal experiences into policy issues. I used Emiliana's views to orient the analysis of ethnographic interviews, which in turn generated surveys of the study sample and public dialogues with policy groups. The informants' needs assessments and policy recommendations provide a context for evaluating resource allocation for the Latino elderly in the United States.

Major Problems Facing the Elderly: Emiliana's Proposals for Government Solutions

Emiliana viewed the major problems faced by elderly Puerto Ricans as affecting everybody in *El Barrio,* including the elderly. Consequently, Emiliana's suggestions for government solutions are based on framing the problems confronted by the elderly as policy issues affecting the people of *El Barrio.*

Problem 1: Housing Cost

Alternative Solution A: Continue Income Maintenance Programs

According to Emiliana, the government should not modify welfare while there is no available work with which to pay rent. Emiliana interviewed me as much as I interviewed her, as the passage below shows:

Judith: You asked me what I think of welfare.
Emiliana: That is because they are talking about that [subject] out there and I say that it is not good that it is taken away [*que lo sacan al welfare*], because it would be on top of everything else [i.e., it would add to other bad conditions of living for the poor] because there are so many people living from that [welfare], so if they take it away . . . Because the Mayor wants to put people to work, but he cannot pay them

the same [amount] as [what] they get from welfare, and people do not agree with that.

Judith: So if they send them to work, they will pay them less?

Emiliana: Yes, that is the problem. So you tell me! Because they say that a person that starts to work now will earn $4.50 an hour. You tell me! A poor person making $4.50 an hour, would not get to three hundred dollars [at the end of the month], and what will he pay rent with? If they do that [abolish welfare], they need to lower the rents.

Alternative Solution B: Price Housing According to Personal Income

To prevent as well as to eradicate poverty, Emiliana believes government should supply housing according to personal income. She notes the discrepancies between housing affordability and employment earnings by means of the following example:

Emiliana: Do you know what it is when they [people] go to rent three rooms and it is eight hundred dollars? This is to cry in God's eyes [*es llorar a los ojos de Dios*]. And this is everywhere. Even projects charge nine hundred. So you tell me: a poor person who earns $150 a week and has two or three children, you tell me. He can't. That is why you see homes with three families splitting the rent. [Take] the apartment above this one, for four rooms they paid eight hundred. And in addition if they give them a new refrigerator, they have to pay separately; if they give them a new bathroom, they have to pay [additionally] too. Here they brought a new refrigerator, a new bathroom . . . and we had to pay nothing. Only the rent. How much is that you pay here, Jovino?

Jovino: We pay little here, $255 a month. The rents are higher in the private homes [i.e., tenements].

Emiliana: That is because we are old. And also because we were here from before when nobody paid too much rent.

Jovino: We have been here in this building for thirty-six years.

Emiliana: Thirty-seven years, almost thirty-eight, because Emily was born here and she is thirty-eight already.

Alternative Solution C: Provide Housing for the Elderly Living Alone

According to Emiliana, housing needs are different for those elderly poor who live alone and have few daily contacts. Government should provide specific solutions to specific needs.

Emiliana: I would say the government should set up a house for those who have nowhere to live, and who have no family, who are alone, who have nobody to take care of them [*no tienen quién sea por ellos*]. That house would be shared by men and women. I would put staff to take care of them day and night . . . not false persons who say they would take care of them and then they don't. In this a patient and an elderly person are alike, because if an old person cannot take care of himself you need to have a person dedicated to his care [*una persona al pié que lo atienda*], who cleans him and feeds him on time. So that is what the government should do so that the elderly do not suffer: give them what they need and have responsible people caring for them. . . . The check the government would give him, be it from social security or welfare, that check would go to the director of this home and whatever remains would be for him [the elderly person] . . . in case he wants to go out or buy something. There is one like that in New Jersey, there is where my granddaughter's mother-in-law lives. They have her there like a millionaire and they give her money to have fun and she comes here [to *El Barrio*]. She does not want to live here because there she has everything. She does not have to wash or iron, or anything.

Judith: Is it like a nursing home?

Emiliana: No, it is like a community.

Problem 2: Housing Maintenance

According to Emiliana, daily life for people of *El Barrio,* regardless of age, is more adversely affected by housing disrepair than by their ability to pay rent.

Alternative Solution A: Curb Landowner Abuse

Judith: So what would you say are the most important problems that the [other] elderly have with housing around here?

Emiliana: It is not the elderly, but the nonelderly that have problems with housing—for example, my granddaughter who lives on 116th in an apartment which is broken up [*desbaratado*]: the hall is broken, the door is broken, and she has complained and nobody comes to fix anything. I told her she should call the owner and they came and told her they would send somebody to fix the place. That was six months ago and they have not sent anybody. Then I told her: "Go to the

Department of Health and they will come to fix it right away, but [until they do that] do not pay and take the rent to the court [she means, deposit the money in escrow] and see if the problem gets solved that way." But she cannot do that because the welfare sends the rent directly to the owner. She fell the other day and broke a leg. That is a problem: the owners do not respect anybody, even when one complains, they do not come to fix, and people have to get used to living like that. The owners around here are mean, what they want is to get their money and bother [*molestar*] the tenants. They do not comply with their obligations. Why should tenants pay rent for houses that are broken, destroyed, houses with rats running on the floor, and cockroaches that even if you kill them, keep coming? This is what happens to her, but there are millions of people living here in *El Barrio* in all those houses. Not in the projects, there they take care of people. Those old houses are destroyed, but you should see how much worse they have it under Section VIII!

Housing maintenance problems, with important health implications such as those faced by Emiliana's granddaughter, are left unattended by owners unless tenants report them to the appropriate authorities. But, even for those who do, results are often unpredictable. In other words, it takes more than reporting to get results. According to Emiliana, the government agencies involved in delivering services are uncoordinated, which affects their capacity to respond to people's needs. Emiliana goes as far as to question the existence of a democratic political system in the country at present, and she suggests that following up on a claim is the only possible solution to the problem.

Alternative Solution B: Follow Up on Your Claims

Judith: What could she [Emiliana's granddaughter] do to solve the problem?

Emiliana: Well, problems do not end for a number of reasons, because she goes to the owner, the owner leaves her with vague answers [*el dueño la deja con hoy, con mañana*]. If she goes there [to the office] . . . the owner says: "I have decided to repair, but the material has not arrived." And on and on it goes, and one has to go back to the Department of Health, because if one does not move, my daughter, nothing is done! You have to follow up. If I went today, and they did not take care of

me, then I return tomorrow. If there is something that is yours, if you
do not follow it up, you do not get it. This is what I tell my grandson
Alan: "Do not leave things for later, everything is forgotten."

*Alternative Solution C: Focus Attention on an Uncoordinated Government
Structure Rather Than on People's Problems*

Things are worse now . . . the Governor says one thing, the Mayor says another, the President says another, Congress says another, and anyway they
cannot fix things because everything is bad. Have you seen how things are?
Now they accuse the senators, I do not know what is going on, my daughter [*mija*]. Things are so covered up in life [*es tal la envoltura en la vida*]
that it is hard to understand, and that is because there is no democracy!
They have covered up democracy, they have bought it! What the Senate
does is wrong and what the President does is also wrong because one
wants one thing and the other wants another.

Problem 3: Structural Unemployment

Another fundamental problem is lack of employment, which is made
worse by current policies aimed at terminating welfare.

*Alternative Solution A: Discourage Income Maintenance
Programs as a Dead End*

For Emiliana, the government should not provide income to those
below the poverty line to the exclusion of the creation of jobs to assure
decent salaries to people:

People nowadays feel badly, they are not happy, they do damage without
any need, and that is because government helps too much but people cannot find work. People nowadays do not know what work is. As I see it, the
problems people have are that, say, this one [points to a transitory guest]
wants to work, so he goes out to look for work, and he is not given work;
somebody else goes out to look for work, he is given a half day; yet another
looks for work, and he is given two hours. There is no work! Now there is
no work! This is the problem people have, men and women, . . . because
people need the same [things] that people needed in the past, they need
clothing, shoes, medicine, they need a home, they need to furnish the
home, the kitchen, the rooms, and nobody thinks about that. And the

government knows it has to have jobs for the poor. For sure! If before there were jobs for everyone, what is going on now? The government, the mayor, has taken away all the programs that give work to people. I think what is going on today is the bad faith [*mala fé*] because both rich need to eat and the poor need to eat and you need to eat in order to live.

Alternative Solution B: Promote Job Creation

In turn, investing in job creation would be a way to redress the increasing inequity of wealth distribution in the country:

> Now, I will tell you something. Do you know who makes the rich, rich? The poor! It is the poor because here in this country if there were no poor, would there be money in the treasury? Hmm? They give many penalties/fines to innocent people [*multas,* which need to be paid in money], where is that money? How many thousands of *pesos* do they get from those who have vices around there, where is that money? And the money that the rich have in their factories, in their companies, where is that money?

Alternative Solution C: Stop Exploitation of Foreign Workers

In Emiliana's view, all workers are exploited. Native workers are often laid off for a few days and then recalled so that the employer can save their salary for the time they are not needed. In some cases, they are fired altogether and replaced by workers who are willing to work for even lower wages and who have no knowledge of legal hiring requirements. In fact, Emiliana believes that it is the exploitation of foreigners, not their migration in search of work, that harms local workers:

> There is another thing that is happening. Here a lot of people [*público*] come from every country. If they let them come in, it is their duty as well to get them work and not to leave those poor people without work, so then the factories take them. . . . You are working in a factory for many years, and they tell you: "Look, work is scarce, you will have to stay home for some months." This is the way they start with this one and that one, until they leave the factory empty. The foreigners come and they put all those people to work. Why? Because if they gave me three hundred a week, they give those poor people who come looking for work, $150, half, as they see that they are so eager to work, the poor ones, that they take any-

thing because they cannot die of hunger and they do not know anybody here. Right? That is what is happening.

Alternative Solution D: Defend Individual Rights

Emiliana believes individuals have only one solution to redressing the current situation: to persevere in the pursuit of their rights and, if need be, to confront the system legally:

> That is what happened to my niece who was fired last year. Since she came [to New York] she had the same job and the boss tells her: "You will have to stay at home [unpaid] until I call you [because there is no work for you here]." When she [re]entered the factory, it was full! Full with those people who came from abroad! She told the boss: "You give me my job or I will report you.". . . And the boss told her: "If you wish to work, you can work for the same price they work." She told him: "You pay me what you were paying me." "No, I cannot pay you that, you stay at home until I call you." Do you know that he made her wait for months, without work, waiting, waiting. She went to the Labor Department and told them what was going on. He had to give her all the money he made her lose, and he had to take her back, earning what she was earning before. But she did that [was able to do that] because she has an uncle who is a lawyer in the Bronx.

Emiliana proposes that we focus on structural problems affecting *El Barrio* rather than on problems of the elderly. Her alternative explanation to the increase of crime is that government, not *El Barrio,* has changed. She offers holistic explanations to deteriorating environmental conditions: in her opinion, the general state of disrepair is caused by landlords who do not motivate tenants to improve housing conditions; street crime has increased because deteriorated housing shelters delinquents; the streets are not safe due to an increase in crime; and there has been an increase in juvenile delinquency because there are less opportunities for youth employment. Emiliana proposes that these problems could be redressed if the government were more sensitive to people's needs, which have not changed. She believes that government responses to people's needs have changed: she maintains that, in the past, there was not only more work available but also alternative ways to work (recall that she opted for working at home, subcontracting with workshops, during the latter part of her working years). She concludes that the government does not offer enough opportunities for poor youth to lead a good life. Thus, for Emiliana, it is not so much that *El Barrio* has changed but that the government is less concerned with people and the social circumstances affecting them in daily life. This includes understanding how policies are implemented at the local level:

> The government cares, what happens is that some people do not respect, you know? . . . [In other cases], the government cares, but what happens is that there are more people [to be helped] than [available] help. The government is not guilty of what they do out here because government is there, the Governor and the President, but those who are here [in *El Barrio*] are the ones who boss around, doing and undoing, you tell me!

El Barrio as Problem: The Ethnographic Sample's View

What is the view of Emiliana's cohort on changes in *El Barrio*? To compare Emiliana's views to those of her cohort, informants were encouraged to reflect on *El Barrio* in time and space before they were engaged in suggesting solutions to perceived problems. As they put *El Barrio* in historical perspective, there was no agreement as to whether it has changed all that much, and if so, whether for the worse or the better. Most informants, however, maintained that current problems confronted by the people of *El Barrio* had worsened the moral value of relationships across generations:

> Life was much better here then, oh yes! This has gone down tremendously [*esto ha bajado de una manera terrible*]. In those times, my daughter, one went to the street at midnight and nobody bothered you [*uno se tiraba a la calle a medianoche y nadie se metía con uno*]! You could have the doors open to get air, nobody came to do you harm. From time to time there was a crime, but not like this! . . . This was in 1927 or 1928. It [a crime] was a coincidence, now it is all around us, now we do not know who's who. And the crime that is happening, the mothers who are suffering, you do not know how much we [church brothers and sisters] suffer when we see those mothers who come to pray and cry and scream because their children are into drugs, and they do not know what to do! They have to call the police to take them to prison so they stay out of the street in case they kill somebody or something like that. There is a tremendous amount of suffering here!
>
> —Matilde

I came in 1936. . . . . I say that the situation now is worse: there is corruption, the youth is lost, the kids drop out of school, there are crimes, the elderly are afraid with the situation here in *El Barrio.*

—Dora

In the past, elderly people helped us [younger generations], but nowadays things have changed too much and nobody wants to help anybody. The drugs expose all of us [to danger] and this is one of the worst problems [in *El Barrio*].

—A social club owner

Yet other informants supported the view that *El Barrio* had not changed that much, and that people needed to focus on coping with the problems rather than complaining about them:

We were talking about *El Barrio.* Well, *El Barrio* in the past, there were always little gangs, you know, things like that, but I have no complaints about *El Barrio.*

—A man watching domino players on the sidewalk

I have lived in *El Barrio* for forty-two years but I did not stay at home much [*no paraba en casa*], so I do not know how things are. But I have always maintained morals and seriousness. I know everybody here. If you live as a decent person, minding your own business [*si no te metes con nadie*] [you are fine, nothing happens to you].

—Felix

We have been living here for forty years, here in this house, and I thank God, I thank the Sacred Spirit, our Immaculate Mother Mary, that nothing has ever happened to any of us. . . . And yet, look, there were bandits here in the past . . . but thank God. . . . And I worked at night and came home at three in the morning, [but] I do not complain about anybody, I do not complain about anything, thank God.

—Emiliana

Synchronic views of *El Barrio* in space—"here" versus "there"—were elicited by comparison to the ecology of social class in other urban neighborhoods. What they said while visualizing their space not only validated the public knowledge that *El Barrio* is a poor neighborhood but also contextualized this knowledge with perceptions of its marginality within the larger society. In response to photos of *El Barrio*, informants pictured social class by saying that "people [here] cannot live very well . . . cannot afford things . . . in *El Barrio* everybody is on welfare." Conversely, they believed that elsewhere in the city—identified broadly as "downtown"[1]—people "live better," they "have better jobs," they "are not on welfare," they can "afford things." Thus, in response to a series of photographs taken in a middle-class neighborhood in New York City [the informants were not told the specific location], they perceived their lot to be marginal with respect to what they understood as social norm. They correctly assessed that the people they recognized as not being like them lived better, inhabited larger apartments that were well maintained, could afford more consumer household items, and had steady and well-paying jobs that prevented them from falling from grace and down into welfare. In their words:

> They are mansions for the upper class [*son mansiones jaitonas*]. . . . It is not *El Barrio*. These people live better, you can see it from the outside of the house. They can afford things, maybe they are doctors who earn good money.
>
> —Dora

> Here there are some hotels but they are falling down. . . . It has to be a hotel because nobody around here lives that elegant. . . . Around here everybody is on welfare . . . you cannot live well today.
>
> —Florentino

> They live a pleasurable life. It is a condominium, each family has a whole floor. It is downtown, where people live well.
>
> —Monchito

Conversely, in response to photographs of a slum neighborhood in Buenos Aires, Argentina,[2] informants detected differences and similarities in the human condition:

> This looks worse, it looks too poor, it is worse there, it is dreadfully poor.
>
> —María

> But it is the same, here in [*El Barrio*] dogs open up garbage bags as well.
>
> —Dora

There are poor everywhere, there are rich everywhere, depending on the situation of people . . . how they are educated . . . and the will of the people.

—Aurelia

The informants understand the problems they face—concern with public safety, increase in juvenile delinquency, and pervasive poverty—as well as their interconnections in daily life. But they differ in their approaches to solutions. What can be done with the problems faced by *El Barrio?*

Alternative Solution A: Get Politically Involved

Some informants believe people should support democracy by looking after their rights; pressuring politicians through the political system; voting to change politicians, particularly those unresponsive to the elderly and poor Latinos; and lobbying through community organizations.

I am president of the Council for Seniors. Our board meets with . . . [the executive director of the Institute for Puerto Rican and Hispanic Elderly] to see what we want to do, if we should see somebody in Washington, what are the needs of the elderly. . . . We also help [the Institute] organize their conference in October [on the elderly].

—Petra

I am very busy now that elections are near. . . . Yesterday I went to a workshop in Astor Place where they invite representatives of both parties to ask questions. Then I went to the corner of my house on 103rd Street to distribute leaflets for the Democrats. People are very confused because they have the radio, TV, and newspapers but not face-to-face information.

—Dora

The only thing that can fix [this situation] is a president like Roosevelt. . . . I have spent many years in this country and I know how things are: Whites do not want to live with Blacks because their houses go down in price. Why, if we are all human and we all have to live?

—Dominga

What fails the elderly is that they do not want to get involved, they are afraid they would be used, like with their children.

—Andrea, a regular at a senior citizen center

Many believe in the efficacy of casting votes to express their dissatisfaction with some areas of public policy:

> I lived on 112th and Second Avenue. I got this apartment [in a housing project for the elderly] seven years ago because of [my involvement with] politics, veterans, and Red Cross. I am a voter and here [in East Harlem] with Del Toro and Olga Méndez: I went to her office to fill papers out and they wrote me a letter.
>
> —Telesforo

> I was one of the first persons to get Social Security. I gave [my vote] to Roosevelt, I am in politics, I like to read. . . . Olga Mendez's father-in-law helped me get into the hospitals to take nursing courses.
>
> —Dora

For others, however, voting is no solution for problems:

> It has been eighteen years since I have voted. When I moved here, I did not know where the schools were [to go vote]. Sixty years in the U.S., why vote anyway? The poor always get the same, whether they vote or not. Politicians change after being elected. The only change is in power.
>
> —Angela

Alternative Solution B: Elect Politicians Who Represent Residents' Rights

For the informants, an important factor for positive social change is the election of politicians committed to addressing housing and sanitation needs. For example, politicians could monitor the present uses of public space and recommend more efficient ones, such as building housing on vacant lots presently infested with garbage:

> Around here there are a lot of uninhabited places. It is not that there is a housing problem, it is that they put garbage [in the uninhabited places]. There are people that have to sleep in the streets.
>
> —María

Existing housing conditions could be improved by renovating tenements or having politicians support rent control legislation:

There is a lot of housing for the elderly, yet there is not one politician who defends us from rent raises even if our check stays the same, after we have spent our lives suffering for the community and the American government, after we have paid our taxes and still continue paying taxes.

—Dora

The delivery of public sanitation services should be improved:

There is too much garbage, *Ave María!* the garbage piles up, they [people] are so careless, they throw a lot out. The city picks it up but there is a tremendous fly haven [*se hace un mosquero tremendo*] here, [because] they leave it [the garbage] there many days and sometimes they do not even come to pick it up.

—María

Politicians could also raise civic consciousness about the role people need to play in improving sanitary conditions:

The politicians do nothing. When the salaries of the department to pick up garbage went down, thousands and thousands of workers were laid off. And we are so abusive in putting out furniture, any filth, bottles. . . . Because it is only one man: the driver has to go down to help him. This the borough president nor anybody else sees, those men need to work like donkeys.

—Dora

Alternative Solution C: Consult with the People of El Barrio

Dora, looking at her own photo, reflects that the elderly who have lived in *El Barrio* for a long time have knowledge about the problems and can provide ideas on how to address them:

This is me, paying attention to what I am being asked about the life of the community, housing, and how we can face this situation in *El Barrio*. She thinks a lot before answering, is very well known, has lived here in *El Barrio* for a long time. She is among the old-timers so she has the privilege since she came in 1926 to answer the truth. She speaks of the corruption there is in *El Barrio*, about lost youth, about children dropping off from school, about crimes and the abuse that nowadays even an older person suffers from the situation. But this person is sure of herself and strong to withstand the situation in this district of Manhattan, in East Harlem, by giving advice to youth and trying to fight for housing for us, because it is not possible that we who have an advanced age cannot have a politician, a person who defends us from this discomfort/uneasiness [*malestar*], to suffer from drugs, with such a reduced check we receive, after we have given our life, our strength, struggling for the community and the American government. To start with we have paid taxes and we continue to pay taxes. Does a person who is seventy years old need to suffer the injustice that we are suffering? That is why I am supportive of the vote, that I speak my mind at open forums [*conferencias*]. I speak my mind and what the heart dictates. Injustice with the elderly, with the young, now with medicines, with hospitals, what will it be [*que va a ser*] for the poor Latin American population here in the United States, especially in the state of New York which is corrupt to the core [*corrupto por los cuatro lados*]?

Consulting with residents would help policymakers identify residents' most important needs: housing, protection from crime, and safety:

Everybody complains about housing, it is the most important problem.

—Susana

We have no safety [*seguridad*] nowadays.

—Matilde

Consultations would also provide policymakers with knowledge about how the residents themselves explain the interrelationship among their various needs. For example, the state of housing is perceived in direct relationship to personal safety:

This [photograph] is the Bronx [where] houses are falling apart [*destartaladas*]. There are always housing problems because we are many, there is not enough housing. For the elderly, housing is bad [also] because they are getting people with vices in. For example, this [building] was for elderly before and now it is for anyone. People come who have grandchildren who have vices, they say they go to see grandpa, and they take over the elevators.

—Aurelia

This has to be in *El Barrio*, in projects that are not cleaned up and where the maintenance is not very good. It has to be a project just built because you can still see the old houses and the garbage waste around, but at least he has a house where he can sleep calmly and protected, because there has to be protection in that project.

—Dora

Deteriorating housing conditions contribute to an environment conducive to increased drug sales and consumption, and can also heighten people's sense of social isolation:

Housing is terrible [*fatal*], bad, it is due to all those old buildings that have been all broken up by the drug addicts [*desbaratados por los tecatos*], who do not let one pass by, if you tell them any little thing, they attack you. I do not like that around here, from 105th to up there, 110th, 109th. On 109th, it is terrible, it is full of drug addicts who want to get one's money. On 103rd, it is full of elderly. They wait until they cash [their money] and then they take it away.

—Florentino

These conditions also directly impact on individual health status:

Asthma cannot be cured. I think it probably got worse in this apartment because it is very humid, water comes down the pipe. Also there is no ventilation and I am afraid to leave windows open at night or when I go out for fear that they will rob me—and this is spite of having bars! I did not suffer from asthma in the past. I think it is dampness [*la humedad*]. I need to change, would like to move to 119th, those are nice [he refers to Casabe], but I do not know how to go about it, I do not wish to bother anyone [*no quiero molestar*]. Sometimes I would like God to take me with him, this sickness has killed me [*me ha matado esta enfermedad*].

—Juan

Housing, health and income are perceived in close interrelationship:

Things are terrible. We have little food left.

—Vicente

They used to give us a supplement for heat [$100–$200] and they called me from the office to tell me they had discontinued it [*lo han tumbado*]. Things are bad [*está mala la cosa*].

—Julia

| 255 |

This lady does not seem to be very sick, she might have some ache [*achaque*] but she looks thoughtful [*pensativa*], and by the way she is talking to the social worker, who is somebody who probably investigates [*investiga*] her welfare. She has to work for the government, because she answers with her expressions, with her hands, with her thought, about her poverty, that they have reduced her check, that they have not sent her Medicaid, even if she has no Medicare. She is asking the social worker how she can live if she does not have sufficient money. . . . She might live from Social Security Income, yet anyway the check she is sent is too low. Then the hospitals are very aggressive with the medicines. She is asking [the social worker] what she will do if she does not have [medical] insurance with what she gets? Then the conversation with the investigator [*el coloquio con la investigadora*] continues and she will tell her not to worry, that she will try to solve her problem. We will see what will happen in the future with the elderly.

—Dora

Finally, the poor state of housing compromises the people's feeling of safety in the public space, and thus indirectly inhibits them from a healthy level of activity:

I almost never go out. Only to do shopping.

—Telesforo

I went down and came back quickly. I am waiting for my grandson's call because I do not give the keys to anybody.

—Augustina

I used to go to Joint Diseases [a hospital in the area] but I find it is very difficult to go out with street violence.

—Aurelia

Consulting with informants can enhance the information contained in the statistical population descriptions on which program planning is based by providing the lived experience, for example, on how employment and education interrelate, the importance of entertainment to youth, or the strategies people use to feel safer:

There are people here who have good jobs because they have good education and there are people who are living on the street because they have bad education, they did not want to learn anything. If they do not have any education, they have to do the worst jobs and they are not going to be taken [offered a job] wherever they want either. . . . Even if you are poor, you can get a good education. Look at Serrano who is now a government employee, he was born in my hometown, in Puerto Rico, in Mayaguez. He came here when he was twelve years old and now he is a lawyer and an accountant. And he was born in Puerto Rico. He had no father nor mother but he had an aunt who gave him an education.

—Aurelia

There are so many things happening today that one does not dare. . . . I blame government, so much crime, so many things are happening, youth nowadays is what is most dangerous today. The culprit is the government, which is too lenient with youth [*le da mucho realce a la juventud*] but does not have [money] to take youth out to play ball.

—Antonio

There is drug trafficking. As one is so alone, at night, one needs somebody to look after one [*se necesita alguien que vele por uno*], and an animal knows if somebody comes. The best friend is the dog. I talk [to a dog] as a person. Without them I would feel tremendously alone. I buy them meat, I take them to the hospital, I take care of them as a person.

—María

By focusing on the elderly as individual service recipients rather than on *El Barrio* as context, the elderly's vulnerability to exploitation is overlooked. Dora concludes that if

all the young are in the street, they do not go to school, they do not work, they are on drugs, then, it is the elderly who are supporting government [*es el viejo el que está manteniendo el gobierno*].

There are two ways of changing the socio-cultural condition of aging. The first is to participate in community organizations to raise people's awareness of social problems. Susana, for example, believes in education as an instrument to change housing conditions for the elderly:

Health? Yes, it is important, but housing is the most important. They have put homeless in projects and they have no idea of cleanliness. . . . The problems of people in projects [like herself] is that politicians think that buildings fall down [*los edificios se vienen para abajo*] because people do not take care of them. But the elderly people are tired, it is the young that do not want to work. One needs education for people living in projects so they take care. More than one person needs to sit down to give ideas. Youth nowadays do not worry about anything. They have a bad interpretation of what it is to live together [*convivir*]. They have no love for people. . . . I belonged to the Federation of Puerto Rican Parents of Aspira and was president of a chapter, Julia de Burgos. We had education meetings for parents.

—Susana

A second way to participate in changing life conditions for the elderly is to get involved in playing informal politics to influence elected officials as well as potential voters. Petra, for example, lobbies for elderly rights and holds office in organizations that support their rights. For example, as president for the East Harlem Coalition of Senior Citizen Centers, she coordinates monthly meetings at which three senior representatives per center discuss common problems and evaluate alternative solutions. Another example is Dora, for whom a typical day includes activities ranging from volunteering with established organizations to committing personal time to registering undecided voters:

I woke up early, as is my routine, I went to the Council, I went to report to the centers. I visited a lady [as a volunteer]. I went to [a senior citizen center] and took them an invitation for the conference [on the elderly, organized by the Institute for Puerto Rican and Hispanic Elderly]. I went to UPACA [Upper Park Avenue Communtiy Association] where there was an open house . . . because they are thinking of opening a community office. There is fear that the seniors would be attacked. The police [said at the meeting] that they have nothing to do with drugs. That there is a hotline for drugs, a federal agency. Then I went to see Ms. C. at Casabe to see if she got the invitation for the conference. She takes a busload of people from [Public Housing Projects for Seniors].

There are also the isolated, unconnected elderly who remain invisible to society—those whose needs not only remain unaddressed but also unheard by policymakers and program implementers:

Even when services are available, it is so complicated to obtain services! The red tape . . . to get benefits if you were not already in the system, you do not qualify. There are social workers who have no conciousness of the elderly who are sick . . . alone and have problems. That is why we find elderly who have been dead for three or four days. There is always a loophole in the regulations but there are persons who do not really wish to help. This is the greatest weakness people have.

—Petra

Among the invisible elderly are those who are dissuaded from participation by physical disability or who are discouraged by the difficulties inherent in negotiating the system.

Problems and Solutions: A Survey of Perceived Needs

To return to this chapter's title, where do informants think *El Barrio* will end up? Which problems are assigned the highest priority for action? What suggestions can be made to government? What are the similarities and differences over time?

I incorporated in my ethnographic survey two questions asked by Johnson [1974] in her 1968 survey of East Harlem. The first question asked: "Here are some things that may be important to have from life. Can you tell me which is most important to you?" As can be seen in Figure 11.1, the ranking for some categories can be generalized (e.g., health ranks first), while some describe a culturally specific population (e.g., religion is awarded more importance than education). Comparing the rankings, however, the changes undergone by *El Barrio* through the eyes of its inhabitants are evident: for example, housing was assigned ten times the importance it was given in 1968 [20 percent versus 2 percent], confirming the ethnographic sample's views about the importance of good housing for safety. Money has almost doubled in importance, reflecting a concern with increasing poverty and unemployment. Although this study has shown that family is not always available, social interaction with family members has slightly increased, and is highly preferred to friends, who have decreased in importance to almost half.

Johnson's second question asked: "The City government, as you know, spends money on a lot of different things. I would like to ask you: Which of these things do you think the City government should be giving most attention to?" Here the first two categories reverse in the two surveys (see Figure 11.2): in 1968, housing was thought to need the

Category	1968 (N = 143)[a] Percentage	1989 (N = 30)[b] Percentage
Health	58.7	33.6
Housing	2.0	20.7
Family	11.1	13.8
Religion	14.1	10.3
Money	4.0	9.5
Education	1.1	5.2
Friends	9.0	5.2
Employment	0.0	1.7
	100.0	100.0

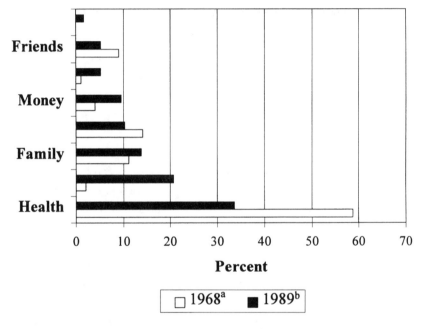

□ 1968[a]   ■ 1989[b]

[a] Source: L. Johnson, 1974. The People of East Harlem. Department of Community Medicine, Mt. Sinai School of Medicine, City University of New York. Survey results for Latinos of all ages.
[b] Source: Survey conducted for this research.

Figure 11.1. What Are the Good Things to Have in Life?

Category	1968 (N = 143)[a] Percentage	1989 (N = 28)[b] Percentage
Health	24.8	32.8
Housing	37.6	27.1
Public Protection	17.2	11.1
Education	7.5	21.3
Welfare	7.5	5.8
Consumer Protection	5.4	1.9
Transportation	0.0	0.0
	100.0	100.0

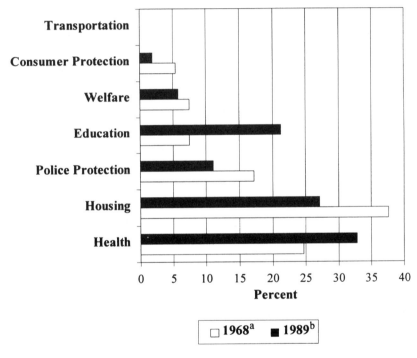

[a] Source: L. Johnson, 1974. The People of East Harlem. Department of Community Medicine, Mt. Sinai School of Medicine, City University of New York. Survey results for aged Latinos.
[b] Source: Survey conducted for this research.

Figure 11.2. What Should the Government Spend Money On?

most attention, while health is prioritized in the most recent study. Twenty-one percent of the study population thought education should be paid more attention, a 200 percent increase in twenty years, making it the third most important demand on the government.

Examining survey results over two decades allowed for historical comparisons of this information. Bringing in the human perspective of the changes undergone in East Harlem adds to demographic, economic, and political profiles necessary for policymaking.

Implications for the Policy Process

A unique contribution of anthropologists to the policy process might be to apply their expertise in eliciting problem areas, providing suggestions for solutions, and prioritizing intervention recommendations. Yet a comparison of the needs allocated by the national budget to the needs assessed by these ad hoc policy groups reveals that their opinions often remain unaddressed by policymakers. The policy process itself should be submitted to scrutiny, most particularly the methods currently in use to generate population information. Assuming that the political goal of policy formulation is to arrive at the maximum consensus between the need priorities of such disparate interest groups as service beneficiaries, program planners, policymakers, and the public and private sector, to name the most important ones, what methods could be used to engage the study population's opinion formation and assure that their recommendations will be communicated across groups?

Anthropologists, who have proven that observational methods lead to understanding program beneficiaries' cultural and social articulation, could apply their expertise to eliciting presumably unintelligible languages spoken by a variety of opinion groups and interpreting them to one another. In so doing, they would contribute to transforming the necessarily descriptive generalizations of policy directives intended for general populations into population-specific statements that are both more flexible to local risk factors and more attuned to population diversity, both in the general population and in the study populations.

Using cross-sectional and longitudinal methods, this case study shows that generalizing elderly Puerto Ricans in *El Barrio* as uniformly poor is misleading. Thus, while we can safely state that being Latino and elderly in a low-income urban enclave carries equal risks of being poor, we should note the important differences among subgroups by age, gender, and living arrangements, which are significant enough to qualify the initial statement to more accurately describe the subpopulation at highest risk of poverty: elderly minority females living alone.

This chapter has explored the role of collaboration in policy planning by having anthropological study populations engage in policy conversations about the problems of *El Barrio* and noting their degree of consensus. For Emiliana, the major problems are housing cost and maintenance, and unemployment. Although she suggests solutions for both government and the people of *El Barrio*, she strongly advocates changes in government policies. The ethnographic sample provides historical and ecological explanations for changes in major problems—public safety, juvenile delinquency, poverty, housing—and strongly feels that consultations with the people of *El Barrio* could provide information to policymakers, not only on their perceived needs but on their interpretation of the interrelations among these needs. The people of *El Barrio* have changed over twenty years: health has decreased in importance, while housing, education, and employment have increased. However, more resources continue to be allocated to health care facilities than to social issues in the community, and the ability of the elderly to remain independent at home is severely curtailed (Fisher and Julius 1987).

But even this characterization falls short of an understanding capable of generating plausible short-term solutions to this population's life circumstances (e.g., poverty) unless an effort is made to contextualize findings within issues affecting the larger society (e.g., unemployment). For example, the most vulnerable elderly subgroups in *El Barrio* confront an added risk of poverty when younger relatives, constrained by structural unemployment, need to share their more predictable resources. Conversely, contextualizing the risks affecting subgroups within larger populations contributes to the examination of trends that can generate long-term policy decisions and thus help plan preventive interventions for generations to come. One such larger population is the elderly in the United States, a group that has increased in size and become more heterogeneous in the last two decades. How will their needs be addressed by our current policy climate regarding the aged? Policy alternatives are constrained by both the size of the national budget and the lack of consensus among decision-makers and between decision-makers and other groups. In addition to the analysis of policies' impact on vulnerable populations, anthropologists can contribute to the examination of the disparities in the policy agenda of various groups as predictors of the feasibility of solutions to social problems. Finding out how various public and private interest groups construct knowledge about "problems" in different policy contexts can help lead to policy solutions that are both cost-effective and responsive to neighborhood priorities. What information is collected? How are needs identified? Who prioritizes them? What are the alternative solutions proposed? Which of those are most feasible?

As this view from *El Barrio* indicates, while the allocation of resources is based on the knowledge of population needs provided by clinical, epidemiological, and demographic data collected on individuals, anthropologists could elicit information on policy issues framed by interest groups that value equity and common well-being differently (Estes et al. 1993). Then, the disparities between the funding allocated to health care (referred to the "biomedicalization of aging," which accounted for almost 30 percent of the federal funding on older people in 1992 as compared to the less than 1 percent spent on social services) and the amount allocated to address people's other concerns could be explained by reference to socio-economic conditions affecting the aged, rather than to the process of aging in and of itself. Interventions could then be geared to ameliorating the conditions faced by vulnerable elderly subgroups whose lot has not improved proportionally to the expansion of services for the elderly during the 1960s and 1970s, and who might fare even worse as a consequence of program reductions in the 1980s and 1990s.

What are the implications of current policy based on age for service delivery to elderly poor Latinos? Although median income of the total elderly population has more than doubled since the 1950s, by 1992 poverty rates were still higher for elderly Blacks (33 percent) and Hispanics (22 percent, but 33 percent if the near-poor are included) than for Whites (11 percent) (U.S. Bureau of the Census 1996). Program planning, a structured response to population problems defined on the basis of information collected on individual characteristics, primarily through the Census, should incorporate needs assessments at the neighborhood level. Although there is still little ideological consensus in the United States as to whether policy agendas should be based on individual characteristics, such as age, or on need, the case study presented here shows how incorporating the perspective of the population into program planning would facilitate the understanding of a problem, crucial for formulating policies, and the effectiveness of social interventions, crucial for implementing such policies. Moving from the individual ("what affects me") to social ("what affects people like me") frameworks, encouraging analysis of interrelationships among needs ("what leads to what"), and suggest solutions ("what should be done") would influence resource allocation on the basis of the used space.

Ethnographic Findings
and Policy Recommendations

Anthropology and the Policymaking Process

What are the policy implications of the research findings in this study for Puerto Rican and other Latino elderly in inner-city neighborhoods? Does existing policy address the needs of these vulnerable populations? Can guidelines for policy research on Latino elderly with similar profiles be generated from the case study? In sum, does an ethnography have implications for planning service delivery programs and formulating policy for the general population?

This book has attempted to show that the conditions under which people grow old are influenced by how they grew up; that their mode of incorporation into the labor market during their working years affects their available resources upon retirement; that their major concerns of daily life are addressing health care needs, availability of social connections, income sufficient to cover perceived expense needs on a daily basis, and assuring their personal safety in both the public and private domains. Since these are social issues affecting general populations, they were understood by interweaving ethnographic, social history, and political approaches in an effort to demonstrate (1) that there is a need to understand how policy issues affect the Latino elderly in low-income urban enclaves as populations at risk; (2) that in order to understand these policy issues, the process of aging needs to be looked at from a double perspective, as a local and as a personal experience; (3) that in order to understand the process of aging as personal experience, a specific population should be selected and its experience examined through time and space to discover the similar and the diverse (typical/atypical); and (4) that to account for the similarities and differences within the population, the population experience—the ethnography—needs to be understood in the context of history and political economy.

Implications of Research Findings for Policy Formulation for *El Barrio* Elderly

Ethnographic findings on specific domains were to be applicable to policy development, specifically on health care access, social networks, income, and safety domains, as follows:

On Health Care Access. Tracing the health-seeking process over time provided knowledge on the timing and the context that contributed to determining whether health symptoms were defined as problematic. This finding suggested the need to explore the extent to which these ethnomedical assessments coincided with the biomedical assessments found more commonly in health care planning, and to discriminate between health care access and service utilization. Health care policies that include information about the career of a person as a patient at the local level will contribute to planning health care interventions that are both available and accessible.

On Social Networks. The availability of daily contact was found to be significant for health care utilization: people with stronger social networks were better equipped to address their perceived needs and to use the medical system with more regularity. The composition of strong networks was not limited to biological family members. There was an increased reliance of the elderly on a variety of nonfamily networks for daily contact. These findings are relevant to service providers, and suggest the need to revise policies.

On Financial Status. Knowledge about the distribution of household income is important in understanding how people address their basic needs. Policies that address the amelioration of poverty pay an enormous amount of attention to personal income, but the extent to which scarce resources are allocated to population-based needs should be understood to assess major deficits in poverty-reduction policies. For example, even if housing and health care of the elderly is partially subsidized, those residing in low-income enclaves often spend a disproportionate amount of their income on food since they assign high relevance to feeding network members. Programs that reduce these out-of-pocket expenses, such as food cooperatives, need to be considered and established as policy alternatives, or as complements to housing and health programs.

On Personal Safety. Analysts have collected and analyzed information on the increase of violence among youth, but little on its impact on the elderly. Although crime reported by the elderly is low, fear of crime is high. This fear constrains their ability to address everyday needs that require going out, such as cashing checks, shopping, using common housing areas, going to a clinic, or socializing outside of the house. Adequate programs are needed to provide special protection for the elderly (chaperons, alternative ways of disbursement of funds, etc.) and transportation to entertainment places they enjoy (churches, senior citizen centers, cultural programs outside of the neighborhood, etc.)

Implications of Research Findings for a Policy Ethnography

Rendering ethnographic results only as written text might limit the potential of ethnography to influence policy formulation: often the anthropologist's analytical understandings are presented in a fashion not intelligible for policymakers. Ethnographic data that is presented both as narrated personal stories and quantitatively allows for a comparative interpretation to larger populations, the goal of public policy. Similarly, a "user-friendly" approach to disseminating ethnographic findings to the public can sensitize general populations to social issues. Relying on visual media, for example, can enhance the potential of ethnographic findings to transfer knowledge to the general public and to engage public audiences in reflection and debate on social issues.

Have Informants Define Policy Issues. Two useful strategies point to having informants define the current state of a problem and what they believe its solution ought to be. In the process, information is elicited regarding the concerns of the elderly, as well as how they addressed these concerns and which ones were not dealt with. Problems and alternative solutions are better articulated when informants are prompted to react to the social experiences of others, not just their own.

Give Informants Access to Policymakers. Informants can also make specific proposals for action if they are afforded the opportunity to engage in dialogue and debate with the general public, providers of health care and social services, and government agency representatives. Mingling informants with policymakers and general publics to exchange information through visual media (museum audiences, public forums, and workshops involving social service and healthcare providers, university teachers, and researchers, etc.), discussing and debating their concerns, and making suggestions for the formulation of local-level policy can be useful in developing and validating policy directives at the grassroots level. Facilitating public forums can make the experiences of a specific population available to policymakers who usually do not have knowledge of what people define as needs and what they do about them. Conversely, the public should have easier access to providers to fully understand their entitlement rights. This consultation with target populations might then generate further research on social issues.

How people experience the impact of public policies and how they utilize programs tells a lot about the success or failure of interventions designed to induce change. Since interventions are programmed to address human needs, planners may need to further their understanding of local population's beliefs and practices when these affect the design and outcome of an intervention. To the extent that people are consulted as informants, by observation, interview, and debate their needs can be made public and programs can better adjust to their actual expressed needs. In addition to the existing programs to educate the population, we need to expand our efforts to find appropriate mechanisms to disseminate useful information about local-level needs and practices to policymakers and providers.

Public Policies/Private Lives

My research corroborated that the Latino elderly in *El Barrio* are not a homogeneous population, leading me to conclude (1) that a full documentation of the human condition of this population lies within the interconnectedness of variables as they affect special groups; (2) that individual variables, such as income, need to be interpreted within the realm of broader social issues, such as poverty; and (3) that it is probably more effective to plan for needs experienced by specific populations, such as the social mechanisms Latino elderly employ to address medical needs, than for population categories, such as age strata.

The existence and recognition of intragroup diversity should deter the formulation of public policies on the basis of stereotyped populations, and encourage culturally sensitive research on how these policies affect them. A survey conducted to formulate policy that elicits information based on the cultural assumptions of the investigator will be less useful than one that is ethnographically based. Thus, asking whether a person lives alone does not provide information on the nature of transient or unplanned stays of relatives, which are necessary to predict the availability of help.

The major insight resulting from this research is that assuming that the hiatus between public policies and private lives is not problematic, may lead to faulty policy decision-making for program planning and intervention. I suggest two strategies to explore the boundaries between public policies and private lives.

Public Policies Informed by Private Lives. Population information can be collected through long-term anthropological research, but also through rapid assessment methods that involve group consultation (e.g., focus groups, public forums, group interviews, consensus meetings at community organizations) in which the community, together with program planners, service providers, and policymakers, can contribute to the public debate on alternative solutions to perceived problems.

Private Lives Made Public. Informants can be invited to reflect on and react to anthropological interpretations of their life conditions and unaddressed needs, and their responses can be disseminated widely to a variety of audiences in ways that engage the general public in dialogue. Exhibits, anthropological visual documentation of life conditions, artifact collections, and video productions are examples of mechanisms that generate opinion exchange across diverse sectors of society.

During the last few decades, anthropologists in the United States have explored ways to utilize the knowledge they produce (Ervin 2000; Cernea 1991; Van Willigen 1991) by applying it to practical problems (Poggie, DeWalt, and Dressler 1992; Van Willigen 1993; Reed 1997; Eddy and Partridge 1978; Wulff and Fiske 1987) to influence social change (Stull and Schensul 1987; Moran 1996) and the policymaking process (Belshaw 1976; Goldshmidt 1986; Chambers 1985; Heyman 1995; Hackenberg and Hackenberg 1999). However, our understanding of the middle ground between public policies and private lives requires further work.

If we can "look," but also "see"; if we can "hear," but also "listen," it becomes possible for the anthropologist to mediate between proposals for action based on the informants' experience and those based on data for general populations. For example, it is not the same to be an elderly woman suffering from arthritis in wealthy New York as it is in *El Barrio*. By bringing personal experience to bear on the construction of data that form the basis for programmatic planning, anthropologists can play an important role in implementing directives based on differences as well as similarities.

An understanding of locally generated knowledge systems and proposals for action can contribute to narrowing the hiatus between macrostructural policy directives and the micro-organization of daily life within a neighborhood. People have the ability to identify public problems and consider which policy options ought to address and solve them. Their perceived needs can enhance local-level providers' ability to evaluate alternatives before implementing policies. A challenge for contemporary applied anthropology might well be to explore ways of articulating local-level policy thinking in the policy process. It is important to understand not only how policies impact people, but also how people can become actors and impact on policies.

Policy development and the process of aging are complex, and both are historically and socially constructed. The historical and life-course approach taken here makes clear the difference between aging policies that assume an inactive and dependent population, and policies based on knowledge about the actual environment which the aged live. Many elderly make productive contributions to society, and they could be even more productive if daily life in *El Barrio* were more predictable and humane. People's experiences validate programs that work and provide useful information for understanding why some fail. People's experiences of daily life, anchored in time and space, should drive the development of policy ethnography.

NOTES

Notes to the Introduction

1. "Hispanic" is the term most commonly used by agencies such as the Bureau of the Census, that collect and publish population data, that is then disseminated by the media and is most readily recognized by the general public. The term designates "individuals [who] immigrated to the United States or are native-born U.S. citizens who self-identify under any of several national origin designations (e.g., Mexican American, Puerto Rican, Cuban, Guatemalan) or racial/ethnic group (e.g., Chicano, Latino, mestizo, Hispanic)" (Padilla 1995, xii). Although in current usage the terms "Hispanics" and "Latinos" are interchangeable (Furino 1992, 6), in this book I will use "Hispanic" only when referring to Census data and "Latino" in other instances.

2. Latino elderly exhibited a significantly higher mean level of functional impairment than White and African-American elderly. In a 1993 survey, 20 percent of Latino elderly were severely dependent, as compared to 12 percent of Whites and 13 percent of African-Americans (New York Center for Policy on Aging 1993, 21–25).

3. A *bodega* is a grocery store, usually individually owned.

4. The exhibit was *Growing Old in Spanish Harlem*, which I curated for the Museum of the City of New York in 1992.

5. Specialized sites holding historical records of relevance to this search include the New York Historical Society; the Casa de la Herencia; the Schomburg Library, Center for Research on Black Culture and St. Agnes Branch, of the New York Public Library; the Museum of the City of New York; and the Center for Puerto Rican Studies at Hunter College, CUNY, among many others.

6. An example of a survey of the same-age population in the same city used in this study is *Growing Older in New York City in the 1990's* (New York Center for Policy on Aging 1993). An example of a national survey on populations facing similar constraints to the study population is *Elderly People Living Alone* (Commonwealth Fund Commission, 1989).

7. For Puerto Ricans, see especially Benmayor, Torruellas, and Juarbe 1992; Lewis 1966; Padilla 1958; and Harwood 1977. For Dominicans, see

especially Grassmuck and Pessar 1992; Duany 1994; Garrison and Weiss 1979; Georges 1990; Hendricks 1974; and Pessar 1995. For Brazilians, see Margolis 1998. For Salvadoreans, see Mahler 1995. For ethnographic collections, see especially, Freidenberg 1995; Sutton and Chaney 1992; Mullings 1987; and Foner 1987.

Notes to Chapter 1

1. Competition for space, a symbol of access to resources, helped redefine the various ethnic groups. "Irish gangs attacked Jewish immigrants on the streets of East Harlem in 1900. Conflict between the Irish and the Italians seems to have been particularly fierce" (Orsi 1985, 16).

2. By 1890, Las Dos Antillas, a Latino club affiliated with the Partido Revolucionario Cubano, was founded with the collaboration of the Puerto Rican intellectual Arturo Schomburg.

3. Since 1917, when Puerto Ricans were granted citizenship, entry restrictions to the United States have been waived.

4. Fiorello La Guardia, a labor lawyer of Italian-Jewish background from East Harlem, was a U.S. Congressman 1917–1921 and 1923–1933 and mayor of New York City 1934–1945. During his administration, the New York City Housing Authority was created to provide a safe and clean living environment for the working poor.

5. Vito Marcantonio, also a native of East Harlem, occupied the congressional seat for East Harlem from 1936 to 1950.

6. The press connected massive Puerto Rican migration to populist strategies: "Marcantonio's principal strength comes from hordes of Puerto Ricans enticed here from their home island, for the value of their votes, and subjected to pitiful poverty, which Marcantonio has done nothing to alleviate—except force thousands on city relief." (*Daily Mirror*, 1950, cited in Bookbinder 1989)

7. Hometown clubs, located in storefronts or basements, organized social activities and were instrumental in the politicization of Puerto Rican ethnicity in New York City (Freidenberg 1978).

Notes to Chapter 2

1. Virtually all Puerto Ricans, even those who are pro-statehood, defend the continuity of Puerto Rican culture and values (E. Padilla, personal communication).

2. "I embroidered, I did raised work on the festoon."

3. In Puerto Rico, *corsos* are descendants of Corsicans. Emiliana, however, defines a *corso* as a "man who comes from another place [a foreigner], one who speaks Spanish badly."

4. "There was a stone used to hit the cobs and separate the kernels."

5. Potatoes, yautía (an edible root vegetable), bananas, plantains, and yams.

6. She means that her father farmed the land.

7. Literally, "I had to work even with my nails."

8. Although the literal translation is "I learned to do everything thanks to Providence, the meaning could also be construed as "Thanks to the Virgin" or "Thanks to God" (Consuelo Corretjer, personal communication).

9. "Distinguished dances" were attended by "decent people" who were "society people," according to Emiliana.

10. An edible root vegetable.

11. Seeded breadfruit, or breadfruit that has seeds in it instead of pulp; avocado; mamey (a fruit) (Consuelo Corretjer, personal communication).

12. "Mary, Mother of God."

13. Formal or black-tie dances.

14. *Jíbara*—from the countryside—is the literal translation, but it implies someone who lacks education and is scorned by the more educated urban middle classes (Santiago 1993).

15. A *madre* or *padre de crianza* is a foster parent.

16. A technician who makes artificial teeth and dentures.

17. Shaved ice with fruit-flavored syrup.

Notes to Chapter 4

1. Sources that depict daily life in Spanish Harlem include Thomas 1972; Galíndez 1969; and González 1973.

2. *El Barrio* concentrated working-class was the destination of the poorer Puerto Ricans.

3. Major sources on the migrant colonies in Spanish Harlem for this period are, in addition to those cited in the text, Mills, Senior, and Goldsen 1950; Handlin 1959; Padilla 1958; Rand 1958; Lewis 1966; Fitzpatrick 1971; Glazer and Moynihan 1963; and Wakefield 1959.

4. Hernández Alvarez delineates the social contours of a *colonia* thus: "Most Puerto Rican residents of the United States live in a '*colonia*,' an urban nucleus marked by dense settlement, provision for manifestation of the Puerto Rican social identity and way of behavior and by frequency of internal activity and dependence" (1968, 41).

5. Meyer (1992, 82) argues that the popularity of Marcantonio with the Puerto Ricans in East Harlem rested on his support of the *independentista* movement, which sought to sever ties with the United States, in addition to his responsiveness to their daily needs.

6. The bulk of the Whites were Italian, mostly elderly (Cordasco and Bucchione 1973, 183).

7. During the 1950s and 1960s, housing units for private dwellings, institutional buildings, and houses of worship increased. By 1965, "there were more churches—some 135 in all—than all other public and private institutions combined, except businesses" (Benson n.d.).

8. Boarded-up tenements were rehabilitated during the postwar population growth (Wakefield 1959, 235; Padilla 1958, 2).

9. East River House, opened in 1941, was the second federal housing project in New York City (Benson n.d.)

10. Families that did not qualify for a project but lived in condemned tenements were moved to other tenements. "A new category of citizens is created—those people who move from condemned site to condemned site, in a seemingly endless round. These government-propelled travelers are referred to as 'Site Migrants'" (Wakefield 1959, 242).

11. Income gains often conspired against an individual since projects had fixed incomes that could not be exceeded. "If a man with a family in a private home or apartment gets a raise, it means he has the chance to improve his home. If a man in a project gets a raise, it means he may have to move out of his home" (Wakefield 1959, 245)

12. The two largest antipoverty organizations operating in *El Barrio* at that time were MEND (Massive Economic Neighborhood Development) and the East Harlem Community Corporation. They stressed community organizing to solve human needs at the local level.

13. The Puerto Rican Leadership Alliance and the Puerto Rican Community Development Project organized strong registration drives that partly reversed voter apathy. The Young Lords, originally a Puerto Rican protest movement that later diversified into a "rainbow coalition," also contributed to the political socialization of the Puerto Rican newcomer.

14. "Many of them join regular Democratic clubs, because they see those clubs as the safest way to make it politically: a man like Tony Méndez, the regular boss of East Harlem, remains a powerful man politically" (Hamill 1973, 212).

15. "The decrease is due in part to a smaller number of habitable dwelling units" (Johnson 1974, 12).

Notes to Chapter 5

1. La Marqueta is the open-air market under the elevated train on Park Avenue.

2. Although Fifth Avenue is an expensive shopping area, it was associated with profitable prostitution at the time my informants arrived in *El Barrio*.

3. "You can only get a wild animal out of the forest with good manners."

4. Olga Méndez, currently an elected politician for *El Barrio*, is married to the son of Mr. Méndez, considered together with his wife Isabel, Danny Caballero and many others as the pioneers of the Puerto Rican community in New York City.

5. The following categories were used to classify the sample: blue-collar and service workers were craftsmen, foremen, operatives, laborers, service workers, and farm workers. White-collar workers were professional and technical, workers; managers and administrators; sales workers; and clerical workers.

6. Movement into white-collar occupations occurred through training (for the three females, two clerical workers, and one teacher) and ownership (for the male, a restaurateur).

7. These figures fail to reflect entire households engaged in agricultural work, as well as females who sew at home for U.S.-based workshops.

8. One-fifth of all of New York's workers were employed in manufacturing, but over two-fifths of Puerto Rican workers held factory jobs (U.S. Department of Labor 1974).

9. "Two-thirds of the men did semiskilled or unskilled blue-collar and service work, nearly twice the proportion of all of the City's male jobholders." (U.S. Department of Labor 1974, 356-59)

10. In 1957, as a result of several indictments by the New York County District Attorney and other law-enforcement agencies, together with public exposure by the Association of Catholic Trade Unionists of the widespread operations of racket unions, the major New York City labor unions established the AFL-CIO Committee on Puerto Rican Affairs. In 1958, the Mayor's Committee on Exploitation was established with representation from the AFL-CIO Central Labor Council, the International Ladies' Garment Workers Union, and other powerful labor organizations. These committees, whose leaders publicly pledged to drive labor racketeers out of New York almost a decade ago, have had little or no effect (Hill 1974, 385).

Notes to Chapter 6

1. *Coraje* can be translated as both: "anger" and "courage."

2. Susana Martínez has participated actively in community activities in *El Barrio* for over thirty-five years and has published two books of poems in Spanish and a work of fiction in English.

3. Susana founded the group with Encarnación Ramírez, a Pentecostal *reverenda* [female minister], also a published poet.

4. Petra Allende, an East Harlem resident for over forty- five years, has devoted herself to helping the elderly through participation in various civic and cultural organizations: Advisory Committee of the Older Americans Act of the State of New York, Advisory Committee of the Department of the Aging of the City of New York, Action Council of the Puerto Rican and Hispanic Council for Elderly Persons, the East Harlem Interagency Council, and the Gaylord White Senior Citizen Center.

The other collaborator was Dora Delorisses, a resident of East Harlem for over fifty years, who has also been active in various organizations, including the Action Council of the Puerto Rican and Hispanic Council on Aging, the Church of St. Cecilia, the Archdiocese of New York and the Casita María Senior Citizen Center.

5. To analyze how the elderly in the sample allocated their time (Gross 1984; Johnson and Johnson 1987), I conducted ethnographic observations during a year and then conducted systematic interviews at random about the previous day. Ethnographic analysis of activity logs provided the periodization of activities, the physical space where activities were carried out, and the social connections who were present during the activity.

Notes to Chapter 7

1. Emiliana refers to her grandson Alan, her primary care supervisor.

2. The hot-cold dichotomy is a folk categorization of illness prevalent among low-income Latin Americans (Harwood 1977).

3. "Florida water" is a cologne sold at *botánicas* to cure ailments of the body (like arthritis) and the soul, and to attract good luck.

4. I am using *curandero,* following Snow (1993), for a healer who treats physical disorders as *empacho* [indigestion] using touching and massage.

5. *Empacho* [obstruction or upset stomach] is caused by excessive food intake, particularly of heavy or starchy food, attributed to a bolus of food in the intestine (Harwood 1977).

6. Shark pills [*cartílago de tiburón*] are advertised as an effective treatment for all ailments.

7. Deriving from *santo* [saint], *hacer el santo* refers to costly rites performed to influence the spirits in *santería,* an Afro-Caribbean religion blending Catholic,

Spiritist and Yoruba beliefs (For further reading, consult Stevens-Arroyo, Anthony M. and Ana Maria Díaz-Stevens, 1994).

8. See Freidenberg and Jiménez-Velázquez 1992.

Notes to Chapter 8

1. Giving the *bendición* means blessing someone so that God goes with that person and guards her or him from evil.

2. See Freidenberg and Hammer 1998.

3. Five network variables—(size, reciprocity, daily contact, reciprocal daily contact, and number of connected pairs—were used to classify strong (at or above the median on all network variables) or weak (below the median).

Notes to Chapter 9

1. Morales and Bonilla (1993) argue that Puerto Ricans are a minority within a minority, since economically they lag behind other Latinos in the United States.

2. "*Vividores* are exploiters": men who live off women.

3. See Chapter 4 above about *ambiente*.

4. A *numerito* is a bet for *la bolita*, the illegal lottery.

5. Information about this insurance payment is not always shared with network members. In other cases, the relevant paperwork is not found after death. Thus, in many instances the money invested for burial expenses is lost to funeral or insurance companies that collect monthly payments.

6. "Meals on Wheels" is a food program for disabled elderly.

Notes to the Introduction to Part IV

1. *Casitas,* small wooden houses replicating those of peasants in Puerto Rico, are constructed in unused or empty building lots and rented out for parties.

2. *Mofongo* is made of fried green plantain that is mashed with garlic and served in the shape of a bowl.

Notes to Chapter 11

1. Informants used the worked English word "downtown."

2. Informants were told it was in Latin America, but not the specific geographical location.

REFERENCES

Abraido-Lanza, A. F., C. Guier, and T. A. Revenson. 1996. "Coping and Social Support Resources among Latinas with Arthritis." *Arthritis Care and Research* 9 (6): 501–8.

Administration on Aging. 1996. *Aging into the Twenty-first Century*. U.S. Department of Health and Human Services. Bethesda, MD: National Aging Information Center.

Agar, M. 1973. *Ripping and Running*. New York: Academic Press.

Angel, R. L., and J. L. Angel. 1992. "Age and Migration, Social Connections and Well-Being among Elderly Hispanics." *Journal of Aging and Health* 4 (4): 480–99.

———. 1997. *Who Will Care for Us? Aging and Long-Term Care in Multicultural America*. New York: New York University Press.

Annals of the American Academy of Political and Social Science. 1989. *Hispanic Elderly in Transition: Theory, Research, Policy and Practice*. Westport, CT: Greenwood Press.

Antonucci, T. C. 1990. "Social Supports and Social Relationships." In *Handbook of Aging and the Social Sciences, ed*. R. H. Binstock and L. K. George, pp. 205–26. San Diego: Academic Press.

———. 1995. "Convoys of Social Relations: Family and Friends within a Life Span Context." In *Handbook of Aging and the Family*, ed. R. Blieszner and V. Bedford, pp. 355–71. Westport, CT: Greenwood Press.

Applewhite, S. R., ed. 1988. *Hispanic Elderly in Transition*. Westport, CT: Greenwood Press.

Arellano, A. 1990. *The Health Status of the Hispanic Elderly*. New York: New York City Department of the Aging.

Atchley, R. 1997. *Social Forces and Aging: An Introduction to Social Gerontology*. Belmont, CA: Wadsworth.

Auslander, G., and H. Litwin. 1991. "Social Networks, Social Support and Self-Ratings of Health among the Elderly." *Journal of Aging and Health* 3 (4): 493–510.

Baer, H., M. Singer, and I. Susser. 1997. *Medical Anthropology and the World System: A Critical Perspective*. Westport, CT: Bergin and Garvey.

Balán, J., and E. Jelin. 1979. "La Estructura Social en la Biografía Personal. Buenos Aires, Argentina: *Estudios CEDES* 2 (9).

Barsa, B. R. 1997. "*The Physical Health of Hispanic Elderly in an Urban Setting, Its Relationship to Activities of Daily Living and the Need for Social Networks.*" Ph.D. dissertation, Columbia University.

Basch, L., N. Glick-Schiller, and C. Szanton Blanc. 1994. *Nations Unbound: Transnational Projects, Postcolonial Predicaments, and Deterritorialized Nation-States.* Amsterdam: Overseas Publishers Association.

Bean, F. D., and M. Tienda. 1987. *The Hispanic Population of the United States.* New York: Russell Sage Foundation.

Behar, R. 1993. *Translated Woman: Crossing the Border with Esperanza's Story.* Boston: Beacon Press.

Belshaw, C. 1976. *The Sorcerer's Apprentice: An Anthropology of Public Policy.* New York: Pergamon Press.

Benmayor, R. 1991. "Testimony, Action Research, and Empowerment: Puerto Rican Women and Popular Education." In *Women's Words: The Feminist Practice of Oral History, ed.* Sherna B. Gluck and Daphne Patai, pp. 159–74. New York: Routledge.

Benmayor, R., R. Torruellas, and A. Juarbe. 1992. *Responses to Poverty among Puerto Rican Women: Identity, Community, and Cultural Citizenship.* Joint Committee for Public Policy Research on Contemporary Hispanic Issues of the Inter-University Program for Latino Research and the Social Science Research Council. New York: Centro de Estudios Puertorriqueños, Hunter College, City University of New York.

Benson, K. n.d. *Radical East Harlem: An Exhibition Proposal.* Submitted to the Museum of the City of New York.

Bertaux, D. 1981. *Biography and Society: The Life History Approach in the Social Sciences.* Beverly Hills, CA: Sage Publications.

Bookbinder, B. 1989. *City of the World: New York and Its People.* New York: Harry N. Abrams.

Bourgois, P. 1996. *In Search of Respect: Selling Crack in El Barrio.* New York: Cambridge University Press.

Brink, T. L, ed. 1992. "Hispanic Aged Mental Health". *Clinical Gerontologist* 11 (3–4).

Cantor, M. H., M. Brennan, and A. Sainz. 1994. "The Importance of Ethnicity in the Social Support Systems of Older New Yorkers: A Longitudinal Perspective (1970–1990)." *Journal of Gerontological Social Work* 22 (3–4): 95–128.

Carnoy, M., H. Daley, and R. H. Ojeda. 1990. *Latinos in a Changing U.S. Econ-*

omy: Comparative Perspectives on the Labor Market since 1939. New York: Research Foundation of the City University.

———. 1993. "The Changing Economic Position of Latinos in the U.S. Market." In *Latinos in a Changing U.S. Economy*, ed. Rebecca Morales and Frank Bonilla, pp. 28–55. Newbury Park, CA: Sage Publications.

Centro de Estudios Puertorriqueños. 1979. *Labor Migration under Capitalism: The Puerto Rican Experience*. New York: Monthly Review Press.

Cernea, M. 1991. *Using Knowledge from Social Sciences in Development Projects*. Washington, D.C.: World Bank.

Chambers, Erve. 1985. *Applied Anthropology: A Practical Guide*. Englewood Cliffs, NJ: Prentice-Hall.

Chenault, L. 1938. *The Puerto Rican Migrant in New York City*. New York: Columbia University Press.

City of New York, Department of City Planning. 1992. *Socioeconomic Profiles: A Portrait of New York City's Community Districts from the 1980 and 1990 Censuses of Population and Housing*. New York: Department of City Planning.

Collier, J., and M. Collier. 1986. *Visual Anthropology: Photography as a Research Method*. Albuquerque: University of New Mexico Press.

Colón, J. 1975. *A Puerto Rican in New York and Other Sketches*. New York: Arno Press.

Commonwealth Fund Commission on Elderly People Living Alone 1989. *Poverty and Poor Health among Elderly Hispanic Americans*. Baltimore: Commonwealth Fund Commission on Elderly People Living Alone.

Community Service Society. 1987. *Poverty in New York City: 1980–1985*. New York: Community Service Society.

Cordasco, F., and E. Bucchione. 1973. *The Puerto Rican Experience: A Sociological Sourcebook*. Totowa, NJ: Rowman and Littlefield.

DeHavenon, A. L. 1990. "Charles Dickens Meets Franz Kafka: The Maladministration of New York City's Public Assistance Programs." *New York University Review of Law and Social Change* 17 (2).

DeLeaire, R., 1994. *The Inner-City Elderly: How Effective Are Their Support Structures?* New York: Garland Publications.

Delgado, R., and J. Stefancic. 1998. *The Latino Condition: A Critical Reader*. New York: New York University Press.

Duany, J. 1994. *Quisqueya on the Hudson: The Transnational Identity of Dominicans in Washington Heights*. Dominican Research Mongraphs. New York: City University of New York, Dominican Studies Insititute.

Eddy, E., and W. Partridge, eds. 1978. *Applied Anthropology in America*. New York: Columbia University Press.

Ernst, R. 1949. *Immigrant Life in New York City: 1825–1863.* New York: King's Crown Press.

Ervin, Alexander M. 2000. *Applied Anthropology: Tools and Perspectives for Contemporary Practice.* Boston: Allyn and Bacon.

Estes, C. L., and J. H. Swan, et al. 1993. *The Long-Term Care Crisis.* Newbury Park, CA: Sage Publications.

Fischer, C. S. 1982. *To Dwell among Friends: Personal Networks in Town and City.* Chicago: University of Chicago Press.

Fisher, E., and N. Julius. 1987. *The Elderly of East Harlem: People, Resources and Service Needs.* New York: Department of Community Medicine, Mount Sinai School of Medicine, City University of New York.

Fitzpatrick, J. 1971. *Puerto Rican Americans: The Meaning of the Migration to the Mainland.* Englewood Cliffs, NJ: Prentice-Hall.

Flores, J. 1987. Introduction to *Divided Arrival: Narratives of the Puerto Rican Migration 1920–1950.* New York: City University of New York, Centro de Estudios Puertorriqueños.

Foner, N., ed. 1987. *New Immigrants in New York.* New York: Columbia University Press.

Freidenberg, J. N. (published as Herbstein, J. N.). 1978. *"Rituals and Politics of the New York Puerto Rican Community."* Ph.D. dissertation, City University of New York.

Freidenberg, J. N., and M. Hammer. 1998. "Social Networks and Health Care: The Case of Elderly Latinos in East Harlem." *Urban Anthropology* 27 (1): 49–87.

———, ed. 1995. *The Anthropology of Low-Income Urban Enclaves: The Case of East Harlem.* Annals of the New York Academy of Sciences, vol. 749. New York: New York Academy of Sciences.

Freidenberg, J. N., and I. Z. Jiménez-Velázquez. 1992. "Assessing Impairment among Hispanic Elderly: Biomedical and Ethnomedical Perspectives." In *Hispanic Aged Mental Health,* ed. T. L. Brink, pp. 131–44. Binghamton, NY: Haworth Press.

Fry, C. L., J. Dickerson-Putman, P. Draper, C. Ikels, J. Keith, A. P. Glascock, and H. C. Harpending. 1997. "Culture and the Meaning of a Good Old Age." In *The Cultural Context of Aging: Worldwide Perspective,* ed. J. Sokolovsky, pp. 99–124. Westport, CT: Bergin and Garvey.

Furino, A., ed. 1992. *Health Policy and the Hispanic.* Boulder, CO: Westview Press.

Galíndez, J. de. 1969. *Puerto Rico en Nueva York: Sociología de una Migración.* Buenos Aires: Editorial Tiempo Contemporáneo.

Garrison, V., and C. Weiss. 1979. "Dominican Family Networks and the United

States Immigration Policy: A Case Study." *International Migration Review* 12 (2): 264–83.

Gelfand, D. 1994. *Aging and Ethnicity: Knowledge and Services.* New York: Springer Publishing Co.

Georges, E. 1990. *The Making of a Transnational Community: Migration, Development and Cultural Change in the Dominican Republic.* New York: Columbia University Press.

Ginzberg, E. 1991. "Access to Health Care for Hispanics." *Journal of the American Medical Association* 265: 238–41.

Glazer, N., and D. P. Moynihan 1963. *Beyond the Melting Pot: The Negroes, Puerto Ricans, Jews, Italians and Irish of New York City.* Cambridge: Harvard-M.I.T. Press.

Glick-Schiller, N., ed. 1997. *Transnational Processes/Situated Identities.* Special Issue. *Identities* 4 (2).

Goldshmidt, W. 1986. *Anthropology and Public Policy.* Washington, DC: American Anthropological Association.

González, J. L. 1973. *En Nueva York y Otras Desgracias (In New York and Other Misfortunes).* México City: Siglo XXI.

Grassmuck, S., and P. Pessar. 1992. *Between Two Islands: Dominican International Migration.* Berkeley: University of California Press.

Groger, L. 1992. "Tied to Each Other through Ties to the Land: Informal Support of Black Elders in a Southern U.S. Community." *Journal of Cross-Cultural Gerontology* 7 (3): 205–20.

Gross, D. 1984. "Time Allocation: A Tool for Cultural Analysis." *Annual Review of Anthropology* 13: 519–56.

Gurock, J. 1979. *When Harlem Was Jewish, 1870–1930.* New York: Columbia University Press.

Hackenberg, R. A., and B. H. Hackenberg. 1999. "You CAN Do Something! Forming Policy from Applied Projects, Then and Now." *Human Organization* 58 (1): 1–15.

Hamid, A. 1996. *The Political Economy of Drugs,* vol. 2, *The Cocaine Smoking Epidemic of 1981–1991 in New York City's Low Income Neighborhoods.* New York: Guilford Press.

Hamill, P. 1973. "Coming of Age in New York." In *The Puerto Rican Experience,* ed. F. Cordasco and E. Bucchioni, pp. 199–209. Totowa, NJ: Rowman and Littlefield.

Hammer, M. 1983. "'Core' and 'Extended' Social Networks in Relation to Health and Illness." *Social Science and Medicine* 17 (7): 405–11.

Handlin, O. 1959. *The Newcomers: Negroes and Puerto Ricans in a Changing Metropolis.* Cambridge: Harvard University Press.

Handlin, O. 1965. *The Newcomers: Negroes and Puerto Ricans in a Changing Metropolis*, rev. ed.. Cambridge: Harvard University Press.

Hareven, T. K., and R. Langenbach. 1978. *Amoskeag: Life and Work in an American Factory-City*. New York: Pantheon Books.

Harwood, A. 1977. *RX: Spiritist as Needed*. Anthropology of Contemporary Issues. Ithaca: Cornell University Press.

Haslip-Viera, G., and S. Baver, eds. 1996. *Latinos in New York: Communities in transition*. Notre Dame: University of Notre Dame Press.

Hazuda, H. P., and D. V. Espino. 1997. "Aging, Chronic Disease, and Physical Disability in Hispanic Elderly." In *Minorities, Aging, and Health, ed.* K. S. Markides and M. R. Miranda, pp. 127–48. Newbury Park, CA: Sage Publications.

Helman, C. 1994. *Culture, Health, and Illness: An Introduction for Health Professionals*, 3d ed. Oxford: Butterworth Hinemann.

Hendricks, G. 1974. *The Dominican Diaspora: From the Dominican Republic to New York City. Villages in Transition*. New York: Teachers College Press.

Hernández Alvarez, J. 1968. "The Movement and Settlement of Puerto Rican Migrants within the United States: 1950–1960." *International Migration Review* 2 (spring): 40-52.

Heyman, J. M. 1995. "Putting Power in the Anthropology of Bureaucracy: The Immigration and Naturalization Service at the Mexico–United States Border." *Current Anthropology* 36 (2): 261–87.

Hill, H. 1974. "Guardians of the Sweatshops: The Trade Unions, Racism, and the Garment Industry." In *Puerto Rico and Puerto Ricans: Studies in History and Society*, ed. A. López and J. Petras, pp. 384–417. New York: Wiley.

Hooyman, N., and H. A. Kiyak. 1996. *Social Gerontology: A Multidisciplinary Perspective*. Needham Heights, MA: Allyn and Bacon.

Iglesias, C. A., ed. 1984. *Memoirs of Bernardo Vega: A Contribution to the History of the Puerto Rican Community in New York*, trans. J. Flores. New York: Monthly Review Press.

JAMA (Journal of the American Medical Association). 1991. *U.S. Hispanics: Health Issues*. Special Issue. *JAMA* 265 (2).

Jencks, C., and P. Peterson, eds. 1991. *The Urban Underclass*. Washington, DC: Brookings Institution.

Johnson, A., and O. R. Johnson. 1987. "Time Allocation among the Machiguenga of Shimaa." In *Cross-Cultural Studies in Time Allocation*, vol. 1. New Haven, CT: Human Relations Area Files.

Johnson, L. 1974. *The People of East Harlem*. New York: Department of Community Medicine. Mount Sinai School of Medicine, City University of New York.

Jones, D. 1976. "Applied Anthropology and the Application of Anthropological Knowledge." *Human Organization* 35: 221–29.

Jones-Correa, M. 1998. *Between Two Nations: The Political Predicament of Latinos in New York City.* Ithaca: Cornell University Press.

Kleinman, A. 1995. *Writing at the Margin: Discourse between Anthropology and Medicine.* Berkeley: University of California Press.

Kleinman, A., P. Kunstadter, E. R. Alexander, and J. L. Gale, eds. 1978. *Culture and Healing in Asian Societies: Anthropological, Psychiatric and Public Health Studies.* Cambridge, MA: Schenkman.

Lacayo, C. G. 1980. *A National Study to Assess the Service Needs of the Hispanic Elderly (Final Report).* Asociación Nacional Pro Personas Mayores [National Association for Hispanic Elderly]. DHHS Publication No. 0090-A-1295. Washington, DC: U.S. Government Printing Office.

Lewis, O. 1966. *La Vida: A Puerto Rican Family in the Culture of Poverty: San Juan and New York.* New York: Random House.

Liebow, E. 1967. *Tally's Corner.* Boston: Little Brown.

Lindenbaum, S., and M. Lock, eds. 1993. *Knowledge, Power and Practice: The Anthropology of Medicine and Everyday Life.* Berkeley: University of California Press.

Lomnitz, L. 1977. *Networks and Marginality: Life in a Mexican Shantytown.* New York: Academic Press.

López, A., and J. Petras, eds. 1974. *Puerto Rico and Puerto Ricans.* Studies in History and Society. New York: Wiley.

Los Amigos del Museo del Barrio. 1974. *Quimbamba* (bilingual education quarterly, September issue). New York: Los Amigos del Museo del Barrio.

Mahler, S. 1995. *Salvadoreans in Suburbia: Symbiosis and Conflict.* Needham Heights, MA: Allyn and Bacon.

Maldonado, D. 1979. "Aging in the Chicano Context." In *Ethnicity and Aging: Theory, Research and Policy,* ed. D. E. Gelfand and A. J. Kutzik. Pp. 175–183. New York: Springer Publishing Co.

Margolis, M. 1998. *An Invisible Minority: Brazilians in New York City.* Needham Heights, MA: Allyn and Bacon.

Markides, K. S., and C. Mindel. 1987. *Aging and Ethnicity.* Newbury Park, CA: Sage Publications.

Markides, K. S., and M. Miranda. 1997. *Minorities, Aging and Health.* Newbury Park, CA: Sage Publications.

Markides, K. S., L. Rudkin, R. J. Angel, and D. V. Espino. 1997. "Health Status of Hispanic Elderly in the United States." In *Ethnic Differences in Late Life Health,* ed. L. J. Martin, B. Soldo, and K. Foote. Washington, DC: National Academy Press.

Massey, D., and N. Denton. 1993. *American Apartheid: Segregation and the Making of the Underclass.* Cambridge: Harvard University Press.

Meléndez, E. 1996. "Hispanics and Wage Inequality in New York City." In *Latinos in New York: Communities in Transition,* ed. G. Haslip-Viera and S. L. Baver, pp. 189–210. Notre Dame: University of Notre Dame Press.

Mencher, J. 1958. Growing up in Eastville. Ph.D. dissertation, Columbia University.

———. 1995. "Growing Up in Eastville, a Barrio of New York." In *The Anthropology of Low-Income Urban Enclaves: The Case of East Harlem,* J. N. Freidenberg, pp. 51–75. Annals of the New York Academy of Sciences, vol. 749. New York: New York Academy of Sciences.

Menéndez, E. *Alcoholismo.* 1987. Cuadernos de la Casa Chata. México, D.F.: CIESAS.

Meyer, G. 1989. *Vito Marcantonio: Radical Politician: 1902–1954.* Albany: State University of New York Press.

———. 1992. "Marcantonio and El Barrio." *Centro* 4 (2): 66–87. (Published by Hunter College, City University of New York, Centro de Estudios Puertorriqueños.)

Mills, C. W., C. Senior, and R. K. Goldsen. 1950. *The Puerto Rican Journey: New York's Newest Migrants.* New York: Harper and Row.

Mintz, S. 1996. "The Anthropological Interview and the Life History." In *Oral History: An Interdisciplinary Anthology,* ed. D. Dunaway and W. K. Baum, pp. 298–305. Walnut Creek, CA: Altamira Press.

Miranda, M. R. 1991. *Preface to Empowering Hispanic Families: A Critical Look of the Nineties.* Milwaukee: Family Service of America.

Mohr, E. V. 1982. *The Nuyorican Experience: Literature of the Puerto Rican Minority.* Westport, CT: Greenwood Press.

Moore, J., and R. Pinderhughes, eds. 1993. *In the Barrios: Latinos and the Underclass Debate.* New York: Russell Sage Foundation.

Morales, R., and F. Bonilla, eds. 1993. *Latinos in a Changing U.S. Economy: Comparative Perspectives on Growing Inequality.* Race and Ethnic Relations, vol. 7. Newbury Park, CA: Sage Publications.

Moran, E. 1996. *Transforming Societies, Transforming Anthropology.* Ann Arbor: University of Michigan Press.

Mor-Barak, M. E., L. M. Miller, and L. S. Syme. 1991. "Social Networks, Life Events, and Health of the Poor, Frail Elderly: A Longitudinal Study of the Buffering versus the Direct Effect. *Family Community Health* 14 (2): 1–13.

Mullings, L., ed. 1987. *Sterilization among Puerto Rican Women in New York City: Public Policy and Social Constraints.* New York: Columbia University Press.

Myerhoff, B., and A. Simic, eds. 1978. *Life's Career Aging: Cultural Variations on Growing Old*. Newbury Park, CA: Sage Publications.

Navarro, V. 1994. *The Politics of Health Policy: The US Reforms: 1980-1994*. Oxford: Blackwell.

New Museum of Contemporary Art. 1994. *Testimonio*. New York: New Museum of Contemporary Art.

New York Center for Policy on Aging. 1993. *Growing Older in New York City in the 1990s: A Study of Changing Lifestyles, Quality of Life, and Quality of Care*. New York: New York Community Trust.

New York City Department for the Aging. 1992, *The Older Population in New York City: Changes in Race, Hispanic Origin and Age, 1980 to 1990: An Analysis of Census Data*. New York: Bureau of Research and Planning.

———. 1994. *Chartbook on the Income of the Elderly in New York City*. New York: Office of Management and Policy.

Omi, M., and H. Winant. 1988. *Racial Formation in the United States*. New York: Routledge and Regan Paul.

Orsi, R. A. 1985. *The Madonna of 115th Street: Faith and Community in Italian Harlem, 1880–1950*. New Haven: Yale University Press.

Ortiz, A. 1996. *Puerto Rican Women and Work: Bridges in Transnational Labor*. Philadelphia: Temple University Press.

Padilla, A. M., ed. 1995. *Hispanic Psychology: Critical Issues in Theory and Research*. Newbury Park, CA: Sage Publications.

Padilla, E. 1958. *Up from Puerto Rico*. New York: Columbia University Press.

Palinkas, L., D. Wingard, and E. Barret-Connor. 1990. "The Biocultural Context of Social Networks and Depression among the Elderly." *Social Science and Medicine* 30 (4): 441–47.

Paulino, A. 1998. "Dominican Immigrant Elders: Social Service Needs, Utilization Patterns and Challenges." *Journal of Gerontological Social Work* 30 (1–2): 61–74.

Peattie, L. 1968. *The View from the Barrio*. Ann Arbor: The University of Michigan.

Penn, I. 1990. *Other Ways of Being: Ethnographic Photographs 1948–1971*. New York: Pace-MacGill Gallery.

Pessar, P. 1995. *A Visa for a Dream: Dominicans in the United States*. Needham Heights, MA: Allyn and Bacon.

Poggie, J. D., B. R. De Walt, and W. Dressler, eds. 1992. *Anthropological Research: Process and Application*. Albany: State of New York University Press.

Population Bulletin. 1995. *Older Americans in the 1990's and Beyond*. Washington, DC: Population Reference Bureau.

Portes, A., and R. Rumbaut. 1990. *Immigrant America: A Portrait.* Berkeley: University of California Press.

Rand, C. 1958. *The Puerto Ricans.* New York: Oxford University Press.

Reed, M. C., ed. 1997. *Practicing Anthropology in the Post-Modern World.* Bulletin 17. Washington, DC: American Anthropological Association.

Richards, E. 1990. *Below the Line: Living Poor in America.* Washington, DC: Consumer Report Books.

Rodriguez, J. 1994. *Spanish Harlem.* New York: Art Publishers.

Safa, H. 1981. "The Differential Incorporation of Hispanic Women Migrants into the United States Labor Force." In *Female Immigrants to the United States: Caribbean, Latin American, and African Experiences, ed..* D. Mortimer and R. Bryce-Laporte, pp. 235–67. Research Institute on Immigration and Ethnic Studies. Washington, D.C.: Smithsonian Institution.

Salgado, S. 1986. *The Other Americas.* New York: Pantheon Books.

San Juan, E. 1992. *Racial Formations/Critical Transformations.* Atlantic Highlands, NJ: Humanities Press.

Sánchez-Ayéndez, M. 1988. "Elderly Puerto Ricans in the United States." In *Hispanic Elderly in Transition,* ed. S. R. Applewhite. Westport, CT: Greenwood Press.

Sánchez Korrol, V. 1983. *From Colonia to Community: The History of Puerto Ricans in New York City: 1917–1948.* Westport, CT: Greenwood Press.

Santiago, E. 1993. *When I Was Puerto Rican.* New York: Random House.

Sassen, S. 1990. *The Mobility of Labor and Capital: A Study in International Investment and Labor Flow.* New York: Cambridge University Press.

Schepper-Hughes, N. 1992. *Death without Weeping: The Violence of Everyday Life in Brazil.* Berkeley: University of California Press.

Sexton, P. C. 1965. *Spanish Harlem: Anatomy of Poverty.* New York: Harper and Row.

Singer, M., and H. Baer 1995. *Critical Medical Anthropology.* Amityville, NY: Baywood Press.

Snow, L. F. 1993. *Walkin' over Medicine.* Boulder, CO: Westview Press.

Sokolovsky, J. 1997a. "Bringing Culture Back Home: Aging, Ethnicity and Family Support." In *The Cultural Context of Aging: Worldwide Perspectives,* ed. J. Sokolovsky, pp. 263–75. Westport, CT: Bergin and Garvey.

———. 1997b. *The Cultural Context of Aging: Worldwide Perspectives.* Westport, CT: Bergin and Garvey.

Sotomayor, M., ed. 1991. *Empowering Hispanic Families: A Critical Issue for the Nineties.* Milwaukee: Family Service America.

Sotomayor, M., and A. García, eds. 1993. *Elderly Latinos: Issues and Solutions for the 21st Century.* Washington, DC: National Hispanic Council on Aging.

Stack, C. B. 1974. *All Our Kin: Strategies for Survival in a Black Community.* New York: Harper and Row.

Stevens-Arroyo, Anthony M., and Ana María Diaz-Stevens. 1994. "Religion and Faith among Latinos." In *Handbook of Hispanic Cultures in the U.S.,* ed. Felix Padilla. Sociology, Vol. 3. Houston: Arte Publíco Press.

Stewart, D. 1972. *A Short History of East Harlem.* New York: Museum of the City of New York.

Stull, D. D., and J. J. Schensul, eds. 1987. *Collaborative Research and Social Change: Applied Anthropology in Action.* Boulder, CO: Westview Press.

Susser, M. 1993. Health as a Human Right: An Epidemiologist's Perspective on Public Health." *American Journal of Public Health* 83: 418–26.

Sutton, C., and E. Chaney, eds. 1992. *Caribbean Life in New York City: Sociocultural Dimensions.* New York: Center for Migration Studies.

Thomas, P. 1972. *Down These Mean Streets.* New York: Knopf.

Tienda, M. 1989. "Puerto Ricans and the Underclass Debate." In *The Urban Underclass,* ed. C. Jencks and P. Peterson. pp. 105–119. Annals of the American Academy of Political and Social Science. Washington, DC: Brookings Institution.

Torres, A. 1988. "Explaining Puerto Rican Poverty." *Centro Bulletin* 2 (2). Winter 1987–88: 9–21.

Torres-Gil, F., and E. P. Stanford. 1992. *Diversity: New Approaches to Ethnic Minority Aging.* Amityville, NY: Baywood Press.

Tran, T. V., P. Fitzpatrick, W. R. Berg, and R. Wright. 1996. "Acculturation, Health, Stress and Psychological Distress among Elderly Hispanics." *Journal of Cross-Cultural Gerontology* 11 (2): 149–65.

U.S. Bureau of the Census. 1996. *65+ in the United States.* Current Population Reports, Special Studies (P23-190). Washington, DC: U.S. Government Printing Office.

———. 1998. *State and Metropolitan Area Data Book 1997–1998,* 5th ed. Washington, DC: U.S. Government Printing Office.

U.S. Department of Health and Human Services. 1991. *Healthy People 2000: National Health Promotion and Disease Prevention Objectives.* Publication Number (PHS) 91-50213. Washington, DC: U.S. Government Printing Office.

U.S. Department of Labor, Bureau of Labor Statistics, Middle Atlantic Regional Office. 1970. *Some Perspectives on New York in Transition.* New York: Bureau of Labor Statistics.

———. 1971. *The New York Scene.* New York: Bureau of Labor Statistics.

———. 1974. "The New York Puerto Ricans: Patterns of Work Experience." In *Puerto Rico and Puerto Ricans: Studies in History and Society,* ed. A. López and J. Petras, pp. 347–84. New York: Wiley.

References

Van Willigen, J. 1991. *Anthropology in Use: A Source Book in Anthropological Practice.* Boulder, CO: Westview Press.

———. 1993. *Applied Anthropology: An Introduction.* Westport, CT: Bergin and Garvey.

Wakefield, D. 1959. *Island in the City: Puerto Ricans in New York.* New York: Citadel Press.

Waldinger, R. 1985. "Immigration and Industrial Change in the New York City Apparel Industry." In *Hispanics in the U.S. Economy,* ed. George J. Borjas and M. Tienda. Orlando, FL: Academic Press.

Waterston, A. 1993. *Street Addicts in the Political Economy.* Philadelphia: Temple University Press.

Williams, B. 1988. *Upscaling Downtown: Stalled Gentrification in Washington D.C.* Ithaca: Cornell University Press.

———. 1992. "Poverty among African Americans in the Urban United States." *Human Organization* 51 (2): 164–74.

Williams, T., and W. Kornblum. 1995. "Public Housing Projects as Successful Environments for Adolescent Development." In *The Anthropology of Low-Income Urban Enclaves: The Case of East Harlem,* ed. J. N. Freidenberg, pp. 153–76. Annals of the New York Academy of Sciences, vol. 749. New York: New York Academy of Sciences.

Wilson, W. J. 1997. *The Truly Disadvantaged.* Chicago: University of Chicago Press.

Wolf, E. R. 1984. *Europe and the People without History.* Berkeley: University of California Press.

Wulff, R. M., and S. J. Fiske. 1987. *Anthropological Praxis: Translating Knowledge into Action.* London: Westview Press.

Wydle, L., and A. Ford, eds. 1999. *Serving Minority Elders in the 21st Century.* New York: Springer Publishing Co.

Yoder, P. S. 1997. "Negotiating Relevance: Belief, Knowledge, and Practice in International Health Projects." *Medical Anthropology Quarterly* 11 (2): 131–46.

AUTHOR INDEX

Abraido-Lanza, A. F., 153
Administration on Aging, 3
Agar, M., 240
Alexander, E. R., 124
Angel, J. L., 10, 154, 181
Angel, R. L., 10, 154, 181
Annals of the American Academy of Political and Social Science, 182
Antonucci, T. C., 154, 176
Applewhite, S. R., 4, 10
Arellano, A., 181
Atchley, R., 101, 122, 181, 182
Auslander, G., 153

Baer, H., 150
Balán, J., 9
Barret-Connor, E., 154
Barsa, B. R., 10, 154
Basch, L., 4
Baver, S., 10
Bean, F. T., 182
Behar, R., 8
Belshaw, C., 272
Benmayor, R., 8, 10, 275
Benson, K., 13, 278
Berg, W. R., 154
Bertaux, D., 9
Blanc, C. Szanton, 4
Bonilla, F., 178, 182, 281
Bookbinder, B., 276
Bourgois, P., 10
Brennan, M., 10
Brink, T. L., 4, 181
Bucchione, E., 71, 278

Cantor, M. H., 10
Carnoy, M., 182
Centro de Estudios Puertorriqueños, 47, 178
Cernea, M., 272
Chambers, Erve, 272
Chaney, E., 276

Chenault, L., 15, 18
City of New York, Department of City Planning, 4
Collier, J., 8
Collier, M., 8
Colón, J., 14
Commonwealth Fund Commission, 181, 275
Community Service Society, 182
Cordasco, F., 71, 278

Daley, H., 182
DeHavenon, A. L., 240
DeLaire, R., 10
Delgado, R., 10
Denton, N., 182
DeWalt, B. R., 272
Díaz-Stevens, Ana María, 281
Dickerson-Putman, J., 121
Draper, P., 121
Dressler, W., 291
Duany, J., 276

Eddy, E., 272
Ernst, R., 13
Ervin, Alexander M., 272
Espino, D. V., 181
Estes, C. L., 264

Fischer, C. S., 154
Fisher, E., 263
Fiske, S. J., 240, 272
Fitzpatrick, J., 277
Fitzpatrick, P., 154
Flores, J., 65
Foner, N., 276
Ford, A., 10
Freidenberg, J. N., 10, 72, 148, 240, 276, 281
Fry, C. L., 121
Furino, A., 275

Author Index

Galíndez, J. de, 47, 64, 277
García, A., 4, 10, 181
Garrison, V., 276
Gelfand, D., 10
Georges, E., 276
Ginzberg, E., 182
Glazer, N., 277
Glick-Schiller, N., 4
Goldsen, R. K., 277
Goldshmidt, W., 272
González, J. L., 277
Grassmuck, S., 276
Groger, L., 154
Gross, D., 280
Guier, C., 154
Gurock, J., 14

Hackenberg, B. H., 272
Hackenberg, R. A., 272
Hamid, A., 240
Hamill, P., 69, 278
Hammer, M., 10, 72, 153, 281
Handlin, O., 15, 277
Harwood, A., 275, 280
Haslip-Viera, G., 10
Hazuda, H. P., 181
Helman, C., 124, 126
Hendricks, G., 276
Hernández Alvarez, J., 277
Heyman, J. M., 272
Hill, H., 71, 279
Hooyman, N., 3

Iglesias, C. A., 15, 16, 17, 63

JAMA (Journal of the American Medical Association), 181
Jelín, E., 9
Jencks, C., 182
Jiménez Velásquez, I. Z., 148, 281
Johnson, A., 280
Johnson, L., 69, 70, 259, 260, 261, 278
Johnson, O. R., 280
Jones, D., 240
Jones-Correa, M., 10
Juarbe, A., 10, 275
Julius, N., 263

Kiyak, H. A., 3
Kleinman, A., 124, 151

Kornblum, W., 72, 182
Kunstadter, P., 124

Lewis, O., 275, 277
Liebow, E., 240
Lindenbaum, S., 150
Litwin, H., 153
Lock, M., 150
Lomnitz, L., 154
López, A., 21
Los Amigos del Museo del Barrio, 14, 69

Mahler, S., 276
Maldonado, D., 4
Margolis, M., 276
Markides, K. S., 10, 181
Massey, D., 182
Meléndez, E., 182
Mencher, J., 68, 94, 97
Menéndez, E., 150
Meyer, G., 16, 17, 18, 67, 278
Miller, L. M., 153
Mills, C. W., 277
Mindel, C., 181
Mintz, S., 9
Miranda, M. R., 10, 181
Mohr, E. V., 47
Moore, J., 182
Morales, R., 178, 182, 281
Moran, E., 272
Mor-Barak, M. E., 153
Moynihan, D. P., 277
Mullings, L., 276
Myerhoff, B., 121

Navarro, V., 150
New Museum of Contemporary Art, 115
New York City Center for Policy on Aging, 3, 275

Ojeda, R. H., 182
Omi, M., 4
Orsi, R. A., 14, 276

Padilla, A. M., 275
Padilla, E., 277, 278
Palinkas, L., 154
Partridge, W., 272
Paulino, A., 10
Peattie, L., 10
Penn, I., 8

Pessar, P., 276
Peterson, P., 182
Petras, J., 21
Pinderhughes, R., 182
Poggie, J. D., 272
Portes, A., 21

Rand, C., 277
Reed, M. C., 272
Revenson, T. A., 154
Richards, E., 8
Rodríguez, J., 10
Rudkin, L., 181
Rumbaut, R., 21

Safa, H., 94
Sainz, A., 10
Salgado, S., 8
Sánchez-Ayéndez, M., 10
Sánchez Korrol, V., 15
San Juan, E., 4
Sassen, S., 71, 96
Schensul, J. J., 272
Schepper-Hughes, N., 150
Senior, C., 277
Sexton, P. C., 66, 69
Simic, A., 121
Singer, M., 150
Snow, L. F., 280
Sokolovsky, J., 121, 177
Sotomayor, M., 4, 10, 181
Stack, C. B., 154, 240
Stanford, E. P., 4
Stefancic, J., 10
Stevens-Arroyo, Anthony M., 281
Stewart, D., 13, 14, 17, 70

Stull, D. D., 272
Susser, I., 150
Susser, M., 150
Sutton, C., 276
Swan, J. H., 264
Syme, L. S., 153

Thomas, P., 10, 277
Tienda, M., 182
Torres, A., 178
Torres-Gil, F., 4
Torruellas, R., 10, 275
Tran, T. V., 154

U.S. Bureau of the Census, 179, 264
U.S. Department of Health and Human
    Services, 150
U.S. Department of Labor, 71, 95, 96,
    279

Van Willigen, J., 272

Wakefield, D., 12, 13, 14, 15, 17, 18, 66,
    67, 68, 277, 278
Waldinger, R., 94
Waterston, A., 240
Weiss, C., 276
Williams, B., 203, 240
Williams, T., 72, 182
Wilson, W. J., 182
Winant, H., 4
Wingard, D., 154
Wulff, R, M., 240, 272
Wydle, L., 10

Yoder, P. S., 151

SUBJECT INDEX

actual needs, 189
AFL-CIO Committee on Puerto Rican Affairs, 279n.10
African-Americans: Hispanic East Harlem merging with, 67; Latinos as second-largest minority after, 4, 10; moving into Harlem, 13–14, 17, 69; poverty rate for elderly, 264; in the projects, 218; as segregated from Puerto Ricans, 70
aging: biomedicalization of, 264; continuity theory of, 122; cross-cultural variability in, 121–22; cultural construction of, 108–9; of immigrants, 3–4; inversion of age pyramid in 1980s, 71–72. *See also* elderly, the
Albizu Campus, Pedro, 17
Andrea, 251
Angela: on faith, 236; on her daughter, 236; on limits on her activity, 109; on politics, 252; statuettes of, 234
antipoverty programs, 69, 278n.12
Antonio: on crime in the projects, 224; going back and forth between New York and Puerto Rico, 62; going to Chicago before New York, 64; on government as the culprit, 257; on home remedies, 143; illness of, 123; on pets for the elderly, 172; on *respaldos,* 234; on working in Puerto Rico, 33
apparel industry. *See* garment (apparel) industry
Armando, 147, 171, 192
Asians, 71
Association of Catholic Trade Unionists, 279n.10
Augustina: on crime, 223; education of, 35; on home remedies, 142, 143; reasons for migrating, 58; on safety, 256; on Society of Saint Rosary, 230
Aurelia: on aging as sad, 116; on biomedical health care system, 149; on drug addicts, 225; on the elderly working, 115; on employment and education, 256–57; on home remedies, 142–43; on housing and safety, 254; on illnesses of the soul, 146; on life as worse in New York, 62; on loneliness of the elderly, 173; on mugging the elderly for their checks, 224; on old age as the end, 117; on pets for the elderly, 172; on photograph of Buenos Aires slum, 251; reasons for migrating, 58; on safety, 225, 256; on sex and the elderly, 117

bingo, 114, 194–95, 215
biomedical system: anthropological knowledge applied to, 151–52; barriers to seeking care from, 130–32, 137–38; biomedicalization of aging, 264; central strategy of, 138; congruence with ethnomedical system, 126, 145–50; educating providers in, 151; ethnomedical system contrasted with, 123–26, 137–45, 151; and health-seeking process, 124; hypothetical "cracks" in health behavior from perspective of, 125, 150; prescription medications, 131–32, 184, 187; problems with, 141–43; and social networks, 153–77; utilization of, 137, 139, 149; for vision problems, 151
bolita, 114, 215–16, 281n.4
borrowing, 198
botánicas, 135, 143, 189, 195, 231, 233
budgets, 190–98
burial, 197, 201, 281n.5
businesses: commercial real estate, 221; flight of Latino-owned, 219; Puerto Rican immigrants starting, 16

Caballero, Danny, 91, 279n.4
candles, 195, 228, 235

Carmen: brother Antonio's illness, 123; on home remedies, 143; on out-of-pocket medical costs, 196; on pets for the elderly, 172; on playing bingo, 114; on private physicians, 145
cashing checks, commissions for, 197
Casita María Senior Citizen Center, 113, 280n.4
cataracts, 151
Central Harlem, 13–14
checks: commissions for cashing, 197; delivery problems, 211; the elderly mugged for, 224
children: child abuse, 34; child care, 82, 84, 86; child labor in Puerto Rico, 34; the elderly caring for latchkey youngsters, 202; intergenerational transfers, 175, 197, 202–3, 263; structured after-school activities needed for, 211–12. *See also* education
churches, 215, 278n.7
class, social. *See* social class
commercial real estate, 221
commissions for cashing checks, 197
companionship, 105–6
construction industry, 96
consumer protection, as what government should be spending on, 261
continuity theory of aging, 122
Council for Seniors, 251
crime, 223–26; causes of, 211–13; as constraint on the elderly, 215, 237; drug addiction associated with, 225; fear of, 211, 239, 269; government policy in increase of, 247, 257; increase of, 248; progressively violent nature of, 210
Cubans, 3, 14
curanderismo, 134, 280n.4

"death insurance," 197, 201, 281n.5
Democratic Party, 69, 91, 278n.14
doctor privado (private physician), 144–45, 196, 201
dogs, 171–72, 257
Dominga: on bingo, 215; on crime, 223; on health care decisions, 138; on her son asking for money, 197; on Medicare and Medicaid, 195; on politics, 251; on private physicians, 145; on public sanctuaries, 216; spiritual artifacts of, 234;

on working and taking care of her children, 84
Dominicans, 3
dominoes, 114, 209, 215, 238
Dora: on activity during retirement, 109–10; on bringing her mother to the U.S., 85; on cheap housing for immigrants, 87; on conditions in East Harlem as worse than before, 248; connections used to get a job, 83; on "downtown," 250; education of, 36, 37; on the elderly living alone, 168; family responsibilities of, 86–87; on health status and income, 149–50, 256; on homelessness, 222; on home remedies, 143; on housing, 254–55; on impact of poverty on others, 192; income as not keeping pace with expenses, 193; on *La Marqueta*, 221; occupation of, 80–81; on parking lots, 225; on pets for the elderly, 171; on photograph of Buenos Aires slum, 250; on policymakers consulting with residents, 253–54; political activity of, 92, 110, 196, 251, 252, 258, 280n.4; purposeful activity as work for, 111; racism experienced in New York, 59; reasons for migrating, 57; on rents, 219, 253; Social Security benefits received by, 92, 196, 252; on social usefulness of activities of the elderly, 113, 257; on work in personal identity, 88
Dos Antillas, Las, 276n.2
drug addiction, 210–11, 225–26, 238

East Harlem (*El Barrio*): being old in, 99–203; census data for 1980, 4; census data for 1990, 4; center of, 17; as *colonia*, 67, 277n.4; commercial real estate in, 221; in eighteenth century, 13; four issues affecting peoples' lives, 217; during Great Depression, 17–18; growing up in Puerto Rico affecting life in, 22; homelessness in, 222–23; *La Marqueta*, 16, 79, 221; low-income population of, 70; median income for, 4; as metaphor for social issues in New York City, 208–39; from 1950s to the 1970s, 67–70; from 1970s to 1990s, 70–72; perceived needs for, 259–62; as place with soul, 215; population change between 1950 and 1957, 67; population in

1890, 13; population in 1970, 70; population in 1980, 71; population in 1990, 71; present and past compared, 209–14; private space in, 227–37; Puerto Rican population in 1936, 18; riots of 1926, 16; searching for a better life in, 46–65; social history of, 12–19; as socialist center, 17; Spanish as lingua franca in, 3, 206; the streets of, 208–27; as tenement district, 13; urban renewal, 68, 70. *See also* Latino elderly
East Harlem Coalition of Senior Citizen Centers, 258
East Harlem Community Corporation, 278n.12
East River House, 278n.9
economy, informal, 82, 193–94, 198
education: crime and lack of opportunities for, 212; and employment, 256–57; household economy affected by, 25; as perceived need, 260, 263; in Puerto Rico, 35–37, 40; as reason for migrating, 57; as what government should be spending on, 261, 262
El Barrio. See East Harlem (*El Barrio*)
elderly, the: an active life for, 102–5; capacity for happiness of, 116; companionship as necessary for, 105–6; cultural construction of aging, 108–19; culturally constructed as handicapped, 100–101; expansion of services for, 264; happiness as right of, 105–8; as increasing during 1980s, 72; infantilizing, 113; as living alone, 2; the meanings of being old, 100–122; median income rise of, 264; Older Americans Act, 177; and poverty, 179–80; sexuality for, 107, 117; social visibility lacking for, 127, 258–59. *See also* Latino elderly
Elsie: daughters not visiting, 168; on home care attendants, 170; on not knowing English, 63–64; and religion, 230
Emiliana. *See* Moreno, Emiliana
employment, 73–97; age restrictions on, 112; child labor in Puerto Rico, 34; crime and lack of opportunities for, 212; in cultural construction of aging, 109–16; as declining in 1970s, 70–71; and education, 256–57; as an entitlement, 111–12; exploitation of foreign workers, 246–47; of first contingent of

Puerto Rican immigrants, 16–17; gender differences in Puerto Rico, 24, 33, 40, 42; gender disparity in wages, 89; housing trends as related to, 72; immigrant networks transmitting information about, 67; as income source for Latino elderly, 199; informal economy, 82, 193–94, 198; job creation, 246; job discrimination among Latinos, 83–84; labor racketeering, 76, 96, 180, 279n.10; in 1950s in East Harlem, 69; as perceived need, 260, 263; personal identity defined by, 88; piecework, 95; as reason for migration, 63; restructuring of New York economy, 95, 96; social value of work, 31, 84, 112; study population's occupational trajectory by age and gender, 39; sweatshops, 95; unfair labor practices, 74; union benefits, 81, 178, 196, 199; unpaid work, 110; volunteer work, 110, 120, 177; women in the needle trades, 40–41. *See also* retirement; unemployment
English language, 63–64, 75, 81, 180
entertainment: budgeting for, 194–95; music, 216; the streets as, 214–17. *See also* games
espiritismo, 134, 138, 195, 230, 236
ethnicity: competition between groups, 276n.1; and the labor market, 66, 71; as political ideology, 12; residential segregation based on, 70. *See also* Puerto Ricans; *and other groups by name*
ethnomedical system: biomedical system contrasted with, 123–26, 137–45, 151; congruence with biomedical system, 126, 145–50; *curanderismo*, 134, 280n.4; *espiritismo*, 134, 138, 195, 230, 236; as expenditure of Latino elderly, 201; home remedies, 133, 142–44; massage, 134–35; natural medicines, 135–36; *santería*, 138, 230, 280n.6; utilization of, 139
exercise, 134
expenditures, 199–201

family: as adding more problems for the elderly, 167; drug addiction affecting, 225; as income source, 199; intergenerational transfers, 175, 197, 202–3, 263; as perceived need, 259, 260; as social network, 157–59. *See also* kinship

Felicita, 224

Felix: altar in apartment of, 233; on conditions in East Harlem, 248; on crime in the projects, 224; on dominoes, 215; on hanging out in the streets, 216–17; and Medicaid, 196; younger friend taking care of, 167

Florentino: on *bolita*, 216; on "downtown," 250; on drug addicts, 225; on the elderly as easy prey, 226; on the elderly seeking activity, 112; on hotels, 219; on housing, 255; on loneliness of the elderly, 173; as a loner, 115; occupation of, 80; on photograph of Luz María, 193; on private physicians, 144; as rarely bored, 115–16; reasons for migrating, 57; on senior citizen centers, 113; on working in Puerto Rico, 33; as working past retirement, 81, 111, 112

Florida water, 133, 280n.3

food: as actual need, 189; disproportionate amount of income spent on, 269; as expenditure of Latino elderly, 200; at senior citizen centers, 200, 202; social relationships maintained with, 185, 200

food cooperatives, 269

Food Stamps, 182, 199

friends, as perceived need, 259, 260

games: bingo, 114, 194–95, 215; *bolita*, 114, 215–16, 281n.4; dominoes, 114, 209, 215, 238; as keeping elderly connected to outside world, 114; Lotto, 114, 215, 216; played at senior citizen centers, 215; played on the sidewalks, 215

garbage collection, 226, 253

garment (apparel) industry: decline of, 71; Emiliana Moreno's jobs in, 75–76, 77–79; women in, 40–41, 42–43, 71, 94, 96

gender: and age of retirement, 92; disparity in wages, 89; employment differences in Puerto Rico, 24, 33, 40, 42; and time allocation during retirement, 120. *See also* men; women

Germans, 13

government: what people think it should be spending on, 259–62. *See also* state services

Great Depression, 17

Growing Old in Spanish Harlem (Museum of the City of New York), 232, 275n.4

Harlem: Central Harlem, 13–14. *See also* East Harlem (*El Barrio*)

health, 123–52; coping with illness, 132–36; the elderly as concerned with, 121; five perspectives for assessing, 124; health-seeking process, 124, 125; and housing, 244, 255; and income, 149–50, 256; as perceived need, 259, 260, 263; and poverty, 181; self- and medical assessment of, 123; as what government should be spending on, 261, 262. *See also* health care

health care: as actual need, 189; consumer and provider concerns about, 150–51; as expenditure of Latino elderly, 200, 201; funding for compared with social services, 263, 264; implications of this study for, 268; and income, 149–50; Medicaid, 149, 181, 189, 195, 196; medical pluralism, 140; Medicare, 108, 132, 142, 189, 195; out-of-pocket costs of, 181, 195–96; pragmatic syncretism in, 140; private physicians, 144–45, 196, 201; as a right, 150; self-diagnosis, 133; and social networks, 153, 173–77; utilization patterns and planning of, 150–52. *See also* biomedical system; ethnomedical system

health insurance, 181, 201

health-seeking process, 124, 125

heating, 226

heat supplement, 197, 199, 255

Hispanics: term as used in this study, 275n.1. *See also* Latinos

home care attendants, 170, 198, 219

homelessness, 222–23, 225, 238

home remedies (*remedios caseros*), 133, 142–44

hopelessness, 226, 238

hotels, 218, 219

housing: bureaucracy as barrier to obtaining, 2, 220; cheap housing for immigrants, 87; as constraint on the elderly, 215, 217–20, 237; consulting with residents on, 254–56; discrimination against Latinos, 15; doubling up, 18, 173; economics influencing living arrangements, 166; educating people on improving,

257–58; for elderly living alone, 242–43; as expenditure of Latino elderly, 200–201; and health, 244, 255; homelessness, 222–23, 225, 238; hotels, 218, 219; immigrant networks transmitting information about, 67; low-rent housing for the elderly, 182; New York City Housing Authority, 276n.4; in the 1950s, 68–69; as perceived need, 259, 260, 263; policy proposals for cost of, 241–43; policy proposals for maintenance of, 243–45; political and economic aspects of, 12; politicians needing to do something about, 252–53; and safety, 254, 256; segregation in, 12, 64, 70; services lacking in public, 226; sharing, 185–86, 200–201; Title VIII housing reduction, 201, 218; unequal distribution of, 71; as what government should be spending on, 259, 261; worsening conditions in 1930s, 18. *See also* housing projects; rent; tenements

housing projects: crime in, 224; dislocation caused by, 74; Emiliana Moreno demands to live in, 88; housing shortage not solved by, 72; Puerto Rican attitude toward, 218; rents for, 242; as replicating tenements, 68; in urban renewal, 70

immigrants: aging of, 3–4; exploitation of labor of, 246–47. *See also* Latinos; *and other groups by name*

income: decline in retirement, 179, 180–81; health status and, 149–50, 256; implications of this study for, 268; median income in East Harlem, 4; median income of study population, 201; sources of, 199, 201–2. *See also* poverty

income maintenance programs, 241–42, 245

independentista movement, 278n.5

individual rights, 247

informal economy, 82, 193–94, 198

informants for this study. *See* study population

Institute for Puerto Rican and Hispanic Elderly, 251, 258

Irish, 13, 14, 210, 276n.1

Italians: conflict with Irish, 276n.1; conflict with Puerto Ricans, 210; in East Harlem, 14, 16, 69, 70; Hispanic East Harlem merging with, 67; moving out of East Harlem, 15, 17, 19

Jews, 14, 15, 16, 19, 276n.1

jobs. *See* employment

Josefa: in informal economy, 82; migrant network established by, 59; reasons for migrating, 58–59; as satisfied with life in New York, 61; on working in Puerto Rico, 33–34

Jovino: on cheap housing for immigrants, 87; comparing *El Barrio* and Puerto Rico, 53–54; on drugs, 211; education of, 35; on the elderly as thinking about the future, 117; grandchildren and great-grandchildren of, 160; migration to *El Barrio*, 52; on working in Puerto Rico, 34

Juan, 2; altars in apartment of, 233; budget of, 190; on buying candles, 195; as distrusting everyone, 237; education of, 37; on the elderly's fear of crime, 219; on his apartment, 219, 220; on his mother supporting the family, 36; on housing and health, 255; in informal economy, 2, 82, 112, 190, 198; migrating to New York, 55; on out-of-pocket medical costs, 196; paying his sister-in-law to cook, 2, 194; on playing dominoes, 114; on public sanctuaries, 216; on *santeros,* 230; on spiritists charging for their services, 195

Juana, 235

judiciary system, discrimination against Puerto Ricans by, 214

Julia: borrowing money, 198; on commission for cashing checks, 197; on crime, 223; on heating, 226; on heating supplement, 197, 255; housekeeping as work of, 36; in informal economy, 82; on learning English, 81; low wages of, 89; on Medicare, 195; as not feeling old, 116; on not speaking English, 198; as not working after marriage in Puerto Rico, 82; occupation of, 81; on pets for the elderly, 172; on private physicians, 144, 145, 196; purposeful activity as work for, 111; reasons for migrating, 57, 61; on religion, 229, 236; upwardly mobile son of, 167

Julio, 149, 235

kinship: and legal representation of the elderly, 167; obligations entailed by, 175; official versus study population's view of, 174. See also family

labor market: and ethnicity, 66, 71; structural characteristics of U.S., 178–79. See also employment
labor racketeering, 76, 96, 180, 279n.10
La Guardia, Fiorello, 16, 276n.4
language: English, 63–64, 75, 81, 180; Spanish, 3, 130–31, 198, 206
latchkey youngsters, 202
Latino elderly, 99–203; concentration in East Harlem, 6; as easy prey, 226; as four times a minority, 179; functional impairment of, 3, 275n.2; housing for those living alone, 242–43; income decline after retirement, 180–81; in intergenerational transfers, 175, 197, 202–3, 263; as living alone, 3, 7, 166; loneliness troubling, 172–73; lower than average incomes of, 120; neighborhood affecting lives of, 208–27; New York concentration of, 3; as percentage of Latino population, 3; as percentage of total elderly population, 3; poverty among, 178–203, 262–63; poverty rate of, 3, 181; social issues pertaining to, 120–22; social networks for, 153–77; time as used by, 108–19. See also employment; health; housing; safety; study population
Latinos: Cubans, 3, 14; Dominicans, 3; in East Harlem population, 70; Harlem riots of 1926, 16; health insurance for, 181; job discrimination among, 83–84; Mexicans, 3, 71, 221; as percentage of New York population, 4; as percentage of U.S. population, 4; poverty among, 3, 10; as second-largest minority, 4, 10; term as used in this study, 275n.1. See also Latino elderly; Puerto Ricans
Lenox Avenue, 14, 17
Lexington Avenue, 18
lighting candles, 195, 228, 235
Logia Hispano Americana de Oro, 231
loneliness, 172–73
Lotto, 114, 215, 216
Lower East Side, 13
Luz María: on age as not bothering her, 117; on being old and sick, 116; on

crime, 223; education of, 37; on entertainment, 195; family and nonfamily in social network of, 167; on friend spending his money on *bolita*, 216; on her burial, 197; home religious services for, 229–30; on home remedies, 143; on illnesses of the soul, 146–47; migrating to New York, 54, 58; paying her helpers, 194; on paying home attendants, 198; photograph of, 170, 193; spiritual artifacts of, 235; on violence indoors, 237; welfare confused with benefits by, 191

Madison Avenue, 17
Manhattan, 4, 13
manufacturing industries, 94–96
Marcantonio, Vito, 16, 276nn. 5, 6, 278n.5
María, 1–2; budget of, 190–91; on crime, 223, 224; as distrusting everyone, 237; on faith, 236; on garbage collection, 226, 253; on having to move because of children, 84; on home remedies, 144; on housing projects, 218, 224; on illnesses of the soul, 146; income as inadequate to cover basic needs, 2, 192; on learning English, 81; on life as worse in New York, 61–62; as living alone, 2, 166; on marriage, 38; on pets, 257; on photograph of Buenos Aires slum, 250; on private physicians, 145; resource exchange by, 198; on spiritists, 236; on spirits, 230; statuettes of, 234; on uninhabited places, 252; union benefits lost by, 81, 196; as working during retirement, 112
Marqueta, La, 16, 79, 221
marriage: as economic survival strategy for women, 37–38; husbands needed only if they are good to women, 161; losing female labor through, 24–25, 27–28; women not working outside the home after, 36, 41, 82, 85
Marta: giving food to María, 191; going back and forth between New York and Puerto Rico, 43; on pets for the elderly, 172; as rarely seeing her daughter-in-law and grandchildren, 167
massage, 134–35
Matilde: on bringing her family to the U.S., 85–86; on cheap housing for immigrants, 87; on conditions in East

Harlem as worse than before, 248; as doing well, 117; on doing what she can while homebound, 109; education of, 35; on the elderly as easy prey, 226; on heating, 226; on home care attendants, 170; on home remedies, 142; low wages of, 89; on raising her children with no money, 85; reasons for migrating, 56; on religion, 229, 230; on safety, 254; on working after marriage, 85; on working in Puerto Rico, 33

Mayor's Committee on Exploitation, 279n.10

Medicaid, 149, 181, 189, 195, 196

medical care. *See* health care

medical pluralism, 140

Medicare, 108, 132, 142, 189, 195

medicines: natural, 135–36; prescription, 131–32, 184, 187

men: eating at senior citizen centers, 200; income decline with age, 181; as living off women, 188; occupational changes upon migration, 96–97; occupations in Puerto Rico, 33, 40, 41, 42, 43; reasons for migrating, 63; retirement by, 92; in service industries, 94; social networks of, 175; time allocation during retirement, 120

MEND (Massive Economic Neighborhood Development), 278n.12

Méndez, Isabel, 91, 110, 279n.4

Méndez, Olga, 83, 91, 252, 279n.4

Méndez, Tony, 91, 278n.14, 279n.4

Mexicans, 3, 71, 221

Monchito: abusive childhood of, 34–35; on age as not bothersome, 116, 117; on "downtown," 250; education of, 35–36; on homelessness, 222; on housing bureaucracy, 219; on influential contacts, 196; on loneliness of the elderly, 167, 172; on photograph of Luz María, 193; reasons for migrating, 58; on violence indoors, 236

money: as perceived need, 259, 260. *See also* income; poverty

Moreno, Emiliana: age at arrival in New York, 63; aging as viewed by, 102–8; in agricultural economy of Rincón, 1902–1914, 22–25; in Aguada with her family, 1918–1927, 28–30; apartment "purchased" by, 52, 68; arthritis of, 126,

127, 128; barriers to seeking biomedical care by, 130–32; as central voice for this study, 8, 9; on cheap housing for immigrants, 87; on child care, 86; on children as an investment, 84; children of, 32, 49, 52; on coffee plantation in Moca, 1915–1917, 25–28; comparing *El Barrio* and Puerto Rico, 53–54; coping with her illnesses, 132–36; cost of connections to, 162–64; daughter's death, 128, 163; depression of, 126, 127, 155; disease and illness of, 126–36, 137; education of, 22–23; English learned in Puerto Rico, 63; family connections of, 157–59; on getting an apartment in the projects, 88–89; as a giver, 186–87; and her husband, 160–61; home religious services for, 229; in informal economy, 82; interpreting her symptoms, 129–30; on job discrimination among Latinos, 83–84; marriage of, 30; marriage postponed by, 29; before migration, 22–32; migration and first year in *El Barrio*, 48–54; mother's death, 162–63; nonfamily connections of, 159–60; nonpecuniary wealth of, 184–88; personal connections of, 154–65; policy proposals of, 241–48, 263; political activity of, 91; premigratory experience compared with study population, 38; present and past compared by, 209–14, 248; pros and cons of where she lives, 211; reciprocity in connections of, 164–65; religious faith of, 227–29; sewing done by, 20, 23–24, 29, 75–76, 77–79, 103; Social Security of, 90; on sugar plantation in Aguada, 1928–1948, 30–32; value of connections to, 160–62; vision loss of, 74, 78, 100, 103–4, 105, 126–28, 129–30, 137; on work as an honor, 82–83; work trajectory in the U.S., 74–79

music, 216

natural medicines, 135–36

needle trades. *See* garment (apparel) industry

needs, actual, 189

networks, social. *See* social networks

New York City: Central Harlem, 13–14; "downtown" as viewed by *El Barrio* residents, 250; as goal of Caribbean

New York City *(continued)*
migration, 47; Latinos as percentage of
population of, 4; Manhattan, 4, 13; opportunity offered by, 18. *See also* East
Harlem *(El Barrio)*
New York City Housing Authority, 276n.4
nonfamily connections, 159–60, 173–74,
176

Older Americans Act, 177
101st Street, 15
106th Street, 14
110th Street, 17
116th Street, 15, 17, 18
120th Street, 18

Park Avenue, 14, 16
parking lots, avoiding, 225
pensions, 89–90, 108, 178, 180, 181, 199
personal safety. *See* safety
Petra: on biomedical system's problems,
141–42; on Council for Seniors, 251; on
entertainment, 195; on home remedies,
142; on Logia Hispano Americana de
Oro, 231; political activity of, 92,
114–15, 258, 280n.4; on red tape in social services, 258–59; volunteer work of,
110
pets, 171–72, 175, 257
Philippinos, 71
piecework, 95
police protection, as what government
should be spending on, 261
policy: and aging of immigrant population,
10; anthropology and, 5, 267–68, 272;
consultation methods, 241; cost-containment as basis of, 101; and cultural construction of the elderly, 100–101; giving
informants access to policymakers, 270;
implications of this study for, 262–65,
268–70; informants in defining issues,
269–70; local-level policy-making,
240–65; and neighborhood trust,
238–39; policy ethnography, 269–70;
and private lives, 270–73; program planning, 256, 264, 272; recommendations
for, 201–3; social networks and, 174–77
politics: for changing life conditions of the
elderly, 258; Democratic Party, 69, 91,
278n.14; political involvement as solution to social problems, 251–53; Puerto

Ricans' activities, 69–70, 91–92,
278n.13
poverty, 178–203; antipoverty programs,
69, 278n.12; calculating, 188; as experienced in daily life, 188–98; and health,
181; income decline for the elderly,
179–80; income distribution and programs for ameliorating, 268–69; Latino
elderly as at risk for, 262–63; of Latinos,
3, 10; as process, 182–83; rate for elderly
African-Americans, 264; rate for Latino
elderly, 3, 181, 264; War Against
Poverty, 69
pragmatic syncretism, 140
prescription medications, 131–32, 184, 187
private physician *(doctor privado)*, 144–45,
196, 201
private space, 227–37; boundary with public space as blurred, 237; household spiritual artifacts, 231–35; religion, 229–31;
residing in low-income urban enclave impacting utilization of, 238; violence in,
236–37
program planning: bringing personal experience to bear on, 272; consulting with
informants for, 256; needs assessment in,
264
projects, housing. *See* housing projects
public sanctuaries, 216
public services, 215, 226–27, 237
public space: boundary with private space as
blurred, 237; elderly desiring access to,
239; the homeless in, 222; perceived as
dangerous, 122; politicians needing to
monitor, 252; reminders of spirituality in,
233; residing in low-income urban enclave impacting utilization of, 238; the
streets, 208–27
Puerto Rican Community Development
Project, 278n.13
Puerto Rican Leadership Alliance, 278n.13
Puerto Ricans: arriving in East Harlem, 15;
comparing New York and Puerto Rico,
60–62; employment of, 16–17; geographical concentration of, 3; going back
and forth between New York and Puerto
Rico, 62; increased immigration during
1930s, 17; judiciary system discriminating against, 214; large-scale immigration
in 1940s and 1950s, 18–19, 47, 62–63;
leftist intellectuals moving to East

Harlem, 14; migrant networks, 51–52, 60, 67, 85; mortality and morbidity differentials of, 181; paradox of migrants, 50; as percentage of New York Latinos, 3; political activities of, 69–70, 91–92, 278n.13; population in East Harlem in 1936, 18; poverty rates increasing for, 182; social construction of immigrant experience of, 54–62; state services discriminating against, 214; upward mobility as limited, 179; what migrants are looking for, 55–60. *See also* Latino elderly

Puerto Rico: colonial capitalism in, 20–21; gender differences in work in, 24; *independentista* movement, 278n.5; industrialization plans for, 66; pro-migration cycle in, 21; U.S. citizenship for, 21. *See also* Puerto Ricans

Puerto Rico in New York (Galídez), 47

Pura: bad childhood experiences of, 35; on drug addiction and the family, 225; on family problems of the elderly, 167; in informal economy, 82; on living in a single room, 219; marriage of, 37–38; on private physicians, 145; reasons for migrating, 58; on religion, 230; on tenements, 218; on working in Puerto Rico, 34

racket unions, 76, 96, 180, 279n.10
Ramírez, Encarnación, 280n.3
real estate: commercial, 221. *See also* housing
religion, 229–31; churches, 215, 278n.7; *espiritismo*, 134, 138, 195, 230, 236; home religious services, 229–30; household spiritual artifacts, 231–35; lighting candles, 195, 228, 235; as perceived need, 260; public sanctuaries, 216; *respaldos*, 234
remedios caseros (home remedies), 133, 142–44
rent: based on personal income, 242; for commercial real estate, 221; increases in, 219; other household members' contribution to, 202; percentage of income spent on, 200; in the projects, 242; rent control legislation, 252–53; for tenements, 242; and welfare reform, 241, 242
residential segregation, 12, 64, 70
respaldos, 234

retirement: age of in study population, 119; automatic benefits, 195; gender differences in age of, 92; gender differences in time allocation during, 120; income decline in, 179, 180–81; Latino elderly during, 108–19; pensions, 89–90, 108, 178, 180, 181, 199; reasons for, 119; unfair labor practices affecting, 74; working past age of, 81, 92–93, 119–20. *See also* Social Security

Riveras, 43
Rosario: on bingo, 215; on biomedical health care system, 149; on garbage collection, 226; on homelessness, 223; on hotels, 219; on housing projects, 218; independence desired by, 111; retiring for health reasons, 81; on working after marriage, 85

R.S.V.P. (Retired Service Volunteer Program), 110

sábila, 135
safety: as constraint on the elderly, 215, 237, 238; consulting with residents on, 239, 254; environmental conditions and, 225; housing and, 254, 256; imbuing neighborhoods with a familiarity suggesting, 238; implications of this study for, 268; as what government should be spending on, 261. *See also* crime
sanctuaries, public, 216
santería, 138, 230, 280n.6
savings, 25
Schomberg, Arturo, 276n.2
schooling. *See* education
segregation, residential, 12, 64, 70
senior citizen centers: bingo played at, 194; food as available at, 200, 202; games played at, 215; knowledge of networks increasing utilization of, 176; planned activities at, 113
senior citizens. *See* elderly, the
Seniors in Action, 113–14, 280n.3
service industries, 94, 96
sewing. *See* garment (apparel) industry
sexuality, 107, 117
shark pills, 135, 280n.6
"site migrants," 278n.10
Sixto, 210
social class: migrants divided by, 65; and perceptions of East Harlem, 249–50;

social class *(continued)*
social networks affected by, 166–67; underclass, 182; upward mobility, 12, 179.
See also poverty
social networks, 153–77; cost of connections, 162–64; food for maintaining, 185, 200; and health care, 153, 173–77; implications of this study for, 268; migrant networks, 51–52, 60, 67, 85; nonfamily connections, 159–60, 173–74, 176; not all connections are good, 175; and Older Americans Act, 177; paying for services from, 193–94, 202; pets in, 171–72; reciprocity in, 164–65; as resource exchange systems, 187; and the service structure, 176; social class affecting, 166–67; value of connections, 160–62. *See also* family
Social Security: as based on earned income, 181, 182; check delivery problems, 211; the elderly mugged for their checks, 224; employers not paying into, 75, 89–90, 180, 184; as income source for Latino elderly, 199; Puerto Ricans unaware of their right to, 178; retiring in order to collect, 119; sixty-five as age for receiving, 108; some employers providing, 76, 92
social services. *See* state services
Society of Saint Rosary, 230
Spanish language, 3, 130–31, 198, 206
spiritists, 134, 138, 195, 230, 236
SSI (Supplementary Security Income), 181, 182, 199, 224
state services: discrimination against Puerto Ricans by, 214; expansion of services for the elderly, 264; home care attendants, 170, 198, 219; public education on, 203; public services, 215, 226–27, 237; red tape in, 258–59. *See also* policy; Social Security; welfare
streets, the, 208–27; constraints of, 215; as entertainment, 214–17; hanging out in, 216–17; music in, 216; a street scene, 217
study population, 5–9; age at migration, 63; age of retirement in, 119; compared with Census data, 7; emotional attachment to physical surroundings, 238–39; expenditures of, 199–201; income sources of, 199; interviews with, 8; median income of, 201; occupational trajectories before emigration, 39; occupational trajectories in U.S., 80–97; policy proposals of, 248–59; poverty as experienced by, 188–98; poverty of, 183–84; premigratory experience of, 38–43; reasons for migrating, 63; recruitment of, 6–7; searching for a better life in the U.S., 46–48; social networks of, 166–73; time of arrival in New York, 63
Supplementary Security Income (SSI), 181, 182, 199, 224
Susana: altar in apartment of, 233–34; on housing, 254, 257–58; on Masonic lodge, 231; meeting with the author, 205; moving within Puerto Rico, 42; as poet, 113, 280n.2; political activity of, 92; in Seniors in Action, 113–14, 280n.3
sweatshops, 95

telephones, 1, 202
Telesforo: aiding and being aided by exwife, 198; as fearing to go out, 256; on home care attendants, 169; on homelessness, 222–23; in informal economy, 82, 198; on not doing badly in New York, 61; occupation of, 80; political activity of, 252; reasons for migrating, 56–57, 61; on tenements, 218; on visitors making the sick feel better, 169; as working during retirement, 112
tenements: as in disrepair, 218–19; East Harlem as tenement district, 13; as percentage of East Harlem's housing stock in 1938, 18; the projects as replicating, 68; Puerto Ricans moving into, 15; as quickly built to house the poor, 12; rehabilitation of, 278n.8; rents for, 242
Third Avenue, 15, 67
Title VIII housing reduction, 201, 218
Toro, Del, 252
transportation: job losses in, 96; protection for the elderly using, 269; as what government should be spending on, 261

underclass, 182
unemployment: as considered only in relation to youth, 112; housing conditions as related to, 72; policy proposals for, 245–48; rate for Puerto Ricans in 1972, 71; rate in East Harlem in 1960s, 69

union benefits, 81, 178, 196, 199
unpaid work, 110
Upper Park Avenue Community Association (UPACA), 111, 258
upward mobility, 12, 179
urban renewal, 68, 70

Vega, Bernardo, 17
Vicente, 255
Vidalina: death of, 128, 163; husband of, 156, 161–62; marriage of, 51; migration to New York, 49–51; taking care of her mother, 158–59
volunteer work, 110, 120, 177

War Against Poverty, 69
Weckquasgek Indians, 12–13
welfare: income maintenance programs, 241–42, 245; as income source, 199; rent and reform of, 241–42; seen as mark

of social inadequacy, 82–83, 191; Title VIII housing reduction, 201, 218; as what government should be spending on, 261; when work is not available, 213
women: in clerical and sales occupations, 95; in declining industries, 71; eating at senior citizen centers, 200; income decline with age, 181; in manufacturing, 94, 95, 96–97; men as living off, 188; in the needle trades, 40–41, 42–43, 71, 94, 96; occupations in Puerto Rico, 24, 33, 40, 41, 42; reasons for migrating, 58–59, 63; retirement by, 92; risk for poverty for elderly minority females living alone, 263; social networks of, 175; time allocation during retirement, 120. *See also* marriage
work. *See* employment

Young Lords, 278n.13

ABOUT THE AUTHOR

Judith Noemí Freidenberg, who trained in anthropology at the *Universidad de Buenos Aires*, Argentina and The City University of New York (The Graduate Center and The Mount Sinai School of Medicine), has been interested in generating knowledge on social issues affecting immigrants in the United States. The focus of much of her fieldwork has been on the life circumstances of Latino populations in the United States, a subject on which she has also edited "The Anthropology of Low-Income Urban Enclaves: The Case of East Harlem," The New York Academy of Sciences, 1995. She currently teaches anthropology at the University of Maryland at College Park.